In the Spirit of Happiness

Also by
the Monks of New Skete

The Art of Raising a Puppy
How to Be Your Dog's Best Friend

THE MONKS OF NEW SKETE

In the Spirit of Happiness

Little, Brown and Company

BOSTON NEW YORK LONDON

FIRST EDITION

Unless otherwise noted, New Testament translations are reprinted with the permission of Simon & Schuster from *The New Testament in Modern English,* Revised Edition translated by J. B. Phillips. Copyright © 1958, 1960, 1972 by J. B. Phillips.
    Hymns, liturgical texts, and Psalms translated by the Monks of New Skete.

Library of Congress Cataloging-in-Publication Data
Monks of New Skete.
        In the spirit of happiness / the Monks of New Skete. — 1st ed.
            p.   cm.
        Includes bibliographical references and index.
        ISBN 0-316-57851-7
        1. New Skete (Monastery: Cambridge, N.Y.)   2. Monastic and
    religious life — New York (State) — Cambridge.   3. Monasticism and
    religious orders, Orthodox Eastern — New York (State) — Cambridge.
    4. Christian life — Orthodox Eastern authors.   I. Title.
    BX388.N48M65   1999
    255'.81 — dc21   99-22489

    10   9   8   7   6   5   4   3   2   1

    MV–NY

    Book design by Melodie Wertelet
    Line illustrations by the Monks of New Skete

    Printed in the United States of America

If you take my words to heart,
tuning your ear to wisdom,
tuning your mind to understanding,
then you will come to know God,
for the Lord himself is giver of wisdom.
Then you will understand what virtue is,
  justice and fair dealing:
all paths that lead to happiness.

Proverbs 2:1a, 2, 5b, 6a, 9
(translation New Skete)

CONTENTS

Contents

Some twenty-five years ago, an elderly monk was spending the summer with us here at New Skete in preparation for making his own monastic foundation. He planned to stay with us until he settled on a suitable location elsewhere. During those weeks, we had many energetic and enjoyable discussions with him on all sorts of topics concerning the spiritual life in general and the monastic life in particular.

On a few occasions we got into a lively debate on, of all things, human happiness. Though it took a while for us even to realize that we were not using the word in the same way, what was really surprising for us was his sweeping insistence that human beings should not be seeking happiness in this world!

The Bible, of course, states clearly that man and woman were made to be happy in this world. However, they soon enough fell into sin. This "original" sin of disobedience cost them their primeval happiness, drove them from paradise, and brought down on them a life of toil and tears. Since then, life has hardly been a picnic. As a result, it seems, most religious teachers have come to the conclusion that happiness is not attainable in this world. Some even think it *should not* be attainable in this world!

Our elderly monastic guest was certainly of this mind. Life, he insisted, necessarily is a bed of suffering and pain; happiness is out of the question. In fact, according to him, to seek happiness in this world would even be quite possibly a serious offense against the Almighty, as well as a deceptive indulgence of our worst tendencies, precisely because it is a refusal to accept "our lot" in this life. And to boot, it is a hindrance and distraction from trying to be good.

Most people probably understand happiness in very earthly and materialistic terms, ranging from having no responsibilities or cares to having two beautiful cars in the garage. For others, it means enough prestige, power, money, and health that they need never worry.

According to such meanings, it would seem correct to say that happiness is not what people should be after, that there is more in human life to think about than merely material possessions and earthly considerations. It in fact does not seem right that such preoccupations should be the sole focus of human life. But is this what happiness means?

All this is doubtless the reason our discussions became quite heated. Our elderly monastic friend's thinking did not resonate in us at all. The very fact that human beings always and everywhere (barring some kind of psychological dysfunction) desire and try their best to attain some kind of happiness is proof enough for us that the traditional religious stance which he so forcefully defended was anything but true. To thirst to attain some degree of happiness in this world seems to be an inherent part of human nature. The universal human desire for happiness is itself evidence enough that it should in fact be pursued. It would seem somewhat disingenuous to say that although human beings have all kinds of desires, that doesn't mean we should pursue them. The desire for happiness, and not just in the next life, is the very essence of the pursuit of anything.

Is it really possible to conclude that, since desire is what caused the fall of Adam and Eve, all desire must be eliminated from a thoughtful and wise life? And furthermore, would it be out of place to point out that the human desire and capacity for happiness seems entirely consonant with the goodness of God? Where did we get this drive to be happy if not from God himself? To think it improper (or worse, destructive!) to pursue happiness is intrinsically unreasonable for the simple fact that it goes against reality.

When the summer was over, we were still deadlocked; he maintained his own position and we ours. So much for theological discussions.

For our part, we understand happiness as a deep and lasting interior peace. It is one that comes only with the struggle to search out and accept the will of God in our lives, one that demands of us a faith, hope, and love upon which and through which we strive to elevate the quality of all human life. It is the same peace of which Jesus spoke, the same inner tranquillity and serenity we see in him throughout his life. We think this is what human beings were created for, so that our lives become a knowing and loving service of God and each other in this world, which will be completed in the world to come.

Happiness, then, is ultimately what this book is all about. It is about attaining happiness, true happiness, not only in the world to come, but in this world as well, even in the midst of the worst suffering. Through this book, we offer the reader an inside look at how to go about attaining true happiness in life, in the midst of and by means of all the myriad of things that happen to us in the short span we have on this earth, by doing the good and the right because it is good and right. After all, isn't that what God, too, is all about?

Attaining happiness is indeed the struggle of a lifetime. Yet, the difficulties and all the stumbling blocks aside, we can honestly see that we were indeed created to be happy, that happiness arises from its very pursuit.

AUTHORS' NOTE

This is a book on the spiritual life from a monastic perspective, which we hope will be of help to anyone seriously interested in pursuing the spiritual life. It has been said that monasticism is "rooted in the blood, not the ink." If this is so, it is only because monasticism emphasizes the way spirituality is lived out in everyday life over against a purely theoretical understanding of the subject. The monk is not interested in accumulating facts in some purely academic manner; he is interested in obtaining wisdom, and learning how to manifest it in everyday living. We believe this is the key to living a full life, which is why it concerns each of us, whatever our religious affiliation happens to be.

As the reader will soon discover, this is not a scholarly or academic treatise. It is written for the interested lay person (though we have reason to believe that a scholar might profit from it, too!). Our goal is to introduce the reader to a real way of deepening and enriching the quality of his or her everyday life, in language that is straightforward and clear.

At the start, it is important for the reader to understand that when we use the pronoun "we" throughout the book, we do so in the name of the whole monastic community of New Skete. While the actual writing was done by a group of monks, the ideas presented reflect the convictions of the entire community and have been discussed at length among us all. Similarly, the character of "the Seeker" is a composite, constructed from the real-life experiences of a number of us, to describe the struggles involved in honestly pursuing the spiritual life.

In the chapters that follow, we discuss the principles that underlie any authentic human life and its movement toward God. We want to make the riches of the Christian tradition accessible to ordinary people who may have been turned off in the past by overly cerebral or technical treatments of faith, or who simply may never have had the opportunity to delve into these matters. Because monasticism is a subject that many of our readers may be unfamiliar with, we have included a number of short "interludes" positioned between chapters, which provide background information on New Skete, monasticism, and the ancient desert fathers. The hymns and texts at the head of each chapter are from Eastern Orthodox divine services and were translated by us from the Greek. A glossary is provided at the end of the book to clarify foreign terms, as well as unfamiliar concepts.

We hope to be that voice in the wilderness that reminds you to take care lest you forget God and your eternal destiny in the course of everyday living. In these pages we are going to share some of our insights, common to us and to the monastic tradition in general, with you the reader, for your enrichment, reflection, and growth. We are not setting out to convert anyone. True conversion takes place in the heart of the individual. It is not something anyone else can do for you. Nonetheless, before we can talk about real growth, there are very serious and necessary considerations that must be clearly understood.

Thus, the reader should be prepared to be challenged, provoked, goaded, perhaps even angered. These issues will not be taken lightly. There have been some retreatants who have gone home from a visit to our monastery highly disturbed because their experience here did not pander to pious religious presumptions, but instead confronted them with the need to look at things anew. Such a process can be threatening and painful, especially when it forces us from the warmth and security of what we had taken for granted into the wilderness of new understanding. This is what the thrust of this book is about. Paths to wisdom and true life are to be found here. If you are looking to reinforce the status quo of a satisfied life, then this book will surely disappoint you. But if you are determined to pursue spiritual understanding and wisdom no matter how difficult the quest, then this book will be of help to you. It is born of our own struggle, and of our own journey in the wilderness.

In the Spirit of Happiness

Saint Theodore of Studios describes the monastic life as the journey of a soul. But, this journey of each human being, if it is to be done in the spirit of Christ, must be done in union with all people of all times. As Saint Basil the Great points out, monastic living is the struggle of a team of spiritual athletes, involving the common human efforts of individuals who are members of the one great human family, members of the mystical body of Christ. United in such groups, those who profess monasticism make their way, like bands of pilgrims, toward the heavenly Jerusalem.

Monastic Typicon of New Skete

A monk is one who is separated from all and who is in harmony with all.

Evagrius Ponticus

ONE

The Seeker

I T IS MANY YEARS NOW since he first visited the monastery, though the details of that day linger quietly in his memory. On that clear October afternoon he thought upstate New York was among the most beautiful places in the world. He had come from the Far West, sweeping airborne over ten states with barely a cloud in the sky. From the plane, the beauty of the Catskills, the Hudson River Valley, then finally the vague outline of the Adirondacks to the north took his breath away. He had always loved flying, but passing through the vast expanse of space, from one time zone to the next, he sensed a parallel passage taking place inwardly as well, one leading him inexorably into a new life. Were we to give him a name, none would be better than simply "the Seeker."

The occasion for his journey was to meet a monk whom he knew only by the power of his written word: Father Laurence, abbot of New Skete, an Orthodox Catholic monastery in Cambridge, New York. Several months earlier, quite by chance, the young man had come across several of Father's articles on monastic life and spirituality. Reading them occasioned one of those rare moments when words speak unmistakably to our deepest concerns. With freshness and candor, they communicated an authority well grounded in personal experience that attracted him. Somewhat presumptuously, the Seeker initiated a correspondence that the monk could have justifiably ignored; he did not, and when several illuminating letters only multiplied the number of the Seeker's questions, Father Laurence graciously invited him to spend some time at the monastery to delve into them more deeply.

Of the Seeker, little needs to be said other than that he had been stumbling along his spiritual journey for quite some time. He liked to think of himself as serious about spirituality, but honesty would have forced him to concede his ambivalence about monasticism. While attracted by contemplative values, and meditating regularly each day, he was wary of the sacrifice such values seemed to require once they were institutionalized. That was why he had boarded that plane.

In a disarmingly direct manner, Father Laurence's articles and correspondence gave him cause to wonder whether a creative synthesis might not be achievable after all — what Father Laurence described as *monasticism with a human face.* The contention that these values were of importance to all, and not just monks, intrigued the Seeker enough to arrange the visit. Whether it would result in his deciding to become a monk himself, the Seeker did not know; that, he would leave to God. Nevertheless, he had a deep premonition that whatever he might learn would be of value no matter what he happened to do in life.

TRADITIONALLY, it is any aspirant's business to make his own way to a teacher, an indication of the genuineness of his desire and an appropriate act of humility. Distance is never an issue. In ancient times, seekers routinely traveled thousands of miles to mine the wisdom of a renowned elder, as Saint John Cassian had when he and his friend Germanus visited a number of elders in the Egyptian desert in the fourth century. Flying to New York seemed trifling in comparison.

The Seeker had planned on renting a car for the final leg of the journey, but when he spoke with him by phone the previous day, Father Laurence had told him not to bother. The monk had errands to do in Albany and could pick him up at the airport himself. That struck the Seeker as unusually flexible. When he asked what kind of car he should be on the lookout for, Father merely chuckled and replied, "Don't worry, I'll find you. Just wait for me in the pickup area."

When the Seeker arrived in Albany, it was a blue station wagon that pulled up beside him at the pickup area, with a mammoth German shepherd staring out from the side window. All of the monks he had met up to that point were predictably "monkish," always dressed in habits and careful to preserve a traditional image. The man who emerged from the other side of the car was heavyset and dressed in street clothes, his graying beard neatly trimmed. Smiling warmly, he extended his hand and introduced himself simply as Father Laurence. After some amiable chitchat, he unlocked the rear door and signaled the dog to stay. As he helped the Seeker get his luggage into the car, he nonchalantly pointed to his canine companion.

"Meet Ivy. No need for alarm, she's a real sweetheart. Hop in."

The second the Seeker got into the car, Ivy shamelessly started licking his ears, and when Father went to the other side of the car, he tapped on the window and told Ivy to lie down in the back of the wagon. She obeyed without protest.

As they pulled away from the airport, the image that stuck in the Seeker's mind was the deft way in which Father Laurence wove in and out of traffic — quickly, but not recklessly — with no scruples about using his horn when someone seemed asleep at the wheel. Since traffic was heavy, they spent the first few minutes together in a comfortable silence, but when they eventually eased onto the Northway and the relative calm of steady speed, Father Laurence turned and asked casually, "So you're serious enough about this to have flown to New York. How about telling me a bit about yourself?"

The Seeker had anticipated such questions. His letters, while open and sincere, were still just letters and hadn't really offered anything more than a general description of himself; their one conversation on the phone had been about the Albany airport. So, despite feeling mildly awkward, he began to stumble through a more detailed self-portrait, filling in facts that he had either omitted or only briefly alluded to in his correspondence. Father Laurence listened intently, and as they spoke the Seeker quickly began to forget his self-consciousness. The monk would nod his head and smile from time to time, and at several points he laughed heartily, making no effort to conceal his delight. Yet he always seemed one step ahead of the Seeker's last sentence, as if he were listening to a story he already knew. Finally he asked:

"And what have you learned through all of this?"

Somehow the Seeker was hoping that the monk would tell *him* that, though it was clear from the ensuing silence that he had no intentions of doing so. He thought for several moments, vaguely aware of the colorful foliage gliding by. They were no longer on the Northway and the landscape was becoming increasingly rural. At last the Seeker replied, "I've learned that the whole world's asleep — myself included."

Father raised his eyebrows and rubbed his bearded chin. "Well now, that's very interesting." He was quiet for quite some time, weighing a response, until finally he offered his own thoughts. "It's the same for all of us. The real question is how serious we are about waking up." He paused. "How far are *you* willing to go? Life will do its best to rouse you, but you're the only one who can wake yourself up. Nobody else can. Someone can teach, invite, cajole, challenge you, whatever, but no one can make you hear what you're not willing to hear — neither I, your parents, your boss, nor the people you live with, for that matter. It's entirely up to you. But if you listen closely, if you're serious, I promise you you'll hear — and that hearing will change you forever."

The car slowed down and he honked at a black-and-white Holstein standing in the middle of the road. It turned its head casually, then lumbered off into the pasture. Ivy barked at it from the back. The monk calmed her and then turned back to the Seeker and reminded him how important the period was that he was going through. The following weeks at the monastery were a chance to come to terms with himself in a new way, and they needed to be used wisely. Aside from times of meditation and worship, he would be working with various brothers each day and should feel relaxed about asking questions as they occurred to him. But Father Laurence cautioned him against chitchat, advising him to avoid needless conversation. "Pay attention to what is deeper." He stressed that it was vital to get in touch with the rhythm of the life as quickly as possible, and he offered to meet with the Seeker every couple of days if he wished to discuss his thoughts. But Father also made it clear that this was entirely up to him, and that he shouldn't feel obligated to do it.

The Seeker was curious about the monastery, and he asked about its beginnings. Though he had read several issues of *Gleanings,* the community's journal, it was difficult to get anything more than a glimpse from that. Father Laurence explained that the community began in 1966, with a dozen monks under his leadership. They came from a community of Byzantine Rite Franciscans. Dissatisfied with the kind of religious life they had been living, they initially tried to form a monastery within their order based on the principles of East-

ern Christian monastic life. Once it became clear that no pro-
vision could be made for such a life within the Franciscans,
they chose to begin a new community. They felt called to an
authentic Eastern Christian monasticism for *our* day, inspired
by the vision of the early monastic fathers.

They also had a passion for liturgy, seeking to infuse new
life into Eastern Catholic worship. In that spirit, they took the
name "New Skete," after one of the first Christian monastic
settlements in northern Egypt, in the desert of Skete. From
the very beginning, their intention was to incarnate the simplicity of the original principles of monastic life, unencum-
bered by the institutionalized accretions of the centuries, and to
do this in a way that made sense for twentieth-century America.

Considering the magnitude of their ambitions, their path
unfolded astonishingly according to plan. "When I left the
monastery, I had fifteen dollars in my pocket. It's true," Father
said in a tone of self-mockery. Then he raised his finger mischievously. "But I also knew that we had many friends who
believed in what we were doing and who were willing to
help us out until we could get on our feet. Leaving was a calculated gamble."

The group spent their first six months together in western
Pennsylvania, in a hunting lodge made available to them by
Dom Damasus Winzen, OSB, founder and prior of the
Benedictines at Mount Saviour, in New York State's southern
tier. Before actually leaving the Franciscans, Father Laurence
had written to him for counsel, and Dom Damasus had
enthusiastically invited him to Mount Saviour to talk about
the group's plans for a foundation. A pioneer in monastic and
liturgical renewal himself, Dom Damasus proved to be a
sympathetic ally. After listening to Father Laurence's story, he
graciously offered the monks temporary use of a lodge that
belonged to a novice of his community.

Those six months gave the monks the solitude and stability they needed to initiate a serious monastic foundation, as well as the time to look for a permanent home. Within a few months, their search led them to a beautiful piece of property with an old, broken-down farmhouse on Stanton Road near the village of Cambridge, in upstate New York. Within another six months, the monks had transformed it into a suitable monastery, fully renovated and beautifully landscaped.

But paradise proved to be uninhabitable. Sitting adjacent to what had initially seemed to be an isolated country road, the new monastery turned out to have everything but privacy. "Sort of a fish tank," Father mused. Tourists drove by slowly, gawking at the young men clad in medieval robes; on several occasions the monks actually discovered strangers peering in at them through their front windows as they ate dinner or chanted the monastic hours.

The extreme visibility of the monastery also gave rise to bizarre rumors amongst the local townsfolk that their bearded neighbors were actually draft-dodging hippies who had formed a commune to sit out the Vietnam War. Oddly, noise was also a major problem. Beneath the property in the valley below, summer transformed the sleepy little lake community into a busy resort featuring water-skiing by day and rock music by night. In a memorable summer meeting that lasted late into the night, the monks painfully came to the conclusion that they would have to look for a more suitable location in the general area.

In July of 1967, they came across a promising piece of property for sale on the other side of Cambridge: 300-plus acres of dense woodland on Two-Top Mountain, in the town of White Creek. But claiming it for a monastery would require an immense amount of work. There was an old shack on the property, but no road, and since the soil was completely shale or clay, the hilly land was unsuitable for any kind of farming. What the property did offer, however, was a secluded location of profound beauty. Together the monks weighed the pros and cons, and the majority of the monks prevailed: they decided to take the gamble.

With help from friends they were able to get a down payment on the property as well as a mortgage, and they began the enormous task of building the monastery themselves. For seven months they shuttled back and forth from Stanton Road to the new property, and much of the hardest work fell in the dead of winter. The daily liturgical services served as a steady anchor in what was routinely eight to ten hours of heavy manual work each day, coupled with community meetings that lasted well into the night, as they hammered out the principles of the monastic life they were forging. Given such intensity, a couple of brothers left.

"In retrospect, it seems astonishing, impossible to believe," Father remarked. "We started with practically nothing, philosophy majors owning no more than a vision. We relied on sheer enthusiasm and willpower to make things work, to make up for whatever else was lacking." He paused, as if caught in a dream he was reliving. "Yet I wouldn't trade those days for anything. They were filled with great passion and zeal, and they set the tone for the type of monastic life we live now."

In 1969, with the monastery three years old and finally established in its permanent location, another remarkable thing occurred. A small group of contemplative nuns were looking to form a new monastic community, prompted by many of the same ideals that had originally inspired the monks. Having heard about New Skete, they made contact, and, after visiting the monks, decided to settle nearby, eventually becoming a sister community.

"I sometimes wonder whether I wasn't out of my mind to seriously consider such a thing," Father said, his eyes reflecting the recollection of all that was involved in such a step. Though the monks had discussed the idea of a sister community from the very beginning, no one had expected it to come about so quickly. When the possibility arose, the vision of what the benefits of a male/female community could be outweighed the certain risks, and the community decided to move forward with the idea. In the years that have followed the nuns' foundation, the result, though not without difficulties, has been something entirely distinctive, no doubt even prophetic, in modern monasticism. New Skete has demonstrated that monastic life can accommodate men and women in a spiritual communion that is fruitful for all concerned, celibate yet free of unhealthy attitudes toward human sexuality.

Just like the monks, the nuns, too, had a cold baptism. Connecting with New Skete, not to mention becoming part of it, meant integrating themselves into the existing mind-set of the community, no easy proposition. Father Laurence was the founder and leader of the community, and part of their adjustment involved accepting his leadership. Further, they had to find a means of self-support so that they could build their own monastery and stabilize their way of life. They initially took up residence in the workshops of the men's monastery, while looking for property where they could build.

To achieve their hopes, they did whatever work they could find. Several nuns did housework for local people and others performed hospital and secretarial work in Cambridge. Two learned iconography and the fabrication of liturgical vestments for the monastery. One nun even began an upholstery and drapery business.

Next, because the nuns were starting with nothing, the monks agreed to purchase a piece of property for them near

Cambridge, a small farmhouse that was three miles from the monks. Though the farmhouse was far too small to serve as a permanent residence, the property included a hilly pasture across the road with an idyllic view, which was a suitable site for the monastery. This meant that once the nuns' new monastery was habitable, the monks could sell the smaller house to pay off the mortgage. The plan worked. After the monks built the shell of the monastery, the nuns were able to finish the inside. By taking shop courses at a nearby high school, they learned the skills necessary for building, and within a year they had settled into their own monastery. Thus, New Skete acquired the unusual characteristic of being a modern male and female monastic community.

At the time of the Seeker's visit, the community numbered twenty-three between the monks and the nuns. This was before the creation of the married couples' community, the Companions, which began in 1982, adding another eight members to the mix. The Seeker asked if there were limits to how big the community intended to grow, but Father Laurence just shrugged philosophically and said, "We've had many people come and go, so at times the number has been more, but basically we've remained the same size for several years now."

He went on to explain that since their spartan beginnings, the monks had developed several stable means of supporting their community. They breed German shepherd dogs, offer an obedience-training program for dogs of all breeds, run a mail order business specializing in smoked meats and cheeses, and publish liturgical books and music. The nuns, meanwhile, have developed a thriving cheesecake business, and continue to produce liturgical vestments and icons. The Seeker was impressed and said so, but Father Laurence just shrugged and said, "We simply did what we had to do."

When conversation is good, it builds steadily, without self-consciousness; Father's manner, relaxed and open, made it feel natural for the Seeker to introduce more personal concerns, and while Father Laurence could have easily deflected these for another time, he listened patiently and without condescension to what must have seemed the accumulation of years of questioning and ambivalence. There is no need to recount these concerns at length, only to say that they reflected the Seeker's own spiritual confusion and frustration, and his singular desire to break through them, to come to real self-understanding and integration. More than anything Father said, what moved the Seeker was the monk's sincere interest in him, and the fact that the Seeker could talk about these issues openly with him.

He was so immersed in the conversation that he barely noticed the sign that said Cambridge, signaling their approach to the general environs of the monastery. Father noted the hazy outline of the Green Mountains in the distance and mentioned that New Skete was a couple of miles from the Vermont border as the crow flies. Then he motioned to the right toward a distinct pair of peaks, set like beautifully proportioned breasts along the eastern horizon. "The monastery's tucked on the other side of those hills."

They descended into the outskirts of the village, passing through a corridor of flaming maple trees that seemed to glow in the soft light of late afternoon. Cambridge is small, a "one-stoplight town" as the locals will tell you, and passing through it took all of a couple of minutes. Riding by the Cambridge Hotel with its tacky "Home of Pie a-la-Mode" sign, Father noted that the famous chef James Beard once remarked that he had had the worst fried chicken of his life there. Aside from that, the village has precious little notoriety:

an overgrown graveyard marking the site of the second-oldest Methodist church in the United States is about the extent of it. As they traveled eastward out of the village on Ash Grove Road, Father soon pointed out the nun's monastery, half hidden on the hillside, and honked the horn as they drove by two of the nuns walking their dogs along the road.

The Seeker expressed his pleasure at the remoteness of the surroundings, and Father nodded in agreement. "Monastic life requires a certain degree of solitude, and this location has served us well in preserving that." Then he added pointedly, "But we're not hermits." Along the road a local farmer waved to them as he waited to move his herd of black-and-white Holsteins across the road.

Soon, the car slowed and turned onto a narrow gravel road marked New Skete Road. The Seeker also noted a Dead End sign and wondered to himself whether it wasn't some local road commissioner's idea of a joke. Immediately the road began to trace a gradual incline, flanked by rows of white birch — hundreds of them — and brilliant sugar maples. Purple asters and goldenrod blossomed abundantly beneath the trees, composing a pleasing vision of warmth and color. Father pointed toward the top of the mountain, looming up ahead of them and set majestically against the deep blue sky.

"You can't make it out from down here, but when the sun is just right you can see a gilded cross at the top from the road. Brother Stavros tacked it up there near a spot he likes to hike to." They continued to climb steadily up the mountain, past broad oaks and a dilapidated shack that was barely visible through the thick tangles of locust and sumac. Father described it as the decaying testament of the former owner, a local lawyer who kept it as a low-profile getaway. By the time the monks bought the property it was in complete disrepair; all they could use it for was a chicken house, which they did for several years. "You can still smell the evidence even now, years after we've stopped using it."

They passed by a small pond; a lone mallard glided peacefully back and forth. As the Seeker watched its movement, dust clouds from their ascent spread out behind them. Further up the hill a honey-colored doe and her fawn emerged from the woods. They paused momentarily, then bounded across the road and disappeared on the other side.

The Seeker had been so put at ease by nature's welcome and the serenity of the landscape that he was quite unprepared for what he saw next. Rounding the final bend, he was suddenly dazzled by the sight of brilliant gold domes, leaping like candle flames atop a beautifully rustic church. To an American used to typically Western religious architecture the vision was stunning. This edifice wasn't something simply to be admired: its beauty accosted him, becoming the context for whatever else he would experience. Even the landscaping around the church supported the space without diminishing it, integrating juniper bushes, Japanese maples, flowers, and stone. In front of the church, next to where the car stopped, a majestic golden locust grew from a carefully constructed rock island.

Father smiled slightly, as if reading the young man's thoughts.

The Seeker really didn't know what to say. He just stared for a few moments, taking it all in. The church had been designed and built by the monks themselves, in seventy-three days. It was loosely patterned after the wooden churches of northern Russia. The gabled roofs, supporting the smaller domes, were covered with cedar shingles and rose from one another naturally. The principal tent-style support holding up the largest dome reached effortlessly toward the sky, no doubt carrying with it the hopes and aspirations of many a monk and pilgrim. The church stood at the heart of the monastic complex, the first thing visitors see when they visit the monastery. It is an appropriate introduction. Such a sight gives one something to ponder immediately. The other monastery buildings flank it to the north and west sides, partially obscured by concolor firs and Austrian pines.

"Why don't you get out here and look around," Father said. "It's almost time for vespers and I still have a few things to do beforehand. The service will last about an hour and a quarter, and then we'll have some supper with the whole community. We'll get you settled down in the guest house later on."

"Fine."

The priest smiled and patted the Seeker's shoulder. "Wandering through darkness isn't pleasant, but if you're patient, your eyes adjust." The Seeker wanted to say something to him in reply, some expression of thanks, but he drew a blank. Thanks seemed altogether insufficient. After an embarrassed silence, he simply nodded and got out of the car. The monk pulled away and the Seeker walked slowly around the driveway toward the entrance, guided by the low shale walls surrounding the church. The exterior was darkly weathered pine, set off by eaves painted dark red. The front doors were red as well, and above the entranceway was an icon of the Transfiguration, the mystery to which the temple was dedicated. Opposite the doorway was a simple tower with two bells; nearby was a larger bell fastened to its own support. Before he could open the door, a brash chipmunk hopped up onto the shale wall and began chattering away at him. The Seeker removed his cap and entered the temple.

Inside it was dark. Several tinted windows allowed narrow shafts of golden light to reflect off the slate floor. He kissed the festal icon and stood off to the side for a moment to collect himself. Incense-laden air, the subtle legacy of years of worship, mixed with his thoughts, quieting them and permitting the many strands of distraction to settle. He breathed deeply several times. A lone figure in a dark robe was lighting oil lamps for the coming service. One by one the lamps came to life, their warm light reflecting off the gilded icons. Though highly stylized, these images colorfully made the saints present and brought to life the mysteries of Christian faith. The temple was filled with them. On the upper walls surrounding the nave of the temple, the Seeker glimpsed Gospel scenes transformed into iconographic murals. Everything blended gracefully into a harmonious whole. He felt the deep stillness.

From outside, a sudden, sharp rapping on wood rhythmically began to build up momentum. He later learned that this was the *semandron,* a six-foot-long board struck repeatedly with a wooden mallet fifteen minutes before the service. A tradition has it that this was the way Noah called the animals into the ark. Somehow the Seeker felt certain that the monks here wouldn't buy that.

As the hammering slowly died down, he sat on one of the benches lining the narthex and waited. Soon the church began to fill with monks and nuns. Entering from the side vestibule, they made the sign of the cross and bowed reverently, touching a hand to the floor. To touch the floor meant that you had to bow fully, from the waist. It was the gesture a vassal made before an emperor in Byzantine times, and made the Seeker feel a bit uncomfortable when he first observed it. He didn't like the image of a slave. As he thought about it, however, he started feeling foolish and petty: this wasn't any earthly lord they were attending to. They were coming here to worship, entering the presence of the Lord of the universe, the King of the ages, who is infinitely more than some Byzantine despot. How does one say that properly with the body? Perhaps touching the floor wasn't such a silly idea after all.

Despite the increasing number of monks and nuns, the temple remained very quiet — no unnecessary noise, no coughing or hacking. Each took a position in the choir and waited. From the side shadows, Father Laurence entered, now robed in a flowing black *riassa,* with a silver pectoral cross hanging from his neck. He bowed and went into the altar area to vest. As if on cue, the large bell from outside the temple sounded three times, followed by the joyful peal of the other bells, announcing the evening service. This was definitely more impressive than the *semandron*. With the bells outside ringing various rhythmic patterns, the priest began censing inside the church, the gentle jingling of the censer's chains discernible despite the bells outdoors. Rich curls of incense smoke drifted upward toward the ceiling, rising throughout the temple in his wake, first within the sanctuary, then from the nave. He was in no rush. He moved with dignity throughout the whole of the temple, censing each icon deliberately. To finish, he stood on the *solea* and censed the worshippers, who bowed their heads in response. The peal trailed off and three monks entered the temple from the back, taking their places in choir. From the darkness of the sanctuary, the priest returned to the *solea* with a large paschal candle in his hand and intoned, "Wisdom, stand aright! Behold Christ, the light of the universe!"

Immediately the choir responded, in a haunting Byzantine melody, chanting the ancient hymn "Radiant Light." As they were singing, the candles throughout the temple were lit, followed by the ceiling lights, turning the dark temple into a pavilion of light. On the iconóstasis, or icon screen, that separated the sanctuary from the nave, the *Theotokos* and Saint

Mary Magdalene, Saint John the Baptist, and Saints Sergius, Herman, and Nil reverently pointed toward the central icon in the apse which now revealed Christ enthroned in glory. The priest chanted a centuries-old prayer:

> *O great and exalted God, who alone are immortal and dwell in unapproachable light! In your wisdom you created the entire universe. You separated light from darkness, giving the sun charge of the day, and the moon and stars, the night. Now, at this very hour, you permit us, sinful as we are, to approach you with our evening hymns of praise and glory. In your love for us, direct our prayers as incense in your sight, and accept them as a delightful fragrance. Throughout this present evening and the night to come, fill us with your peace. Clothe us in the armor of light, rescue us from the terror that creeps about in darkness, and give us that sleep you designed to soothe our weakness, a sleep free of all evil dreams.*
>
> *For you are good and full of love for all of us, O God, and we give you glory, Father, Son, and Holy Spirit: now and forever and unto ages of ages.*

The six-part choir responded with a resounding "Amen." The Seeker believed they meant it. Throughout the service he stood in the back transfixed, awakened to a new universe. Sight, sound, and scent consorted to invoke the hidden yearnings of the human spirit, the quest he felt so strongly in his own heart. Harmonies blended with seeming effortlessness as the choir chanted traditional Eastern Orthodox hymns that had been translated in a fresh way into modern English:

> *Shadows of the law now fade in the light of divine grace! Like that bush so long ago, unconsumed though the flames raged on, so, O lady, you brought forth your Son, while remaining a virgin as before. Where once there stood a pillar of fire, now the sun of justice shines*

forth for all. Moses, too, now gives way to Christ, the saviour of our souls! (Dogmaticon of Tone Two)

The service was a feast of the senses, as well as the mind and heart, that moved him beyond words. It swept him up into its spirit. He had attended several Orthodox Christian services before, but none quite like this. Here, in this small chapel in upstate New York, he felt the wonder of liturgy in a manner unlike anything he had ever experienced before. Here was his own identification with the story of Prince Vladimir of Kiev, who in the tenth century sent ambassadors to all of the religious centers of his day, trying to find a faith suitable for his kingdom. Unimpressed by excursions elsewhere, when his envoys returned from Constantinople they reported a totally unique and moving experience: "The Greeks led us to where they worship their God, and we knew not whether we were in heaven or on earth. For on earth there is no such splendor or such beauty, and we are at a loss how to describe it. We only know that God dwells there among men. . . ."

Once one experiences this, everything changes.

Life never seems to prepare us sufficiently for epiphanies. By definition they come upon us suddenly, dazzling us by their raw power. They are not magical intrusions from another world, but reality, naked and without shame. Their very ordinariness shimmers with unexpected depth, which is why they take us by such surprise. It does not matter whether they occur in the majesty of Hagia Sophia or in the elegant simplicity of a wooden chapel, the effect is the same. In the Seeker's own case, whatever else he was living with, his confusion and fears, this unmistakable realization leapt out at him: God dwells here among these people. In the very palpability of their worship he knew this was so, and suddenly all of his other questions were put into clearer perspective. They were illumined in a cleansing moment of worship that left him changed. How so he dared not describe at that moment, other than to know it had occurred. "This is what has been missing," he thought. "I've had it wrong all along."

What he encountered transcended all his doubts and confusion: knowing this dynamic beauty would be enough. It hardly surprised him when the Gospel chanted at the end of the service was the story of Thomas, who vowed he would believe in the resurrection only if he touched Christ's wounds. There were no revelations, no visions, just the simple poverty of Christ's words to the apostle Thomas: "Put your finger here and see my hands. Reach out your hand and put it into my side. Do not doubt, but believe" (John 20:27). He wanted to, for the first time in his life.

THAT WAS MANY YEARS AGO. The first days of that stay turned into weeks, which in turn became months. They were the prologue of a journey that Seeker is still making in union with us, as a member of our community. This book is not about him. Nor is it about this monastery per se. Rather, it is about discovering the principles of an integrated spiritual life and authentic happiness. We shall not hesitate to draw from our own experience as monastics to illustrate the ways in which these principles take shape concretely in our lives. Throughout, we shall return often to the experience of the Seeker, as well as that of the other monks and nuns like him. We do this consciously, trusting that this will also be of interest to those who are not monastics. The spiritual journey involves the interplay of the heart with life, and the longer we travel this road the more we are convinced that it is every human being's journey. It is not of the essence that ours takes place in a monastery. If you listen carefully, you realize that the world itself is a cloister, worthy of awe and respect.

Monastics or not, the universal human problem is that we're often too busy to listen. We go about our lives forgetting who we are. Therefore, what follows in these pages is a deliberate attempt to present a spiritual vision that is of relevance to anyone seriously interested in living life in a more abundant, fruitful manner. By reflecting on the ebb and flow of our own monastic life, we also hope to address not simply monastics, but universal needs and desires extending well beyond the confines of the monastic life.

As Father Laurence said to Brother James in the kitchen yesterday while they were making tomato sauce, "We have to be sure to mention that what characterizes a monk's life are the *questions* that consume him, the same questions that all human beings have to face to truly know themselves. After all, there's a monastic, contemplative dimension to every human being's life, monastic or not. We've simply chosen to pursue this in a professional way. Now could I have that garlic, please?"

We don't want everyone to become monks. Nevertheless, we do believe that monasticism has the capacity to speak universally, to monastics and nonmonastics alike, because of its singular concern with ultimate issues, with what real living is about. You need not be a monk to share these questions and reflections. You need not be religious or pious, either! Mull over them patiently, in an atmosphere of silence and thoughtfulness, and you may discover that they are indeed your own.

What Is Monasticism?

The arid desert burst forth in bloom.
Hymn for desert saints

Monasteries have existed since early Christian times, often surrounded by a mystique that makes them seem otherworldly. But beyond the stereotypes, the traditional monastic life of solitude, prayer, and spiritual discipline has remained little understood by most people. Most monasteries lie on the periphery of society, hidden from the attention of mainstream culture, and only those who go out of their way discover its deeper dimensions.

In fact, those who have actually embraced such a life in Western civilization have always been few in number. Nevertheless, monks and nuns have never had an interest in "selling" their life to others, and you cannot find any apologiae trying to lure recruits. Most of the time they have quietly gone about their business, trying to give honest expression to their wholehearted dedication and to the deepest human desire — for meaning, the absolute, the search for God. Still, monks and nuns have always been there, open and welcoming, for those who are truly looking.

In spite of its hiddenness, monasticism has endured, and its perennial appeal to the human spirit still continues. As a Christian movement, this way of life is primarily an attempt to live the Christian life as fully as possible, formally pursuing the Gospel ideal together with those of like spirit. Monasteries prove that it really *is* possible for people to live together and strive to base every action on fraternal charity, on the love of God and his word, without trying to escape the realities of life, but instead learning to embrace them. It really *is* possible to acquire peace, quiet, clarity of mind, self-control, and mutual understanding and cooperation.

The way of the monk or nun is to renounce their worldly goods, and to vow to live in their monastic community in a chaste or celibate way, in obedience to the rule and customs of the place and to its superiors. These are the traditional signs of giving up one's self-will for a higher value and goal. Today they may seem archaic and severe, yet they free those in the monastery to single-mindedly explore the hidden realms of the spiritual life, the ins and outs of the relationships of human beings with each other and with God and the natural world. The monastic rule (or prescribed way of living), though it varies somewhat from place to place or in different times, provides its subjects with the professional opportunities, means, safeguards, and support to follow the Gospel precepts, for service to others, for changing one's ways, for salvation and enlightenment.

Monastics have always tried to share what they have learned not only with the Church but with the world at large, whether in literature, art, philosophy, or liturgical, theological, and spiritual experience. Monks and nuns throughout history have excelled in scientific research, the healing arts, agricultural development, architecture and building, administration, politics, preaching, and social work. Those attracted to monastic life come from many different ways of life, and vibrant monastic communities exist around the world today in the Roman Catholic, Orthodox, Anglican, Lutheran, and Reformed Churches.

Come, brothers and sisters! Let us raise our sights,
contemplating the mercy and salvation God has bestowed on us.
O what a strange and marvelous wonder!
Bending down from the heavens, he came to earth,
that he might lift us out of the misery of our passions
and place us firmly on the rock of faith.
Glory to your condescension, O lover of mankind.

Sunday evening sticheron, Tone Seven

TWO

First Fervor

M ONASTIC TRADITION has an uncommon way of offering its wisdom. Take the following bit of advice from a
crusty old fourth-century desert father as representative:

> After Abba John the Dwarf had prayed to the Lord and the
> Lord had taken away all his passions, he went to one of the
> experienced old men and said, "You see before you a man
> who is completely at rest and has no more temptations." The
> elder replied, "Go and pray to the Lord to stir up your pas-
> sions once again, for the soul is made strong only in battle.
> And when this happens, do not pray that the struggle be
> taken away from you, but only say, "Lord, give me strength to
> get through the fight."

Instead of dangling the carrot before us, slickly assuring us
how wonderful the spiritual journey is and the indescribable
bliss we shall discover on its path, monks weigh in on the side
of sobriety. No flashy, hard-sell, "God will solve all your
problems if you give your life to him" spirituality from the
cloister. Not that monastic tradition is unenthusiastic about
searching for God; on the contrary, this is its most passionate
concern. But it does acknowledge how natural it is for each
of us, monk and nonmonk alike, to use the spiritual life
merely in a self-serving way.

Monasticism presents a healthy skepticism toward our spiritual motives; tale after tale in the desert father stories, for example, reveals a monastic elder challenging his disciple, trying to rid him of any vestige of phoniness or insincerity. This is just the approach Father Laurence employs with us, not out of any mean-spiritedness, but as a means for waking us up. We remember the time he happened to be walking through the laundry shortly before a brother was to make his profession, his lifelong commitment to the monastic life. As the brother was folding his clothes, Father tapped him lightly on the back and asked, "Are you sure you really want to do this?" The brother looked up at him with a startled expression and replied, "What do you mean?" to which Father simply smiled and casually walked on.

Do we really want to do this? Monks and nuns ask themselves this periodically in their daily meditation, as well they should, for wherever one happens to live, the spiritual life will always be a struggle. It cannot be otherwise and remain authentic. There will always be the temptation to flee the struggle. Monastic life chooses to meet this temptation head-on. Instead of touting easy grace, it displays a compassionate realism, patiently and repeatedly setting before us the path of radical change that must occur throughout our lives if we are to learn how really to love, how to engage in the unceasing task of going beyond ourselves. Only such real change indicates serious resolve in the spiritual life.

The rewards of heaven, and what — ultimately — we shall get from our labors, these monastic tradition leaves to God. It knows that whether we are monks or not, each of us is called to happiness — true happiness — the sort that stands up to the tempestuous nature of everyday life. This kind of happiness comes only through the integrity and maturity that

result from sustained spiritual effort, and not from more tran-
sitory pleasures that may come to us in the course of our
lives. And though the particular spiritual path each of us follows will vary according to the context in which we live,
nevertheless, they are all pointed in the same direction.

Monasticism's skepticism toward our spiritual motives expresses itself quite openly. For example, Saint Benedict —
the famous sixth-century monastic father — let prospective
monks wait at the door several days, to test their seriousness.
We've often wondered how each of us would have reacted
had Father Laurence applied that approach when we first
came to New Skete. Would we have had the maturity to simply wait patiently in the guest house? Twentieth-century
products that we are, we cringe at the thought of it. Nevertheless, following this guidance to the letter is not what
counts. Showing human warmth and hospitality to candidates
from the start does not prevent us from following the standard
approach toward them that monks have always used: "When
they are finally accepted into the monastery, an experienced
monk sits the candidates down to explain the many harsh and
difficult experiences they can expect to encounter on the
spiritual way," as the Rule of Saint Benedict puts it.

*"I'm not sure this is going to be for you," the Seeker recalled Father
Laurence saying to him during one of their first talks before he actually entered the monastery. "I mean, it's up to you if you wish to try.
At any rate, don't be surprised when there are days you find yourself
angry at the life, at me, at those you live with, so much so that you'll
question whether you can possibly continue."*

*"I must have had a shocked expression on my face," the Seeker
added, "for Father went on to say that things might actually get even
worse. But he also told me that that would be peanuts in comparison*

to what I'd come to understand about myself if I persevered, if I continually strived to do my best. 'Always keep in mind the reason why you have come,' Father admonished, which is advice I've come back to frequently."

Actually, the early Egyptian fathers were even more blunt toward candidates. When young Pachomius came to the anchorite Palamon asking to be a monk, Palamon told him to go away because he was too weak to endure such a life. "This work of God is not so simple; for many have come but have not persevered." Pachomius took the rebuke in stride and replied, "Just give me a chance, and see!" So Palamon gave him a chance. Pachomius persevered to become the father of cenobitic monasticism.

We might think this approach strange and unsympathetic, but its purpose is to "test the spirit," to marshal the candidates' inner resources, for the spiritual journey will demand everything they possess.

"In my own case," the Seeker recounted, "perhaps because of an overly competitive nature, the fact that Father expressed his reservations about my ability to hack monastic life made me all the more determined to try. But his skepticism was not just pro forma, either. It was entirely honest, born of the experience of seeing many people come and go over the years. His straightforwardness challenged my seriousness, and ultimately provoked a radical decision that marked the real beginning of my spiritual search: the resolve to persevere no matter what, 'to put the hand to the plow' and never look back."

There is wisdom in such an approach. Whether it is to prepare an individual to enter a monastery or to begin a serious spiritual life in the world makes little difference. The spiritual cycles are similar, and we can expect a struggle in either case. Better that we know this ahead of time, that we have some idea of what precisely we're getting into once we embark on the spiritual path. Then we'll be less apt to bolt when things get sticky. For when the way becomes dark, and the interior suffering profound (as, at times, it most surely will), we will not be able to accuse anyone of having led us on, of having duped us by withholding the grim details of the difficulties to come. It was all made clear up front.

The problem is that at the beginning of the spiritual journey (or even once we've begun to take it seriously again after a lapse), it is all too easy to forget this. The novelty of the way and the good feelings it inspires in us literally sweep us off our feet. We need to keep our eyes open, without being paranoid. When we look for a secular counterpart to this, the experience that comes closest is falling in love.

We've all tasted this. When we fall in love, aren't those wondrous first days filled with untold excitement? Everything about the beloved fascinates us and appears idyllic — the look, the color of hair, the scent, his or her very "being" — and fills our lives with a headiness that makes us seem alive in a manner we never knew before. It is as if we have never really lived before this.

"The first time I fell in love" recalled the Seeker, "my dad's reaction to the news was an amused 'Fine, now go mow the lawn,' but even that didn't dampen my enthusiasm. My life had drawn a burst of new energy in the glow of this wonderful girl. When I was separated from her, her image filled my soul with vibrancy and verve. I could talk for hours on the telephone with her without tiring, much to my parents' consternation. Yet I also became quite creative and industrious at school, possessing seemingly endless reserves of energy. For the

duration of that love, nothing was able to get me down, and inwardly I was amazed when friends expressed pessimism and discontent with their lot. 'How can they not see how wonderful life is?' I thought. Several weeks later, after I had fallen out of love, I had my answer. Still, no matter how often I fell in love — a number of times, as it happens — such love seemed always fresh and new, as if it had never happened before, and the cycle repeated itself with an increasingly familiar pattern."

Obviously there is nothing wrong with such experiences. They are completely human, and it is only natural to enjoy them for as long as they last. Indeed, they bear within themselves the possibility of developing into enduring relationships of love and fidelity. But we should not misunderstand such experiences: they are simply first love, untested by the demands of time and reality. The romantic, infatuous quality never lasts. The day comes, often sooner rather than later, when our rose-colored vision of the beloved shifts. In time, the beloved turns very ordinary.

The Seeker continued, "For me, it was that first disinterested rebuff, then a thoughtless, nasty remark which really stung me. From there it was downhill. I started to grow weary of her incessant giggling, and things we had been passionately interested in started to bore me. I began running out of things to talk about. So did she. Soon enough, I sensed the unpleasant drift of my heart away from what I had so recently cherished. In time, I even came to dread the very sight of 'my beloved.' What once filled my soul with boundless joy now left me stale and lifeless. I craved a new experience: I was no longer 'in love.' Yet, paradoxical as it may seem, monastic tradition has taught me that this is the point where real love can begin — if we so choose. Once we get beyond the initial flush of emotions, once the thrill is gone, then we see what we're really about."

I S IT SURPRISING that a similar dynamic takes place in the spiritual life? Is it shocking to discover that these feelings of inner warmth and electricity, indeed even sexual feelings, may accompany initiates when they first set out on the spiritual way? And that things soon fizzle? In retrospect, most monastics concede that they should have anticipated these realities ahead of time, since it would have saved them no small embarrassment. But the fact is it takes going through the experience oneself to understand and accept that this is altogether common and nothing to be disturbed about.

The Seeker, for one, was entirely familiar with this. "The first time I experienced 'tingly' sensations in prayer after I entered the monastery, for example, I didn't know what to think, other than that the experience was definitely pleasurable, one that I hoped would happen again." (He was slightly embarrassed at this confession.) "I wondered if it meant something significant, so I mustered up the courage to ask another monk, Brother Christopher, about it as we worked one day cleaning the boarding kennels. I was relieved to discover that he knew exactly what I was talking about.

"'When I first turned to God seriously, even before I entered the monastery, I experienced prayer very sensually,' he told me quite casually. 'For several months it was filled with all sorts of spine-tingling physical sensations. Then came the deflation. I suppose I hoped these feelings meant something special, but I learned quite quickly that they were merely the product of me — so basic as to be commonplace. They certainly didn't come from God.'

"I asked him how he could be so sure.

"'Because they eventually disappeared as quickly as they came,' replied Brother Christopher, 'and with no apparent relationship to the way I was living. Trying to will them back didn't work. That, combined with talking with Father Laurence and simply reading some classic texts on prayer, helped me to understand that they were

entirely common early on in the life of prayer. If anything, they were a sign that I was only at the beginning. Father told me to relax, and just be faithful to my prayer, no matter what feelings arose, paying close attention to my thoughts.' Brother Christopher smiled at me and added, 'Don't worry, you'll get over it.'"

Judging from the remarks of many monks and nuns that we've spoken with over the years, as well as our own experiences, that assessment is fairly standard. True, some writers have described such feelings more positively as "God's initial favors" in the spiritual life, his way of encouraging us when we begin to change ourselves for the better — his "consolations," to be followed by less sensual, more "spiritually pure" experiences. We're suspicious of such jargon. We prefer to think of them as the natural consequence of the radical break with our former life — of conversion, if you will.

Anytime we deal with profound life changes, on whatever level, the psychological dynamics involved can be extremely powerful, resulting in inner experiences of varying intensity. When the slate of life has been wiped clean, we can begin anew. As happens in any conversion, we feel reborn. Through the joy and relief implicit in such an experience, we discover that we have been forgiven an enormous debt, the accumulation of a lifetime of alienation and denial. How could that not lead to a deep sense of inner joy and peace? Yet it is altogether natural.

Monks, like most sensible people, are wary of discussing such conversions, and we certainly don't intend to go into detail about them here. Suffice it to say that the ways they can occur are numerous, and they can happen more than once in one's life: sometimes they occur quietly, in an unassuming manner; at other times they may be more obvious and dramatic, as when an alcoholic or drug addict finally wakes up to the depths his life has sunk to and seeks help. No matter what the circumstances may be, however, their unifying characteristic is that they trigger an emotionally charged inner experience which we quite naturally characterize as "the touch of God."

A guest at the monastery was speaking with one of the novices one day, describing his recent conversion to Orthodoxy. "It's been such a blessing, you just can't imagine! I feel such support from the people in the parish — totally different from where I formerly went to church. And the services, well, they've made such a difference in my prayer life! For the first time in so long, God feels very, very close."

The novice listened politely, having the good sense to recognize that the individual was on a religious "high," and not wanting to belittle that. He had experienced something similar himself, and he understood that in the context of conversion this is something all of us go through. Yet it illustrates perfectly the dynamic involved whenever we make a serious change for the better. Our emotional reaction is profound and often exaggerated, and we naturally overflow with unbridled gratitude. For a time, we live with a palpable sense of God's presence, as pungent and pervasive as the finest incense. We fall in love with God, and for a while, everything is wonderful.

So this is a legitimate, powerful, inner awakening that always happens at the time of conversion. The temptation here, however, is to think that we have finally arrived when actually we are just beginning. Even in a monastery, novices will encounter this to one degree or another as they begin their new life dedicated to God. It takes a lot of hard work to attain a broader perspective.

The Seeker experienced this intensely: "I barely remember my first months in the monastery, so filled were they with fascinating newness. I was so busy immersing myself in a new identity that the possibility that this high would be short-lived didn't really occur to me. Instead, my thoughts whispered, 'If it feels this good now, just think what it will be like when I really grow, when I really become a mystic.' When I confided this thought to Father one day not too long after my entry, he couldn't keep from chuckling. I was a little annoyed with his teasing, but on a more even note he added, 'It's better for me not to say anything. You'll discover soon enough the real meaning and purpose of these first days.'"

No doubt it is embarrassing to recall such thoughts later in life, but as we have said, there is comfort in discovering that this dynamic is common when starting out on the spiritual path. This is the time of *first fervor,* when the initial emotional response to change manifests itself in unalloyed optimism and vitality. The beginner's desire and determination to embrace a radical change in life — a real conversion — conspires with the complete newness of outlook and circumstances to manufacture a deceptive sense of peace and well-being. God is ineluctably close, and the novice takes on new works and spiritual exercises willingly and joyfully.

The Seeker explained, "When I became a novice, everything about monastic life was new and interesting: overnight, I became one of a group of like-minded people whose chief priority in life was to search for God. The rhythm of the life I had embraced supported this down to the very minute. Life was choreographed for holiness, with set times for work, prayer, and relaxation. A perfect script. Everyone was so decent, so encouraging. From the beginning, I couldn't help being impressed with the community's sense of seriousness and dedication."

He paused. "The monastic culture itself reinforced this sense of newness, too. I took a new name, a new identity, which further distanced me from the awkwardness of a less than comforting past. Instead of secular clothes, I now wore a religious habit to services, the sign of my new state in life. Intellectually, the environment was quite stimulating, as well; we received approximately ten hours of instruction each week on all facets of the spiritual life, and had a library chock full of wisdom at our disposal.

"Then there was the monastery itself. Self-contained and beautiful, its cluster of buildings blended effortlessly in harmony with the wooded landscape, a constant reminder of our new purpose. Another brother with whom I was in the novitiate remembers: 'For me, whenever I felt the need for a spiritual boost, simply walking around the grounds and gazing at the buildings, or looking across the valley as the red-tailed hawks cut patterns in the sky, or walking slowly around the church did the trick, reinforcing for some time the sense of peacefulness I had come to expect.' Each of us has our ways."

The Seeker was now deep in his memories. "Over and above all these things, however, at the heart of the life — supporting everything — was the steady liturgical prayer anchoring the day in the service of God. No parish that I was aware of could match the sheer beauty evoked by the services. In the liturgical offices, everything was brought together. Instead of the fragmented existence I had wrestled with in the world, here everything harmonized effortlessly. As I floated through those first months, I couldn't help thinking I was finally on the way to sanctity, a new creature absolved of the aimlessness of a former existence.

"But soon enough this grace period passed, and almost without realizing it, I discovered myself in a new phase, one pruned of many of the sensuous and mental spiritual comforts I had until so recently come to enjoy. I'm not certain how long it took for them to dry up — maybe six months, maybe longer — but gradually everything became different, more mundane. Nothing had changed, yet everything had changed. When I complained to Father Laurence about this, he looked at me for a moment and then said, 'This is very good.'

"'What do you mean?' I snapped. Did he catch the tone of indignation?

"'Because now you're going to get to know yourself in a new way, closer to who you really are.' I remember him looking at me directly. 'What happens to your dedication when you're not getting emotionally rewarded for it? You didn't forget about the struggle, did you? What do you think we've been talking about in class? Haven't there been enough references to this?' Of course, he was absolutely right."

Once we pass through the honeymoon stage of spirituality, the period of first fervor, our spiritual practice becomes routine, and we start to experience the ordinary ups and downs of life. If we happen to be in the monastery, we have been told repeatedly that this would happen, but our disappointment shows that we really didn't understand: we were secretly hoping that we would be the exception to the rule. Usually the transition happens gradually. Gently, but inexorably, our experience forces us to confront the fact that our new rule of life is no longer emotionally gratifying; at least, not like it used to be.

"You mean to tell me all of this is necessary?" groaned the Seeker.

"This is the real beginning of spiritual life, when the hard work starts," Father continued. "Up to now, everything's been preliminary — and delightful! Forget that now — now there's no candy, no unusual emotional gratification. So what do you do? Did you really mean what you said when you were received into the community, that the search for God is what you really desire? Now is the time to recall the enthusiasm of our first fervor, the determination to offer ourselves unreservedly, and at the same time to let go of the craving for emotional consolation." Father shrugged his shoulders. "If it comes, okay; if it doesn't come, okay."

Monastic tradition teaches that this breaking free from emotional dependency doesn't happen all at once but goes on throughout our lives. It entails a spiritual battle on many fronts, which is supremely challenging whether we are veteran or neophyte. Just how challenging became painfully obvious to the Seeker in those ensuing months, once the novelty of the spiritual life had passed. Father Laurence's counsel notwith-standing, he seemed lost in a very existential question: What does it mean when spirituality no longer *feels good?* . . . What do you do? There were days when everything was normal; yet in experiencing the mundane realities of the spiritual life, he inevitably found his former idealism tempered. Soon, the let-down caused him to become increasingly alarmed. *What do my feelings mean?* When we are in the throes of such a phase, it is small comfort to be told that no matter what our state in life, the echoes of this question within us are a sign that we are finally in the foothills of the spiritual life.

For this young monk, the symptoms of his crisis started to spread like wildfire, and it is the same for all beginners, in or out of monasteries. Suddenly, the "saints" he had been living with started to lose their luster, until finally their roughness began to grate on his nerves.

"I resented their treating me like a newcomer," he said, "always telling me what to do, and correcting me whenever I did things differ-ently from the norm. I began rationalizing such feelings and coming to the dubious conclusion that monastic life was keeping me a depen-dent adolescent instead of allowing me to become a mature adult.

"The work I was doing, often simple manual labor, became boring and monotonous, 'dehumanizing' in my crankier moments. Even worse, where my first attempts at prayer had involved exhilarating moments of transcendence and even physical sensation, now prayer became routine, often dry as a bone. Sitting in God's presence in prayer felt like turning the car key in deep winter and hearing nothing but the sick drone of the starter. I started searching inwardly for what

might be wrong: 'Perhaps if only I were better, this wouldn't be hap-
pening,' assuming this testing was a sign of divine disapproval."

At this point, whether one happens to be in a monastery or in the world, the spiritual landscape, far from being paradise, becomes a roaring wilderness. The former comforts we knew seem remote, almost illusory. Without realizing it, we are reliving the experience of Moses and Israel in the desert. Having fled from our former bondage, our exodus now has us wandering in circles, with no *perceptible* signs that we are getting anywhere. We clamor for the consolations of the recent past, as unchecked thoughts and feelings batter us, insisting that we are wasting our lives in a meaningless pursuit.

The darker the moment, the more we doubt our ability to go on. Though the expression can be somewhat melodramatic, this "dark night" is simply part and parcel of being human, and it is known in every spiritual tradition, though not necessarily by the same name. Without guidance, the novice can easily misinterpret this experience and allow his life to go crashing onto the rocks. Though usually described as a stage that we pass through, it is really a recurring feature of the spiritual trek, threatening us throughout our lives with a stark confrontation with nothingness and despair. It is the terror of the inner wilderness — and of life itself! The truth is that the farther we go in the spiritual life, the more accustomed to and less threatened we are with this "dark night." Early on, however, its utter starkness can easily deceive us into the ultimate mistake — *giving up* the spiritual journey.

Help is crucial at this point, which is why monastics are so fortunate in undergoing this purgation in the monastery. Often when people encounter this by themselves, in the world, there is no incentive to continue, no one to show the way. How many times over the years have visitors to our monastery admitted that the reason they let their spiritual life slide was that it had grown so dry and mundane; they felt they were getting nothing back in return for their effort. "Who needs *this?*" one woman remembered thinking crassly when her daily meditation period proved unbearably boring. Indeed, without the support of other, more experienced practitioners, how many people really have the self-discipline to meditate every day, in and out of season?

Monastic tradition is profoundly conscious of the need for help, both in the form of an experienced elder and the support of our brothers or sisters in the monastery, as well as the broader wisdom accumulated by centuries of monks and nuns. Because we placed so much emphasis on the emotional way we sensed God's presence, we can easily feel betrayed when it disappears, as if we had been suckered into falling for some sort of cruel hoax.

Accordingly, we might attempt to meet the challenge of God's absence by desperately trying to regain the thrill of our former experiences. In vain we strain to practice breathing exercises with our prayer, hyperventilating until we feel that "tingle" again, or reflecting again on Scripture passages that formerly provided us with great insight and comfort. Or we might latch onto cynicism, because we feel that our ideals have been reduced to nothing. Both attitudes are dead ends and are doomed to failure. Cynicism leads us to despair, while fixating on the efforts that seemed to work in the past makes an idol out of spiritual states.

The Seeker reflected on his own struggle: "When I admitted to Father Laurence these attempts at restoring my spiritual equilibrium, he shook his head resolutely. 'All that stuff's futile, counterproductive. It's simply feeding an illusion. What you're failing to realize is that nothing is wrong: spiritual dryness is not a problem. It only seems a problem because it's such a contrast with the good feelings of the honey-moon stage.'

" 'How can I know that?'

" 'Because I'm telling you this. Believe me, this night will continue to go on, often getting worse, throughout our life. But if we persevere in our spiritual journey, we will be able to perceive in it positive meaning and learn to understand it. Then we can move beyond it to the freedom that places our feelings in proper perspective.' "

So our greatest fear proves groundless! God hasn't abandoned us at all! Indeed, there is no place where God is not present. His presence is not contingent upon our *feeling* it. It simply is. We must learn to remember this and calm ourselves. By his apparent "absence," God is leading us to a more mature level of consciousness, self-offering, and love. He is leading us from the love of God for the sake of his gifts to love of God for his own sake. As we progress further in the spiritual journey, we discover that what is really happening to us is more akin to giving birth. Any mother knows the *life* that comes out of the pain of childbirth. The same can be said for the process of being born spiritually.

Despite the profound interior discomfort this entails, we actually discover that this stage is crucial to our growth, for it begins to teach us how to deal with feelings. It leads us to an awareness that feelings are arbitrary and no basis for judging spiritual merit. Instead, we learn to direct our energy to what we can control: beginning again, fresh, every day, with the same determination we possessed at the start, but without the craving to feel good about it. We must habitually let go of "our" spiritual experiences and not cling to them. When we happen to be feeling good, monastic tradition tells us to focus on what has yet to be done. Should we be caught in the throes of boredom and discouragement, we need to look patiently toward our goal. Two of the desert fathers put it in this way:

> Abba Moses asked Abba Sylvanus, "Can a person lay a new foundation every day?" The old man replied, "If you work hard, you can lay a new foundation every moment."
>
> Abba Pimen said, "To throw yourself before God, not to measure your progress, to leave behind all self-will; these are the instruments for the work of the soul."

In fact, this is no different from what Saint Paul says at a pivotal moment in his letter to the Philippians:

> Not that I claim to have reached . . . perfection already. But I keep going on. . . . I do not consider myself to have grasped it fully even now. But I do concentrate on this: I forget all that lies behind me and with hands outstretched to whatever lies ahead, I go straight for the goal — my reward the honor of my high calling by God in Christ Jesus. (Philippians 3:12–14)

To begin again in this manner is really to move forward, to break free of the self and its craving for titillation. In fact, such self-forgetful behavior is characteristic of enthusiasm. Father Laurence likes to remind us that "enthusiasm" comes from the Greek words *en* and *Theos,* which means, so to speak, the quality of being immersed in God; in this case, to be so inspired by and passionately dedicated to the pursuit of spiritual growth that we ultimately come to union with God. Enthusiasm should characterize our fundamental spiritual disposition, independent of emotional ups and downs.

"To be enthusiastic means to be really alive, not in some superficially emotional, bubbly way, but from being possessed by a more intense vision of reality," Father explained recently at a community discussion. "If we look at the Gospels without prejudice, Jesus Christ is clearly a model of such enthusiasm.

Throughout the highs and lows of his life, Jesus lived with a profound enthusiasm that is not to be confused with his very human feelings. Believe me, he felt them all. But it didn't matter; he was literally filled with God — fully alive, because he held back nothing in carrying out his total dedication to the Father. He broke free of self-protectiveness and self-concern — he loved without reserve, with his whole heart, mind, body, and soul."

We shall come back to this theme again and again from different angles, for it is the core truth of our tradition and the basis of all spiritual practice. When we try to live in this spirit, we begin to learn to let go peacefully of our anxieties, fears, resentments, and blindness. We become attentive to the world around us in a new way, aware of other people and their needs in a new way, and vividly conscious not only of the beauty and goodness of everything around us, but of suffering and despair as well. And strangely, to the extent that our focus shifts away from ourselves and our many concerns, instead of disappointment, we receive a fullness that remains with us despite our emotional highs and lows. We become perennially enthusiastic. As we learn these shifts of attitude, we also acquire the wisdom of loving as Jesus loved — *agapê* — without being held back by *our* feelings or by concern for what *we* shall get for *our* trouble. We discover that God fills us to the extent that we *let go of ourselves* and give ourselves in this kind of love. As the saying goes, God cannot fill what is already filled with itself.

NONE OF US is the first to walk this path. We can each draw strength and confidence from the wisdom of tradition, which insists categorically that if we are serious, the only reasonable course is to move forward faithfully, into the depths of our desolation if necessary, trusting in God, getting beyond our need for spiritual highs, and knowing that we shall come through this experience alive in a way we never thought possible.

This is first fervor stripped of all immaturity and sentimentality, which becomes the wholly necessary "zeal for the house of God" that consumed the psalmist. Understood in this sense, first fervor fuels the process of spiritual transformation that Saint Paul said would take us "from one degree of glory to another," transforming us into the image of the God whom we seek. This is why Saint John Climacus, a seventh-century Sinai monk, exhorted his disciples:

> Now who is the faithful and wise monk? It is the one who has all along maintained the ideals of his vocation, who adds fire to fire, fervor to fervor, love to love, and this to the end of his days.

To embrace this path is to go from first fervor to true fervor, from sentimental, romantic love to self-giving love, from the fire of emotions to the fire of dedication, moving in a continuously upward spiral into the fullness of what we are meant to be.

This is the unanimous consensus of monastic tradition. It can be applied to each of our lives, monk and nonmonk alike. Our concern must be with what we are responsible for: transforming our fervor, our behavior, our love. Throughout the spiritual journey we are required to let go of our preoccupation with "what we can get out of it." To do this courageously is one of the principal efforts and effects of authentic and wholesome spiritual practice. Paradoxical as it may seem, this weaning away from the craving for consolations is an essential spiritual process, one that develops in us an inner freedom allowing us to live and love ever more authentically. In this way the spiritual life is teaching us to give of ourselves regardless of what we feel. Through this process of stripping, the bonds of selfishness that enslave us are being steadily transmuted into bonds of union with God and our fellow human beings.

Though we stare at the publican,
we have no incentive to imitate his repentance,
nor do the tears of the harlot move us to sorrow.
It is the hardness of our hearts, O our saviour,
that makes it impossible for us to change our way of life.
O Lord and lover of mankind,
in your goodness, save us.

Monday morning sessional hymn, Tone Seven

THREE

The Discipline of Change

WE HAVE AN INFORMAL CUSTOM in our monastery. At least once during a beginner's novitiate, all of the monks and nuns gather for an evening to watch community slides of the early days of our foundation. Unlike other slide presentations, in which a captive audience fights to stay awake as image after image of a friend's vacation floods the screen, the novices really seem to enjoy this presentation. It allows them to share vicariously in those formative years, helping to root them in the soil of our community. With each slide, the older community members offer anecdotes spontaneously, describing in often uproarious detail the ups and downs of those pivotal first years. "That's the shale hillside we dug out by hand in the dead of winter, for the first bedroom addition. . . . And see, there's a shot of Father bringing hot toddies to keep us warm. . . ." or "Is that *Stavros* with that cow? . . . Is he supposed to be milking her?" . . . or, more soberly, "There's Tom, just before his death. . . ." Images of building projects and other work, community gatherings and liturgical celebrations, vividly imprint in the novice's mind the reality that *ours* is now *his* history, too. Through photography and imagination, the novices become part of the monastery's beginnings and early development. That they are invariably disappointed when the last picture passes and the lights go on shows how important seeing "our" history is for them.

But viewing the slides is equally meaningful for the older members. As well as renewing the enthusiasm of those first years, these sessions bring home how much each of us has changed through the years, not only in physical appearance but inside.

After a recent session, a number of the monks were talking informally when Brother John observed, "Watching the slides the other night was a bit eerie; it was as if I were looking at images of people who no longer exist. And yet I could vividly recall the events, the attitudes and responses of each one of us in the context of the various slides. That really was me then! Yet when I look at myself now, I'm absolutely astonished, and a bit unsure how I've gotten here. . . . I can't believe how ingeniously change slips by our consciousness unnoticed!"

Perhaps without intending it, he was expressing an unyielding law of the spiritual life. By experiencing the reality of change in ourselves, in this case through the evidence of the slides, we see clearly that we cannot prevent change from happening; but we can choose to direct it in positive and life-enhancing ways.

"I think that's because ordinarily we're not conscious of how we change: we're too close to ourselves," replied Brother Marc. "We look in the mirror and see ourselves as no different than we were twenty years ago. We may know in our heads that we've changed — grown older — but emotionally we don't perceive any difference, and so we can easily overlook the meaning of change. We find it hard to admit that no one can ever stay the same, that attempting to keep things the same is futile —"

Brother Luke interrupted. "I was just reading an article about that by a biochemist. He was explaining how our bodies are in a perpetual state of change, literally rebuilding themselves over the course of years by replacing the cells. Change is occurring perpetually."

"That's fine, but how often do we hear that our conscious-ness and our circumstances change, and have changed?" Father Laurence joined in. "The real question here isn't whether we can or will change, but *how* we will change." We can either embrace the inevitable changes of life or become their passive victims. Whether we want them to or not, things change, and wisdom teaches us to direct the changes for the good, for personal growth and maturity.

Accepting change correctly brings us into harmony with reality, and this in turn gives us a certain peace and tranquil-lity, which is what happiness is really about. Being in touch with, in harmony with, reality is being in harmony with God — the ultimate reality. The aim of all spiritual practice is to enable us to experience this fullness and dynamism — if only in a limited way each day — concretely, whether in washing the dishes or chanting the Psalms.

"Remember when I had my heart attack?" Father asked.

The others nodded as Brother Marc spoke for them all, "How could we forget that?"

"Granted, that was dramatic, but it shows what I mean. My heart attack brought to light what's always going on, but some-thing we rarely notice. Instantaneously everything changed, almost violently. And not just for me — the whole commu-nity was faced with a period of new decisions and serious change. Life forced each of us to deal with the implications of that event." He paused, then filled out the thought. "It wasn't simply whether I would live or die — but were I to have died then, what changes would that have meant for the rest of you? You would have adjusted no doubt, but how? . . . As it turned out, I survived, but still the experience initiated a new period of visible change on many levels for the whole community. For me personally, it's made each day since unique."

One of the novices, Brother Gregory, wanted him to elaborate. "How do you mean?"

"By transforming my fundamental outlook. For starters, that brush with death gave me a new appreciation for what the early monks called *memento mori,* remembering that each of us is going to die. There's nothing morbid about that — it's simple reality. Through the shock of the heart attack, I experienced in a new way the fact that each new day was a gift, a plus, an opportunity to grow. This hit home because I experienced how incredibly tenuous life is." The monks encouraged him to continue. "Believe me, knowing that tonight's sunset might very well be your last changes the way you see it. In a way, I had to learn how to live all over again, in light of this new reality: not simply what medications I'd have to take, what diet, how much work, how much stress I'd be able to take, but how to use every new moment as a chance for further growth."

C LEARLY, THEN, change does not always pass unnoticed. We can rise to its challenge by using it as a goad and an opportunity for our good. Yet the process of change is often painfully unsettling, even when it occurs later in our spiritual journey. Our tendency is to imagine that spirituality takes place where life is most stable and secure, yet it is not just novices who are shocked to discover that the principal work of their monastic life is to struggle with unanticipated calls to change. When a guest recently asked what the most difficult aspect of monastic life was, Brother Christopher emphasized this coming to grips with change: "I'd say learning to accept what changing one's life really means . . . that we can never sit back and think that we've finally made it, that we now have the answers . . . that we don't have to perpetually re-examine everything. . . . Change is painful. We crave security and certitude, but that doesn't seem to be God's way. The sur-prise is discovering that in spiritual life there's nothing to cling to, that all one has is naked faith."

Paradoxically, this is the unchanging principle of spiritual life that monastics discover: that each of us must work con-stantly to change every single aspect of our lives in the light of the goals of the spiritual life. It is a perpetual process.

All of us can easily find ourselves resisting this pull, justify-ing ourselves under the logic that we have already changed, we have already been converted. "I'm fine right where I am, thank you very much. . . ." Monastic tradition is not so short-sighted. It says, "A few steps on the road to eternity are a pit-tance," then goes about its business piercing our illusions. It proceeds to provoke change, radical change at the core of our being, by persistently challenging the way we live, the way we think, the way we look at everything. Like a rude alarm clock that spoils the serenity of early morning, monastic tra-dition, often in the form of a teacher, rouses us mercilessly from our life of sleep, throwing cold water in our faces by the truth of its word.

Sometimes the manner in which this occurs can be quite amusing. Once, two monks were sitting at table with their spiritual father, discussing a point concerning monastic life. The one monk, brilliant and highly educated, loved to hold forth, and took issue with the opinion of the other monk, who was of a much more down-to-earth character. As they spoke, the highly educated monk took the other's position apart point by point, skillfully using the principles of logic and argumentation to utterly tie his brother into verbal knots.

Finally, the second monk conceded the point and left the table somewhat humiliated and embarrassed. It did not take a wizard to see that the monk who came out victorious was more than a little satisfied with himself.

During the course of the debate, the spiritual father had remained silent but listened intently. Now he spoke to the winner. "Brother, you've won the battle, but you've lost the war. You set out to win the argument, but let's pray your self-righteousness hasn't lost you your brother."

L IFE ITSELF IS one great teacher, but we must realize that life uses a variety of means to teach. We change ourselves only by changing our consciousness, but a teacher is usually the catalyst. Be they Buddhist, Muslim, Hindu, Christian, or Jew, all authentic teachers function in this way, for they speak unapologetically for, and in the name of, reality, truth without limit.

In our Christian tradition, genuine teaching comes through meditating and reflecting upon the sacred Scriptures and on spiritual classics, by participating in worship within the community of faith, through insight gleaned in silent prayer, and simply through living within the tradition itself. And as crucial as these are to our learning and growth, they often fail to achieve their effect unless they are reinforced by a competent teacher in the flesh, who confronts us face to face.

"I remember going through an unusually bleak period several years back," said the Seeker. "Totally cynical . . . everything was negative, and no one seemed to be able to get me out of my mood. Finally, in frustration, Father Laurence pulled me aside and said, 'We've run out of words. How is anyone going to get through to you? Don't you see, you're like a match with a wet head — you can't be sparked. No

one can live without fire — on every level of life. C'mon now, wake up!' That word took me so by surprise . . . it was as if he had slapped me. I understood immediately; I was so laden with self-pity that I couldn't be sparked. The deadness was my own doing, and I saw that I alone was responsible for it. That challenging insight proved to be the rope that helped me crawl out of that swamp."

One can learn to play the piano by oneself, but one cannot deny the obvious value of a knowledgeable teacher if one really wishes to excel. Books don't talk back to us — a teacher very often will, and this makes all the difference. In some respects, the teacher is like a coach, spurring the athlete to run more efficiently. *"Wake up!" "Pay attention!"* Though the coach cannot do the running for the runner, the runner achieves his best when the coach does his job. So it is with us — if we are open and unthreatened enough to listen and hear.

What about those of us without formal teachers, without the benefit of a discerning spiritual director, roshi, or guru? The principle still stands firm: if you don't have a teacher, you need to look for one, and you won't find one unless you look. Of course, we have many teachers throughout our lives. Yet in any given area of life, the more difficulties there are in mastering something, the more necessary an experienced and expert teacher is. In developing our inner life, where the possibility of deceiving ourselves is so great, a teacher is less useful for obtaining facts than for forming a trusting relationship in which we can draw from his experience, so as to avoid the trap of self-deception. To use an analogy, if one wished to scale Mount Everest, would it not be wise to procure the services of an experienced and knowledgeable guide? One's life might well depend on it. The stakes are hardly less serious in the spiritual life! By entering wisely into such a relationship, the disciple cultivates the openness, trust, and confidence necessary to grow.

Certainly there will always be those who teach us skills and provide us with facts, but here we are speaking of a relationship in which someone can point out something about ourselves that we are blind to, who is experienced enough in life to see where we are going and to provide firm, effective guidance in the wilderness. Sometimes what they tell us will pierce us to the heart. We think of the arrogant monk who never listened or took to heart anything his abba taught him. One day, in the midst of a crisis of faith, he went to the abba and said, "Abba, give me a word." The abba replied, "No." The brother, shocked, retorted, "Why not?" The abba looked at him calmly. "'No' is not good enough?" And the brother repented.

Even in religion many people try to deny it, for whatever reason, but the fact is that inner growth does not take place without at least a minimal formal teaching. This is why it is so valuable to take seriously the roles local religious leaders — pastors, rabbis, and priests — can play in our spiritual growth and development. These are people who should be able to provide teaching that triggers spiritual growth in our lives.

"I've spent fifteen years looking for a decent teacher, and all I've come up with is frustration," a retreatant recently lamented. "Most of the priests I've met don't want to assume the role of teacher, and the one or two that might have . . . well, . . . let's just say I didn't feel comfortable with them. The whole process is maddening. Would to God I could order one at Sears!" This might be a valid complaint, yet our experience leads us to believe that someone who is really looking for a teacher will find one eventually. What is essential is that the searcher have the right attitude. Granted, the search may take time — even years — but in the meantime, the individual has to have his eyes peeled, and other individuals can certainly help in a more limited way. Sometimes a good friend's common sense is just what we need. But more often the real obstacle to finding a teacher is actually our own reluctance to enter into such a relationship.

"The thing to be careful about," replied Brother Marc to the retreatant tactfully, "is subconsciously looking for a teacher who will rubber-stamp your ideas, as opposed to one who knows what he's talking about and who has the gumption to challenge you. Connecting with a teacher demands a great deal of emotional maturity, humility, openness, trust, and finally commitment. And by the way, why commitment? Because any teacher worth his salt will absolutely call us to change, to think and act differently, to become a new person. That frightens far too many of us."

People today are often threatened by the prospect of having a teacher because they presume that this automatically means they are not in control. Furthermore, the knowledge that certain so-called teachers have erred seriously, especially in their own personal moral lives, is often used as a reason to resist the relationship. But such a protest seems disingenuous. Is it reasonable to dismiss the principle simply because there have been failures to live up to the high standards of spiritual guidance? What in life is perfect?

Being a teacher does not mean being authoritarian, dominating, intimidating, or possessing all the answers. In fact, an authentic teacher tells no one what to do. He or she simply points out realities the learner must consider, and helps the learner to overcome obstacles; it is the latter who must decide, or learn how to decide, what to do. This is why the teacher defies stereotypes. Actually, we cannot imagine that there are not many people who could be teachers, whose education, training, personal growth, and insights make them capable of leading others into more abundant life.

Those who look sincerely and search hard should eventually find the teacher they need (though not necessarily the one they may have initially envisioned).

Describing this phenomenon, the Seeker reflected on his own experience: "Before I actually met Father Laurence, my image of what a teacher would be like was straight out of pious literature: a plaster saint — nice, all-knowing, and heroically ascetic. A lot of people I've talked to about this over the years have said similar things. I see now how totally unreal that image was . . . yet I was lucky. Before it really dawned on me how different Father Laurence was from the stereotype, I saw the fruit of his teaching in the monastery itself, and in my own initial response to his words. From the start, I was pretty sure I had found my teacher; my commitment became real, which is a good thing, because he began to challenge me right away, pushing my buttons and trying to get me to see where I had to change."

Once we actually find a teacher whom we can commit ourselves to and trust, we can still easily be tempted to turn our backs on him (or her) when he fails to be "perfect," that is, when he fails to live up to our unrealistic expectations, when we dislike what he says or how he says it — and this happens more frequently than we care to admit. Examples abound of the disciple who turns away from the teacher simply because the teacher told him a truth the disciple could not accept.

We have to keep in mind that we are learners, not judges. Obviously this does not absolve the disciple from thinking for himself, nor is it to suggest that he should be blindly obedient. Nevertheless, there has to be a basic tonality of trust in the learner if the relationship is going to be fruitful. Though hardly infallible, the true teacher suffers no compromise on matters he understands: he or she is radically committed to truth, with an integrity that mocks our ambivalence. It is true that we appreciate the teacher when we are not in his line of fire, or when his eloquence serves our interests. We are the first to accord him tribute and respect. But how we squirm when the teacher highlights our own duplicity, calling us to task as well. Then our smiles vanish; consternation is written all over us, and we resist accepting it. It is all so basic: change is for the other person, not me.

Monks and nuns have always known this scenario only too well. Living with a teacher gives them ample experience. Even when he speaks gently, the abba (or spiritual father) roars! Recently, after witnessing a number of recurring disagreements between monks in the community, Father Laurence confronted all of us on the issue of how frivolously we were taking our life together. "How long are you going to insist on hanging on to your own opinions? Don't you see . . . this is precisely the problem — phony discipleship. The phony disciple is like a dried sponge, a sponge that is so old, that has sat around collecting the dust and grime of life, that when you throw it into a bathtub it simply floats! It doesn't absorb water." Bull's-eye!

Such honesty cuts through the subterfuge and gets right to the point. The teacher worth his salt repeatedly points out the signs of intransigence in us in a most uncompromising and direct way, as when we bristle at a helpful correction, or refuse the olive branch in a difficult situation. How annoying it is to have such faults so baldly pointed out, to be shown that our thinking is wrong, that our emotions are blinding us! Even worse is realizing what these corrections signify: that we are still stuck in self-centeredness, miles from the transformation we are called to make.

In fact, this is the problem in a nutshell: while we might be more than willing to accept teaching on an academic or professional level, when it comes to the way we are as individuals, how we think and act, we don't like being told that there is anything wrong with our mind-set or behavior. Yet that is what the true teacher must point out. That is what true teaching is about.

Shouldn't we be grateful for the teacher's candor, in whatever setting it appears, for a voice that keeps us honest?

A GOOD TEACHER KNOWS that deliberate change for the better always requires repentance, literally changing one's mind. It might surprise us to learn that the Greek word for repentance, *metánoia* (pronounced meh-táhn-ee-ah), means, literally, changing one's mind: *meta* = change, *noia* = mind. Period.

What is the change of mind, the repentance that the Greek is referring to? Certainly not the distorted popular image sentimentalized religion promulgates; even less the choreographed displays of trendy fundamentalist televangelists. Focusing on narrow conceptions that ignore the wider reality, they seem to lack any in-depth understanding of how all-encompassing repentance really is, how radical its commitment. *Metánoia* results in a new way of looking at everything; it is a conscious and conscientious new awareness of life and its implications, beginning, of course, with our own life. As a result of this new way of looking at things, we are spurred on to make the often difficult changes consistent with our new outlook. In our tradition this certainly characterizes the message of Jesus, the teacher par excellence.

The first words Jesus utters in the Gospel of Mark explode with a new authority: "*Metanoîte* . . . repent, change the way you look at things, your whole outlook on life!" *Metánoia* connotes far more than a static repentance. Nor is Jesus talking about "feeling sorry" for our sins — some superficial emotional cleansing whose only real purpose is to rid us of unpleasant guilt feelings (or, possibly, even to increase them!). He means a complete about-face, a spiritual revolution in which our former way of thinking is thrown topsy-turvy, and so, by extension, our behavior as well. What is more, Jesus also speaks of it as a process that never ends: it deepens and spreads into every aspect of our life, like leaven in dough.

Metánoia is not an isolated act of conversion, of coming to "believe in God," which is only the first step in a total transformation of life. To follow the spiritual path authentically is to be immersed, baptized into a river of change, to die to our old rigidities. Jesus tells us from the start that lively, true belief will turn long-cherished opinions and ingrained attitudes upside down, plunging the life of anyone who takes his message seriously into the "insecurity of faith."

> "It is fire I that I have come to bring upon the earth — how I could wish it were already ablaze! . . . Do you think I have come to bring peace on the earth? No, I tell you, not peace, but division. . . ." (Luke 12:49, 51)

Lest we take such words lightly, it is worth remembering how far Jesus was willing to go to engender this understanding: he gave his life for it. Throughout his ministry, Jesus' principal work was to get people to see beyond delusion to reality, to lead them to change, and this meant challenging the way we look at everything: *metánoia* — life turned upside down.

Not everyone was enthusiastic about Jesus' message. Those who weren't — particularly the *religious* authorities — bitterly resented and disapproved of his teaching. Their preconceptions and rigid knowledge of the law allowed them "the place of honor at banquets, and the best seats in the synagogues, to [be] greeted obsequiously in the marketplaces, while in turn neglecting justice and the love of God." In other words, their spiritual understanding was barren. It was all surface, because it went no deeper, no farther than their own self-interest.

Characteristically, Jesus called them "unmarked graves." He spoke this way not because he lacked sympathy or understanding for human weakness; in fact, his compassion knew no limits. But he also had little patience with those who felt no need of mercy or forgiveness, whose arrogant blindness and lack of self-knowledge resulted in a disdain of others. By taking dead aim at his opponents' hypocrisy, Jesus threatened their whole way of looking at themselves. He challenged them to change; this, more than anything, was most responsible for his death.

Not everyone reacted this way. For those who were able to see beyond the turbulence of their own emotions, Jesus revealed a new geography of a human being's inner world. With this came an overflowing fulfillment of the will of God expressed in Scripture: *"I came that they may have life, and have it more abundantly."* (*John 10:10*) Jesus made the bold assertion that following his way would bring the disciple to the source of life. He also showed that it would not be easy. He never hid from his disciples the fact that *metánoia* would involve a wrestling with fear of the unknown, with resistance and opposition on all sides. Yet he always set this against the deeper purpose of our inner transformation and a new way of living together. For Jesus, the change initiated by *metánoia* would be continuous, eternal. Our true destiny is to grow into oneness with all in God.

Thus, the correct understanding of repentance, of changing one's mind, is alien to illegitimate and unreasonable self-interests, whatever they may be. Whether we selfishly exploit and manipulate reality to our own ends — or wallow in self-pity, excusing our stumblings and laziness as the inevitable result of circumstances beyond our control, the teacher's challenge comes in the same irritating package: each of us must change, over and over again.

When asked how he reacted to such criticism, the Seeker was quite candid. "In the beginning, as I look back on it now, especially, I can see that I didn't even get it; the implications of repentance just sailed right over my head. Then as I began to get the picture, I was still distressingly pig-headed. I was so used to presuming the validity of my own way of thinking and acting that I actually started to resent Father's observations (as well as those of some of the other monks and nuns, for that matter).

"Take diet: originally I thought we ate too well, that we weren't ascetic enough. I couldn't see the wisdom in eating a healthy, appetizing diet, and Father confronted me on this a number of times. My tendency was to respond defensively, coming back with pious justifications for my beliefs, indirectly setting myself above him as well as the rest of the community. Looking back at it now, it was a colossal exercise in pride! I was interested only in proving that I was right, that my opinions were correct. I wasn't really interested in discovering the truth."

In fact, this is altogether common in the religious journey. It hurts our pride to think our moral and spiritual lives should be anything other than the way we conceive them. Even worse, we often use our religious beliefs to defend such intransigence. Ironically, religion then becomes the problem — preserving a safe status quo in the guise of "fidelity to tradition." What a smoke screen! We show ourselves more interested in proving we are right, and that our opinions need no corrective, than in spiritual integrity and a more objective awareness of how we really are. Instead of changing for the better, our lives grow all the more smug and self-absorbed.

Fortunately for us, the true teacher will give us no rest. He never appears to be satisfied. Yet his satisfaction has nothing to do with it. He is tireless and uncompromising, relentlessly urging us to go beyond ourselves only because he is concerned with our growth. He is neither fooled nor impressed by false piety — what someone has termed "piosity." He is only too well aware of how easy it is to go through the motions of everyday life, monastic or otherwise, while our hearts remain as hard and cold as stone, and, we might add, as barren. Going through all the motions of spiritual living has no purpose if it does not first teach our inner spirits and outer behavior love and compassion, urge us toward authenticity, and help us to become more God-like.

A dynamic priest-friend of ours shocked his parish at the beginning of Lent with a sermon that ignored the traditional things people tend to "give up" or "do" for the forty days. Instead, he focused on scouring the blasé attitude of their hearts. "Who needs your religiosity, your fasts, icons, prostrations, services, Bible studies, periods of meditation, and good works," he said pointedly, "when they are not rooted in your heart, permeating your thoughts and actions with goodness? And you claim you are good? When is the last time that you really looked at your life honestly?"

Ironically, "religious" people are often the most resistant to change, precisely because they think they have already changed; theirs is the story of seed that falls on barren ground. Change, repentance, already occurred at some point or event in the past that led to a spiritual commitment.

Whether it was at an altar call in a football stadium, or through a private prayer of dedication in a quiet chapel, we might frame that moment so decisively that it becomes a once-and-for-all turnabout, an event never to be repeated: we are saved, we are enlightened. Yet despite the undeniable emotional weight of such experiences, to stop here would be shallow, to miss the point, since all change is only incremental. The pattern, the *habit* of change is what counts. To be satisfied with a one-time conversion is to reduce the turnabout to an event rather than a way of life, and to fall far short of what could be achieved. That it ignores the nitty-gritty of our very uneven and imperfect lives should make us uneasy. Repentance is an ongoing process.

This is the lesson the Seeker learned. "Responding to criticism, being challenged to change, was very difficult at first. But in my own case, as I gradually grew to trust Father and the community, I did start thinking more and more about what they were telling me. From our private conversations, and from observing him in the daily life of the monastery, I recognized that Father had no personal agenda against me, nor were his observations personal attacks. He was simply telling me truths directly. The fact that I finally saw for myself how defensive I was set me to thinking that maybe there was plenty else I wasn't seeing. Gradually, I calmed down and began taking what he said very seriously."

We need not be surprised that this word "change" inspires a stampede of panic within, for change always means a confrontation for us with the unknown. To consider changing at all is itself a threatening confession of dissatisfaction with the present. Given the choice, we would much prefer denying anything is amiss, believing that we have already arrived at the point where no change is needed, that center of eternal stability. Our hearts, however, know only too well that it is not so. Like those pioneers who again and again had the courage to pick up their belongings and go after their dreams, this journey will require the rest of our lives.

H*ow could we be so mistaken about change?* In reality, the summons to change is liberating, which is why a message so allied with change could be called "gospel," good news. True life never develops without change, and ongoing change is at the heart of all genuine spiritual traditions. None of us is exempt from this.

"So how does such change take place? *How do we change?*" asked a guest recently in reaction to a sermon she had heard Father Laurence preach earlier that morning. "He didn't really spell that out for us."

"Nor should he have," replied Brother James. "We each have to apply the teaching to our own lives, in our own situations. But we can say this: Changing doesn't mean becoming some kind of perfect being. Human beings by nature are incapable of being perfect; failure to grasp this truth is fatal, and misguided scrupulosity is as unrealistic as it is unhealthy. When Jesus said, *'Be perfect as your heavenly Father is perfect,'* he meant that we should shape up and do our very best to realize our capacities, just as the Father, so to speak, realizes his."

"That still sounds extremely vague to me," the woman said, visibly annoyed. "How do you expect us to change if you don't tell us how to clearly?"

Brother James answered, "Inner change has to come from the heart, not by simply following someone else's behavioral prescriptions. Only then will it be authentic, and honest. Only then will it be real change. Changing our behavior *is* essential to any true spirituality, but unless it flows from a deeper change at the very core of our being, permeating every area of our life, we'll just be spinning our wheels. We'll never become that new person, because the change will only be cosmetic. To change radically means waking up to reality as it really is, not as we presume it is. This demands a fundamental shift in our thinking: put simply, it means becoming other-centered, instead of self-centered. But here, too, we see the crucial need of a teacher."

Other-centeredness gives shape to the amorphous body of love. If this sounds strange, perhaps it is because we have not understood how thoroughly we as individuals are caught in the illusion of being the center of the universe. We have enshrined ourselves in the kingdom of self and we do not even realize it! We filter everything we experience through the lens of our own mentality — our likes and dislikes, our goals and desires, our beliefs and opinions — and we think that this is how things actually are or should be. The ancient thinkers thought that the sun orbited the earth; we think the world orbits us. We judge everything from only our own perspective.

Unfortunately, that perspective is severely limited. When we die, the world still persists. To change radically, we must let go of the death grip we have on ourselves so we can go on to discover what true life is. We must learn to see anew. This does not happen by knowledge alone; it also demands sustained spiritual practice that focuses the mind, that disciplines our energies and emotions, that functions like a plow digging up the hard, fallow ground of our old ways of thinking and acting.

Tested by centuries of experience, the wisdom of monastic tradition provides rich and practical guidance in implementing this change. It uses specific methods: placing oneself under a teacher, developing a daily habit of study, prayer, and meditation, worship in common, and work and service to others, to mention only the more obvious. We shall be exploring these disciplines later, and how they can be translated into the everyday life of any true searcher. But here we can say that this "other-centered" practice means striving to let go of the old self that is so focused on its own petty concerns. Other-centered practice works to create our new self, a whole and healed person. Within such a dynamic, *metánoia* reorients our being from "me" (self) to "God" (other beyond self). This takes on the strength of a habitual way of living the more we give ourselves to it in earnest. Through courageous and faithful practice, we engage life on progressively deeper levels.

It is true that we often fall short of such ideals. The frenetic pace of everyday life and the stress of competing interests and obligations prevent us from observing the true state of our lives, from self-discipline, and from renewing our minds and ways of acting. But it is always within our power to change. Sometimes the new "me" will manifest itself in something as seemingly banal as listening with complete attention to another, when we'd rather be watching our favorite television show. Each moment, in harmony with our changing spiritual outlook, we must remember to *redirect* ourselves toward our primary intention, for our old ways are still ingrained. Is it for self, or is it other-directed? Any act, even the most virtuous, can be approached incorrectly, egotistically. Our task is to work continuously to clean up our hearts, our intentions, our fundamental stance toward life.

As we advance in doing this, then more and more will our life achieve its purpose, whatever the outcome of our individual actions. There is an irresistible dynamism in *metánoia,* an élan that continually surprises, that creates a larger view of life and refashions us constantly into new people.

What Is a Monk?

You taught us to live in the spirit.
Hymn to monk saints

Though most people probably assume that a monk's life is entirely different from their own, the reality might surprise them. The Russian author Dostoevsky put it best when he claimed that a true monk is nothing other than what everyone ought to be. He was referring to an attitude of heart, *a way of seeing life,* not an appeal for celibacy.

What makes someone truly a monk is his interior attitude, not the practical externals associated with his state of life; externals are cultural and hence relative. Long hair and long beards are "monastic" in one milieu, while shaved heads are the norm in another; some monks don't eat meat while others do, some wear habits while others don't. Trying to determine what is more monastic on the basis of such criteria is futile. Though monks and nuns tend to have strong opinions about how they should live, they usually will concede that the essence of their lives goes much deeper than such banalities.

The questions that consume us, which all human beings must face to one degree or another if they ever hope to achieve maturity and real happiness — these are what characterize monks and nuns. *There is a monastic, contemplative dimension in every human being's life.* Monks have simply chosen to pursue this formally in a full-time, radical way.

"Monk" translates the Greek *mónachos,* which comes from *monos,* one, one alone. Though this etymology has been used interminably to justify the solitary life of the hermit as the purest vision of what a monk is (conjuring up eccentric images of monks as unsociable people-haters), such an interpretation is mistaken and misleading. Monks don't hate people, of course; in fact they ordinarily live together in close-knit communities, not off alone by themselves. Granted that there have always been hermit-monks, yet from earliest times *mónachos* was readily applied to those monks living together and sharing everything in common, and it is entirely gratuitous to presume that solitaries were the more authentic monastics by virtue of their isolation.

Again, *mónachos* implies an attitude that goes beyond pursuing security and the usual goals of any individual or society. It also means unique, one with Christ. It in turn translated the Hebrew word *yahid,* which means "exile," one displaced from one's true homeland. This, more than anything else, is what characterizes the true monk. To discover and encounter the true God and find our real home in this reality is the monk's perennial task, making him by nature a wanderer (though living in one place), a pilgrim (though already tasting the goal), exploring the vast wilderness of the human heart (though guided by those who went before him).

Thus, the monk's deepest reality lies beyond simplistic definitions and the various ways monastic life manifests itself. Instead, a monk tries to embody a particular vision of what life is with an intense singularity of purpose. Specifically, the Christian monk focuses entirely on the relationship of the divine and human, and inspired by the example of Jesus, he is consumed with the meaning and experience of this mystery in each moment of his life. This is his joy and delight, yet it also becomes an unquench-able passion that refuses him rest. This is why Saint Dionysius, a sixth-century Syrian monk, called those people monks whose lives are free of division or fragmentation and who strive for the highest beauty, truth, and unity.

What further motivates the monk, fires his imagination, is a desire to live in such a way that life fully blossoms as it is intended by the creator. This is why monasticism is a universal phenomenon, why it arises so naturally in so many religious cultures and even outside these: it gives voice to something intrinsic to the human condition. Though naturally and intimately linked to religion, monasteries ultimately defy sectarian boundaries. They bear witness to the mysterious something that transcends religious differences and really concerns us all, for it is the source of all that is, of life, goodness, and hope. Traditionally we call this reality God, the Supreme Being and Creator, though we readily acknowledge that the name of the thing is not the thing itself. What is important is each person's response to it.

Give our poor souls the desire for repentance, O Christ,
and a passion for true compunction.
Awaken us from the sleep that paralyzes us,
and soften our stubborn, hardened hearts.
Dispel from us all despair and laziness of spirit;
remove the pall of gloom that wickedness throws over us;
and receive us back into your love, O word of God,
that we may faithfully follow you from this moment on,
doing your will in all things.

Sunday evening sticheron, Tone Two

FOUR

Asceticism and Life

THERE IS A FAMOUS ICON that is widely depicted within our monastic tradition called "The Ladder of Divine Ascent," which features a ladder extending from earth all the way to heaven. On the rungs a procession of monks is prayerfully making its ascent to the heavenly regions, and at the top, Jesus himself receives them into his embrace. At the upper left of the icon floats a chorus of brightly colored angels, cheering the monks on, while to either side of the ladder, buzzing like flies around a summer picnic, are sinister demons shooting arrows at the monks and trying to pull them off as they ascend. In fact, to the ladder's right, a number of monks are tumbling downward and being dragged mercilessly into the pits of hell below.

For those who remain on the ladder, the secret that enables them to continue ascending is, significantly, that their eyes are fixed on Jesus. Totally God-centered, looking neither to left nor to right, and with hands open as a sign of prayer, these monks are on the path of spiritual transformation — what Orthodox tradition calls *théosis,* divinization, the process of becoming like God.

This icon is a powerful symbol beckoning us to the challenges of the spiritual life. Yet life is not a gauntlet with devils ready to ambush us at every moment, so we should not take this depiction too literally. There is certainly enough fear and anxiety in modern life already, without further reinforcing them with pietistic fantasies that would distract us from the real point of the icon: each human being's life is a journey, an "ascent" to God, and we need to give our maximum effort if we hope to reach our goal. The effects of such effort can be revolutionary.

The Seeker remembered one of the novice classes Brother Marc had given to him and a fellow novice shortly after they had entered the monastery. It had opened his eyes to the scope of the spiritual task that lay before him, as well as to the fact that we alone are responsible for our own growth; we can't blame our mistakes on anyone except ourselves, much less legions of demons whose sole task is to make us fall. In fact, this had perplexed the Seeker at first. "What about the realm of demons?" the Seeker had asked. "So much of what I've been reading in the early fathers seems to say precisely that they're omnipresent, ready to ambush us at every step. Are you saying all that's just fiction?"

"It depends on your understanding," Brother Marc had replied. "It doesn't seem that we ought to take it too literally." Apparently the Seeker's expression asked for more, for Brother Marc went on: "Look, we have to be very careful how we take some of what the early fathers wrote. Their teaching contains nuggets that are quite perceptive, and absolutely relevant, but their way of thinking differs from ours in many crucial respects. That's the inevitable result of generation after generation learning new things, in many different cultural settings, often coming to a better understanding of the way reality actually is. Yet a lot of people don't seem to appreciate this at all. For example, if you were a doctor, would you treat your patients with fourth-century remedies? No? Why not? Why should it be any different in the inner life? Imagining that we struggle against demons may be useful as a poetic and psychological device to help focus our attention and motivate us to behave as we should, but that's very different from treating it as an

empirical, scientific reality. Though many people today still believe that demons exist who are constantly harassing us, it seems more likely that the negative and malign forces that we encounter really spring from our own inclinations and weaknesses. Jesus himself stressed that the real evil is that which comes out of our heart.

"Life may not be the stomping ground of demons, but opportunities for distraction, bad faith, and inauthenticity are legion, and they do indeed threaten to trip us up at every step. That means always being watchful of our inner selves and our surroundings, regardless where we might be or what circumstance we might find ourselves in. Evil influences abound around us, and dark, negative forces exist within us. We have the task of overcoming them, using every means at our disposal. This is what God has made us able to do."

This is why genuine spirituality has to be eminently realistic, and not bogged down in superstition and naïve misunderstandings of reality. Father Laurence recounted during a Saturday evening meeting a story he first heard when he was a young monk, about a group of strictly cloistered nuns living in China at the time of the Communist revolution. It was a time when everyone was faced with unusual sufferings, and the nuns were no exception. When they were ordered by the authorities to sweep the streets, the mother abbess, in a state of panic, went to the local bishop and pleaded with a sob, "Your Excellency, what are we to do! The Communists have ordered us to leave the cloister and to clean the streets." The bishop listened sympathetically, then calmly looked at the nun and replied, "Well, then, Reverend Mother, I guess you'll just have to sweep the streets."

"The bishop wasn't being flippant," said Father Laurence. "He knew what was happening, and he wisely perceived that despite what they were being forced to do, nothing external could ever force the nuns to abandon their true task in life.

The new reality demanded a new response, not blind adherence to preconceptions. Their vocation of searching could still take place in harmony with the reality demanded of them by their new situation, even in the midst of such unfavorable circumstances. This can be applied to anyone's life."

Father paused a moment. "Doesn't it seem that when the early Christians referred to their religion simply as 'The Way,' they did so because they were conscious that this path was above all a powerful and concrete means of personal transformation? Through it they strove to elevate every aspect of the way they lived by following in the footsteps of Jesus — every single aspect of life, not merely those we associate with being religious."

A hand went up from the side of the room. "So then how have we come to the point where so many people these days seem to look at Christianity as a tired race horse, the last place one would go to stimulate a personal transformation?" asked Brother Barnabas. "Why has our age been labeled 'post-Christian?'"

"I think that's because for so many people today, Christianity has become so nominalistic," Father responded, "just a set of beliefs to be affirmed and duties to perform. It certainly doesn't seem to be affecting the way we think or live in society at large. Instead, Christianity is too often reduced to the theoretical, the academic on the one hand, or the sentimentally emotional on the other. That's astonishing, since the Gospels present us with, above all, a way of life, a way of being moral and compassionate, and not with a fixed set of religious tenets. Christianity is impossible without dedicated inner spiritual practice; otherwise it's a contradiction in terms. Spiritually mature people have always understood this."

After all our study of Scripture and theology, science and philosophy, we still have to look at life and ourselves as a whole. By seeking ever more understanding, and by training ourselves to see, think, and act correctly, we can skillfully and effectively integrate what we perceive and know — even as that changes — with our ultimate goal. In other words, the spiritual life is above all *praxis* — the Greek word for practice, actually doing it — without being side-tracked by how we might feel at the moment or by other circumstances.

During a visit to our monastery, a theology professor, somewhat discouraged by the state of the contemporary Church and the way candidates were being formed for the ministry, got to discussing at lunch how "knowledge is never neutral." When one of the monks took him up on the remark and asked him what he meant, he replied, "Knowledge can't just sit in our heads like money collecting interest, but so often that seems to be the experience in academia. For example, besides being a scholarly institution, we're also a theological school, preparing our students for various ministries in the church. We turn out competent scholars, perhaps, but not necessarily men and women of mature faith, who use a regular and serious life of prayer and meditation to nourish their understanding. Often that's looked upon as beside the point, at least for them personally. Students aren't led to realize that the key to their ministry isn't just what they've learned in class, but also the inner work they have to do to attain a greater depth and breadth of consciousness. If they don't integrate their book learning with inner development, the results are still darkness."

"Actually," replied Brother Elias, "that's a fair distillation of biblical teaching. It brings to my mind the story of Lucifer, the fallen angel of light. His unwillingness to use his knowledge for universal good resulted in his downfall. It seems to me that what you're saying is that the teaching is only the first step in what should be a deliberate living out of its meaning."

"That's the correct way of seeing it," the professor concurred, "but realistically, our seminaries fall far short in facilitating this. We turn out class after class of what we'd like to believe are relatively well qualified candidates for ordination, but the reality is that they have little or no correct understanding and experience of the inner life. And so, what does that mean, not only for themselves, but for the people they minister to? We seem unable to produce graduates who know how to translate what they learn academically into the nitty-gritty of daily spiritual life. In a lot of ways, so many of my students are still basically adolescents. We can't seem to bring about a real practice of prayer of the heart." He glanced at several of the brothers listening to him. "That's one of the reasons I think monasteries are so important today. Their very reason for existing should be able to provide reliable guidance on how the rest of us can live out spirituality day to day. I know that's the kind of help I've received."

We think the professor has a point. Monastic spirituality is certainly not anti–intellectual, but knowledge alone is not the whole answer. Unless knowledge is integrated into everyday life, challenging the way we think and live, its purpose is frustrated. Knowledge should fertilize practice, and vice versa, in a dynamic process; our correctly trained minds should direct the struggle against personal misunderstanding and fragmentation, a supreme effort at self-control and self-reformation that opens us to new clarity of vision and further understanding. The answers to most of the questions on the meaning of our lives cannot be discovered through abstract knowledge alone. The process of putting into practice what we know deepens that knowledge and in turn enables us to further act in a more profoundly human, wise, and constructive way. It is the struggle of a lifetime to live ever more authentically and universally.

EXPERIENCE teaches us that unfortunately we often allow our feelings and emotions to make us act in a manner at odds with the cool head of reason. Why does this happen again and again? Apparently we do not have the practical skills and strength of character needed to act correctly and effectively. It is one thing to know that the Gospel demands we "love our enemies and pray for those who persecute us," but it is another matter entirely to bring that teaching into the actual reality of our own life. Boss, coworker, neighbor, political adversary? Fellow minister, even, in the service of the Lord? . . . The process of transcending our feelings and impulses in order to act virtuously is a lifelong struggle. This is what our spiritual masters call "the unseen warfare."

This transforming struggle is positive, life-enhancing. It involves our whole being, body and soul, and it actively engages us in a discipline that has its perfect analogy in an athlete's training. As Saint Paul said,

> Do you remember how, on a racing-track, every competitor runs, but only one wins the prize? Well, you ought to run with your minds fixed on winning the prize! Every competitor in athletic events goes into serious training. Athletes will take tremendous pains — for a fading crown of leaves. But our contest is for a crown that will never fade.
>
> I run the race then with determination. I am no shadow-boxer, I really fight! I am my body's sternest master, for fear that when I have preached to others I should myself be disqualified. (1 Corinthians 9:24–27)

Though he does not use the word here, Saint Paul is emphasizing the necessity of *áskêsis* — asceticism — the lifelong training in self-control that is essential to spiritual growth. Admittedly the word asceticism has a checkered past, carrying dark, negative baggage linked with images of all sorts of life-despising practices, but the Greek word simply means "training, practice."

The Seeker was surprised when Brother Marc first clarified the definition of asceticism this way in that important conference on spiritual effort. "I've got to say that even before I entered the monastery," said the Seeker, "this was one of the big things I was leery of. I've never been able to understand traditional descriptions of asceticism that I've come across in my reading. They struck me as bizarre and strange. I mean, isolation, exaggerated fasting, sleep deprivation, abject poverty, how do they really help us? As practices, they seem more at home in a prison camp."

"Sure they do, so long as you limit your conception to those kinds of examples of excess," stated Brother Marc. "Asceticism, in the sense we're using it, has a more positive expression, in which the ongoing practice of self-discipline enables us to live life more efficiently and healthily. Looked at this way, asceticism is the healing regimen, the program of training that we undertake to enable us to pursue the difficult road of spiritual growth. Just as an athlete will never excel in his chosen sport unless he trains vigorously and regularly, so will we fail to grow spiritually unless we live a disciplined life, trimming off spiritual flab by consistent and conscientious practice."

It is vital that we be clear on this. True asceticism can give positive power, vigor, and vitality to our lives. Asceticism is ultimately constructive practice. We tear down bad habits only to replace them with good ones, whether we are athlete or spiritual searcher. It involves making good choices and simplifying our lives, for a specific purpose. The spiritual life is not competing against others, nor is it competing for worldly honors: it is pushing ourselves beyond our own static self-conceptions toward living in an ever-deepening communion with the source of life itself. We are not meant to lose the race; we are meant to win it, but without the proper attention and focus, we can end up deceived and lost.

Brother Marc continued, "When Paul says, 'Run so as to win,' he's encouraging us to give our very best in the challenge of life, so that we may become who God meant us to be. That's a way of looking at asceticism correctly. We've now come to understand that anything that frustrates this process is actually antithetical to the true spirit of asceticism."

T HE NATURE OF MONASTICISM is to provide a healthy context in which such a rule of life is followed wisely and with safeguards and the support of others. By examining our attitudes toward sleep, work, eating, recreation, speech, sexuality, study, worship — to life and death — we can learn to express our dedication tangibly through our total life: body and soul, mind and spirit. We can train ourselves to bring each element of our life into line with our relationship with God, the absolute mystery at the heart of all reality.

Visitors constantly question us about this; they sense the deep need to apply these same principles in their own lives, but usually they are at a loss how to do so. When a college student made a weekend retreat with us, the atmosphere brought him face-to-face with how scattered and hectic his life had become and the impact this was having on his inner life. "The problem is that with all that I've got going on, it's hard for me to see how I can make any more time for the spiritual concerns I'm beginning to see are so important," he complained. "There's just never enough time; so ultimately that's what gets placed on the back burner."

"Without a disciplined spiritual practice, you'll never have enough time," observed Father Laurence. "You'll always be like the dog chasing its tail. Actually, one of the fruits of regular daily meditation is that you begin to use the rest of your time more efficiently, more in harmony with your deepest convictions. That's because you're becoming more conscious. From what you've said, it seems you need to think of your spiritual life more broadly, as affecting every dimension of your life, not just those narrow areas we call 'religious.'

"What does spiritual practice really involve?" When the student remained respectfully silent, Father continued, "Well, wouldn't you say that ultimately it means living life well? Living rightly in all things means correctly perceiving, understanding, evaluating, and acting in regard to ourselves and others, our environment, and all of reality. This demands a lot of self-discipline, but unless we learn how to bring into our spiritual practice the most seemingly insignificant details of our life, we won't achieve the degree of spiritual wholeness we're capable of. This is why such training is relevant to everyone, not simply to monks."

"But it still seems to me that monastic asceticism is going to be hard, if not impossible, to apply to everyday living, at least in my world," said the student.

"Who said anything about *monastic* asceticism?" replied Father. "Whatever particular practices we may do in the monastery are tailored to this specific context. Asceticism will vary according to circumstance: growing in consciousness is what's important; the means are entirely secondary. That's why individually we have to know how to apply the principle correctly in each particular situation of life.

"The purpose of asceticism, discipline, or training is not to make life artificial or miserable through practices that are at odds with healthy human living, or which can become an end in themselves. Neither is it a matter of adding more activities to an already cramped schedule. It is only to help us change ourselves so that we can respond to life as consciously and effectively as possible. Naturally, asceticism involves active self-denial, but it's only self-denial at the service of growth."

The student was quiet for several moments, absorbing what had just been explained to him, so as an afterthought Father added, "To use the analogy of athletic training, what we're talking about here is more than just 'keeping in shape.' In fact, by energetically applying self-discipline to living as we should, the range of ascetic practice is as broad as life itself, extending from picking up after ourselves around the house, for example, to assuming the proper responsibility toward those we love. Or have you never thought of listening with complete attention to a person you're having a conversation with as an ascetic discipline?" The student shook his head. "See what I mean? Our personal asceticism will consist of an infinite number of practices. Whatever reality calls us to do, however trivial, is matter for moral, spiritual, mental, emotional — total growth, when we conscientiously strive to do it well and with awareness. Unlike the specific demands of job or profession, when it comes to spiritual life, we're always 'on duty.'"

This is not a romantic undertaking. It entails a delicate interior balance of self-examination, self-discipline, and time for personal regeneration. A key part of this effort of asceticism is our individual search for the personal weaknesses that can compromise our efforts in times of crisis, or can cause us to be unintentionally hurtful. Such discipline has wide ramifications. For example, one of the most difficult challenges of trying to survive in a global society is the practice today of dialogue, peace-making, and social justice. Unless a majority of us focus our energies in support of this effort, our survival as a species is in jeopardy. But this will be futile unless we get our own lives in order first.

The student's eyes brightened. "Actually, Father, what you're saying reminds me of Dag Hammarskjöld, the former U.N. secretary general. One of the things we had to read this past semester in my political science class was a book of his journal writings. The professor made it optional reading, but he recommended it strongly, because it showed how Hammarskjöld's political activities flowed from deeply held, yet quietly kept, spiritual convictions, which he faithfully practiced throughout his life."

"Exactly," said Father Laurence. "And you can be sure the same is true for a lot of other people who aren't so well known. Asceticism, properly understood, should have a place in any life worth living; basically, it's the dedicated, persistent, and conscious effort we bring to the way we live, no matter what our state in life happens to be. It's no different for us monks. We on our part simply express it through the monastic life we profess. That's monastic asceticism — watchful and disciplined right living carried out in the context of a monastic community — not some weird set of medieval practices.

"I think right-thinking monks of whatever religion would agree with this. Western monasticism terms this 'conversion of manners,' bringing everything in monastic life into harmony with God. We call it repentance. We want to integrate 'head knowledge' with 'heart knowledge.' This means continuously seeking to balance a solid understanding of life and of the doctrines of faith with an equally solid living and practice of that faith."

Father Laurence's eyes lit up mischievously. "You don't have to take my word for it. Look at it for yourself. A firm theoretical foundation is absolutely necessary, but it alone doesn't guarantee that your practice will be effective. On the other hand, just because you do all the traditional practices is no sure sign that your understanding is correct. These things vitally affect each other.

"Right practice should flow naturally from right thinking about reality. For example, our belief that Christ is God incarnate, that he is the perfect icon of both divinity and humanity in a single person, is not just jargon. Yet an incorrect understanding of this leaves us open to despising the physical in favor of the so-called spiritual, flying off into la-la land. On the other hand, a correct understanding gives us a profound insight into the full integration of spirit and matter in the human being. If this insight doesn't affect us in our daily life, it remains merely theoretical. Only when we put our right thinking into practice does it lead to further awakening."

We are given a model of the correct marriage of understanding and asceticism in the example of Jesus himself. What he fleshed out through his own way of life and in his teaching, was intended not only for monks but for everyone. Contrary to what some popular spirituality seems to suggest, Jesus did not give us his life to exempt us from a similar journey. He emphasized that the path to greater life would require us to forge our own "way of the cross" on the way to salvation and resurrection. The question is not "if they put you on the cross," but "when." This is what truly being a Christian is: finding our example and encouragement in Christ, helping one another to do what he did, and changing ourselves in order to realize increasingly through our lives the fullness of life he proclaimed. Spiritual transfiguration implies total transformation; true asceticism is the training each of us uses to help in the process.

THE STUDENT WAS only too quick to bring up an obvious paradox: "Since we are created for life, and if, as you say, Jesus' message is ultimately life-affirming, and even if we understand asceticism in a more positive light, how is it that so much of the spiritual literature in Christianity emphasizes dying, renunciation, and despising oneself? I went to a Bible study on campus a few times last semester, but the texts they were looking at gave me the creeps."

Father reached for the Bible next to him. "Sure, without a proper way of understanding these, you can build up a pretty sick version of Christianity. It's certainly no secret that some of the most well-known of Jesus' teachings focus on these *apparent* negativities:

> "If anyone wants to follow in my footsteps, he must give up all right to himself, take up his cross and follow me. The man who tries to save his life will lose it; it is the man who loses his life for my sake and the gospel's who will save it." (Mark 8:34, 35)

Father flipped quickly to another passage. "Or how about this":

> "I tell you truly that unless a grain of wheat falls into the earth and dies, it remains a single grain of wheat; but if it dies, it brings a good harvest. The man who loves his own life will lose it, and the man who hates his life in this world will preserve it for eternal life." (John 12:24, 25)

"At face value, without proper comprehension and interpretation, this can sound like 'bad news.' But if we understand these passages correctly, we'll see their meaning within the entire context of human reality." Father Laurence went on to point out that dying is part of life. Just as there is biological death, there are other types of death also. And when Jesus talks about death, as in the passages above, he is not dreaming up some new reality, he is simply pointing out what life is about. Before there can be resurrection, there is always death.

It is also true that when "dying" is emphasized one-dimensionally or literally (history is rife with examples of such perverse spiritualities that are supposed to express the "good news"), life can take on a decadent aroma of morbidity and is reduced to a somber program whose primary fruit is to make life as miserable as possible for us. "We can't allow ourselves to be naïve about this. This language of spiritual growth — of 'dying to self' — can shipwreck us even before we leave port unless we understand its true, deeper, intent as a metaphor. Without correct explanation, it reinforces a dour and joyless stereotype of spirituality or religion that says the more we suffer, the more God is pleased. Nothing, of course, could be farther from the truth!"

"Dying to self" is spiritual shorthand for rooting out all manner of exaggerated self-interest, characteristics of ourselves that constrict us in narcissism and blind self-centeredness. This is the self within us that, while all too real, is what none-theless must die, the "false self," which must give way to the new life we are called to attain. The false self embodies the very characteristics we loathe in our better moments. Were we to look at ourselves honestly, we would see how petty, thoughtless, and loveless we can be at any given moment. We might have an occasional, fleeting insight that we will never attain any real happiness unless we come to terms with what really counts in life. One doesn't have to search far to find pathetic examples of individuals who struck it rich by the standards of "the world," yet whose personal lives were utterly miserable. Wealth, fame, and talent alone are not enough to make us happy. When they occur independently of genuine spiritual values, they only throw into greater relief the true poverty and slavery of our lives.

We storm the walls of our own imprisonment when we struggle to overcome self-centeredness, when we stretch to build avenues of communion with reality beyond our own self, whatever it happens to be. One moment it might be helping a friend, the next it might be attending to our job, running an errand, overcoming a persistent manifestation of selfishness, expressing gratitude by writing a thank-you note, breaking out of our own little world enough to notice a beautiful sunset . . . anything. With each step of life comes the background question "What is reality asking of us now?" challenging us to respond wholeheartedly, willingly. We escape and leave behind the self that is holed up with its own concerns, and breathe the fresh air of otherness.

"Dying to self is actually dying to the 'false self,'" Father Laurence explained to the student in concluding their talk, "so that the true self, our new self modeled on the image of life reflected in Christ, can come forth. When we willingly discipline ourselves by giving our full attention to whatever is at hand and responding as the situation warrants, the effect is liberating."

Here, of course, is the rub: since the beginning many have misunderstood Jesus' teaching by presuming that being a believer meant literally viewing the world as evil. To cite only one example, the expression *contemptus mundi* ("contempt for the world") is often used erroneously to justify a divisive, life-negating spirituality. Instead of a literal, categorical rejection of God's creation, it should be understood positively, as a challenge to "worldly (selfish) attitudes" that lead us away from God's call to life. It is ridiculous, if not blasphemous, to believe that God wills us to despise the natural world he created, with its unspeakable beauty, which is available to even the most destitute for the mere price of noticing it. After all, the good news has to do with how life can and should be lived here and now in this world.

Misunderstanding *contemptus mundi* results in a rigid attitude of "I'm going to save myself at any cost whatever," even if that cost is our own full humanity. This has certainly sounded attractive to many throughout the ages, and still does, but the wisdom of healthy monastic experience recognizes how shortsighted it is. It further fragments us because it is based on a false conception of both human and divine nature.

The Seeker remembered Brother Marc's response when he had asked him, "So how then does this vision of asceticism play out concretely in the twentieth century?" Brother Marc replied, "I think the criterion is health, understood in its fullest sense. True áskesis always transforms us in life-enhancing ways, in a manner that respects and elevates the human condition. For example, do you really think it's wise for celibates to starve themselves of food and light in order to destroy the sexual impulse for the sake of a very dubious purity in the sight of God? You've come across that one, haven't you? If that's correct, where's the virtue and value of celibacy? The way it's described, it's not much different from what happened in concentration camps. Isn't it more profound, more heroic, and more intelligent, more consonant with the spirit of the Gospels to utilize every single element of human nature, indeed of all creation around us, correctly? It's a matter of creativity: becoming co-creators and responsible stewards of the glory of God, and for the glory of God and our own greater welfare."

"What about fasting?" asked the Seeker. "We place a lot of importance on it in the Orthodox Church, what with Great Lent and all. That's a form of asceticism, isn't it?"

"From biblical times, fasting has been an important religious practice," replied Brother Marc. *"But unfortunately it seems also to have become something of an idolatry in our church, an end in itself. Like so many external practices, it can easily fail to achieve any internal effect on the hearts of people, and so they remain unchanged. You must have heard the story about the monk who bragged how much he fasted, and the retort his spiritual father came back with: 'Yes, but you eat your brother alive!'*

"Fasting, meaning deliberately cutting back on the general intake of food from time to time for religious motives, and abstinence, refraining from some particular food for the same motive, are two distinct concepts that are frequently mistakenly thought to be the same. Both are valid practices, but they have to be adjusted to the pace and understanding of modern living, like all the ancient practices. Incidentally, it's worth our recalling the wisdom that Pope Paul VI once offered in an encyclical on fasting. He pointed out, among other things, that there are many ways of practicing asceticism today in the modern world, and that we need to embrace its spirit correctly by interiorizing any particular asceticism we engage in.

"For example, isn't it necessary for each of us to know what and when and how much we should eat and drink to live optimally, to know when to abstain from unnecessary food that simply puts on added weight and depletes our energy — hopeless indulgence? And these days isn't regular exercise a healthy and necessary facet of self-discipline and asceticism, that helps us care responsibly for the life that was given to us? Can anyone really afford to ignore this?"

The Seeker watched Brother Marc's demeanor grow increasingly lively as he moved from example to example. *"Don't we need to exercise watchfulness, self-control, and the integration of our emotions with the rest of our lives? Don't we have to look at how dependable we are and how helpful we might be to those we live with, and the extent to which we strive for healthy regularity of living, instead of giving in to self-centeredness and laziness? . . ." The Seeker remembered laughing as he finally replied, "I get the picture!"*

N O ONE IS SAVED ALONE. We all have a responsibility for each other and all things, and we need every ounce of our physical and moral energy to fulfill this task. Correct understanding of *áskesis* is not to cut off unruly energy, but to redeem it by integrating and channeling it for the good of all.

The purpose of ascetic training is exactly this: through regular practice, to bring all of the aspects of our reality under control and subject to right reason. This, in turn, affords us the possibility of plugging into life at its source, which is to say, reality, the only place we shall ever come to know God and ourselves.

This is why we speak of asceticism as a means to being fully alive. The phrase "dead to the world" is responsible for so much misunderstanding that it is almost without value today. For centuries, monks have been the cultural scapegoats who were thought to embody this principle, and unfortunately many did. Hair shirts, bread and water, sleepless vigils, and a host of other bizarre and exaggerated exercises formed a caricature of monastic asceticism. If truth be told, false asceticism has plagued monastic life from the beginning, and does so even today. True monastic asceticism, the bywords of which are moderation, balance, and discernment, just like ordinary human self-discipline, has nothing to do with any kind of extremism or disdain for what is human.

The best of monastic tradition shows us that true asceticism is not centered on *practices* (which are always only a means to an end), but on *practice,* true spiritual striving, *assisted by specific practices.* Spiritual or ascetic practice means finding in every aspect of life an opportunity for our own growth: obedience to those in charge and to each other, chastity, simplicity, stability, prayer, study, work, and hospitality. False, or dead-end, asceticism turns practice into an insidious idol that becomes an end in itself, which sets our whole life askew. Consider: why would God possibly sanction or encourage sadistic practices designed to break us and make our lives miserable? So that monks could masochistically pride themselves on how much they must really love God by putting up with such insanity? Wise monks have always cautioned against this sort of imbalance. Examples of excess abound in monastic tradition all the way back to Saint John Cassian in the fourth century, who chronicles in painful detail stories of monks who wrecked their lives through lack of balance. From Abba Antony of the desert, the father of desert monasticism, we learn the reason for their failure:

> It was lack of discretion alone that prevented them from attaining the goal. No other reason for their failure is evident. Without the guidance of older, more experienced men, they were unable to acquire this sense of discretion that avoids every extreme and instructs the monk always to take the royal road. It keeps him from veering to the right, that is, it keeps him from going, out of crass presumption and fanaticism, past the limits of reason and moderation. It keeps him from going off to the left toward carelessness and self-indulgence — toward a lukewarm dispostion — all under the pretense of self-control.

Cassian says the "royal and safe way" is balance, the key to understanding asceticism in a healthy way. The extremes of both self-indulgence and self-deprivation have equally harmful consequences for human life. They result in a distortion that alienates and even kills the spirit.

Authentic spiritual training tills and tends the soil of our human nature so that real fruit can blossom forth. Whatever can aid in this process is a part of asceticism. To make ascetic training comprehensible for today, we have to broaden its scope and realize that fidelity to reality's demands is itself an asceticism, and therefore sane asceticism can and should play a crucial role in each of our lives.

Asceticism, above all, requires consciousness, for only a person growing in awareness can realize what needs to be done and have the self-discipline to do it. A tale from our community exemplifies this: It was known that the abba loved freshly squeezed orange juice. Once, while working on a very hot summer day, the abba asked one of his disciples, "Please squeeze me some orange juice." The disciple went off, but he lacked a quiet mind and murmured beneath his breath, demanding to know why he should have to be the abba's butler when he already had other work to do. From the other side of the room the abba could observe the disciple and the manner in which he carried out the task. He saw him cut the oranges carelessly, squeeze them even more carelessly, and leave the squeezer and counter a mess. Using a small glass instead of a large one, he also neglected the courtesy of adding ice cubes, and he spilled some juice as he carried the glass to the abba. When the disciple returned to take away the empty glass, he asked how it was. "Bittersweet," replied the abba.

ORDINARILY, the training linked with "dying to self" is not made up of supreme sacrifices, where we actually lay down our life once and for all for someone. Though this can happen in extreme circumstances (such as in war), more commonly dying to self is a process, the accumulation of millions of smaller acts of self-discipline and self-control, which we face every day and which often pass unnoticed. We can look upon this in one of two ways: as akin to a dripping water faucet, the constant drip, drip, drip that slowly wears away the enamel in the sink; or the continual opportunity given to us to grow, to smooth away our rough edges by acting in harmony with what life asks of us.

To discipline and train ourselves correctly requires a willing desire to do what we know should be done, in spite of the negative, self-centered feelings that may accompany such acts. Even these smaller acts, the composite of our daily life, contain within themselves the practice that steadily fosters our interior transformation.

In our stubbornness of heart and lack of faith,
we live in constant fear of what the end will bring.
To the world we show a countenance that is serene and sure,
but the depths of our souls are torn by the turmoil of despair.
Bring us repentance, O patient saviour,
and fill our lives with peace and hope,
that we may cry out to you with the thief:
Remember us, Lord, when you come as king.

Wednesday evening sticheron, Tone Seven

FIVE

What About Techniques?

TODAY'S CULTURE idolizes technique. How-to manuals literally overflow the shelves of bookstores. We are so conditioned to the genre that we automatically seek out books on whatever interests us, fully expecting that we can achieve whatever results we might desire simply by finding the right recipe — learning the technique. Particularly in the realm of spirituality and prayer, an abundance of material either new or extracted from traditional cultures from every part of the world seems to emphasize psychospiritual or physical techniques as the key to spiritual growth.

After skimming through these books, it is easy to conclude that as long as we get the technique right, we will discover the experience that leads us to the heights of spiritual growth. The difficulty is that technique too easily remains detached from the change of mind and heart, from the attitude and behavior necessary for us to grow authentically; how balanced, complete, and compassionate we actually are as human beings seems incidental.

The Seeker explains: "When I first entered the monastery, I was all business, burdened with an unrealistic perfectionism. I was under the mistaken impression that mastering the techniques of the spiritual life would be the fastest route to heightened spiritual consciousness, and that therefore all I had to do was learn the techniques. I didn't realize that I was simply embodying the mentality that had been with me since college. I approached prayer as though I were cramming for a final, memorizing facts — ways of praying — rather than really understanding their meaning, so that I could apply them to my life. Though I read everything on prayer I could get my hands on, I grew impatient with most of it because it seemed so impractical. It was true that these books offered wonderful spiritual insight, but they really didn't tell me how to come to the same insights myself, other than in the most general of terms. When I complained to Father Laurence about this, however, he was uncharacteristically reticent about giving me anything too specific."

"I don't like talking about this," Father said. "It's not that techniques are useless, but each of us has to discover the ones that are helpful for us. I mean, if you ask ten different monks how they pray, you'll get ten different answers. Each of us has to come to this on our own. Now obviously, there are basic guidelines which the beginner needs to be aware of and follow, like doing your meditation at a regular time each day instead of getting it in when you can, but within those parameters, there's a lot of room for personal expression, for seeing what works for the given individual. You've read the books; why do you think they're so general about the way to pray? Doesn't it seem likely that the reason why Christian prayer doesn't limit itself to set techniques for prayer is that ultimately God transcends technique? Prayer is a mystery that goes beyond technique, which is a relief, really. We needn't be worried about getting the techniques absolutely right, so much as being absolutely honest and sincere before God. What happens after that is God's business."

The Seeker pursued the thought further. "But that still doesn't answer the real question, does it? I mean, there's a right way to swing a golf club and a wrong way. Isn't it the same in the spiritual life?"

"Within limits," Father Laurence said, "but there's a lot more room for personal creativity in prayer than in golf. Actually, the real *secret is discovering that no matter how helpful they are, methods and the experiences they produce are always only a means to a deeper reality; that reality is what counts, not the things leading up to it. The reality may be discovered from a number of different routes."*

Father continued, "Let me tell you a story about a novice who was in our community a number of years back. I remember her coming to me one day all enthusiastic about a book she had just finished reading, one I suspect you're familiar with: The Way of the Pilgrim. *Well, after she gushed on about it for several minutes, she declared to me her intention to follow the example of the pilgrim by reciting the Jesus prayer 'Lord Jesus Christ, Son of God, have mercy on me a sinner' as many times as she could during the day. She was more than a little put out when I told her that I didn't think that was a good idea at all, that the book reflected circumstances and a mind-set entirely different from our own, and that she should simply stick with the way of prayer she had been practicing. 'Use the Jesus prayer for your formal period of meditation if you wish,' I told her, 'but for the rest of the day keep your attention directed to whatever else you happen to be doing.'*

"Her response was predictable, I guess. 'But how can you possibly say that?' she sputtered. 'This is a time-honored technique for Orthodox monastics.'

"'And the way it is usually practiced has made it an end in itself, not a means,' I countered. I said that she could do what she wanted, but that I thought she'd end up doing herself more harm than good if she followed her present course, and that if she were wise, she'd steer clear of it.

"Well, she thought she knew better and so she started doing it anyway, despite my warning. And what soon began to happen was revealing. The other nuns living with her started to notice her neglecting her responsibilities and becoming careless and thoughtless in everyday tasks. I don't know how many times she messed up in the

bakery by not paying attention to what she was doing, but I know it was a lot.

"Once, when the superior sent her to do an errand, she actually backed their car into the garage door, forcing the nuns to replace the door, simply because she hadn't noticed that the garage door was closed. She was too busy 'praying.' But the real problem was that no one could get her to see these patterns in her everyday living. Her mind was closed and her consciousness divided; she was so intent on reciting her prayer that she became less and less in touch with everyday reality."

"So what happened?" asked the Seeker.

"Eventually we had to ask her to leave. It was clear that she had no intention of changing, and the course she was following simply made it impossible for her to fit into the community." Father paused, recollecting the pain of the relationship. "It was very sad. But that's what can happen when we make an idol out of a technique. In her case, worshipping the Jesus prayer became more important than the spirit of the beatitudes. She lost perspective, and the unfortunate consequence was that she became more and more distanced from reality."

This is precisely why until now in this book we have not suggested specific techniques to foster spiritual development. It is all too easy to place an excessive value on a formal spiritual exercise before realizing that our real goal is to acquire an attitude of deep faith, reverent attentiveness, unwavering trust, and dedicated love. This insight is fundamental.

Visitors ask the monks and nuns about prayer all the time, but most often what they want is advice on the "way to pray," as if using a particular method was going to guarantee a specific result in their inner life. A better way of thinking about technique and the mystery of prayer is to consider that the value of any technique is only in helping us to be more open to God, of getting us to move beyond ourselves. No technique in itself is a sure lock on that.

"You can do that if you want," Sister Rebecca explained to a retreatant who had questioned her about using a yoga position when praying, "but your legs will have to tolerate the strain of being intertwined for a half-hour or so. Most Americans find that next to impossible — and it can be harmful to one's joints to boot — and probably should use some other posture. But that doesn't mean the value of our prayer will be any less. It's what's in the heart that counts. Certainly prayer doesn't depend on our being able to get into the lotus position."

Sister Rebecca detected some hesitation on the part of the retreatant, so she continued, "You know, since becoming a nun, I've lived all over the world — in the Far East, Europe, and North America, and I've had numerous opportunities to speak with different people on issues of prayer and the inner life. What's been confirmed for me again and again is that spiritual methodology must be subordinate and subservient to the more fundamental intention of the heart. It's so easy to become preoccupied with a particular technique when it actually does lead to some sort of spiritual experience. In fact, if we follow it correctly, for example breathing rhythmically with a prayer word, the experiences may be quite positive, even dazzling, especially in the beginning."

"That's what I mean," the retreatant replied. "I have a friend who spent a lot of time at a Far Eastern monastery putting her life back together after a serious bout with drugs. The few times we talked about the experience, she told me that with all the periods of formal meditation, plus the daily discipline of work she had to do in silence, the interior quiet she experienced was really quite remarkable. But the austerity of the life was too difficult for a more permanent stay, so she returned to college and finished her degree. Several years later, when she was really busy running a restaurant, she'd always think back nostalgically on that year."

"Did she stop meditating?"

The woman shrugged her shoulders. "I don't think so. I believe she still spends some time in silence before going to work, but she complains that it's just not enough time to get really focused the way she was able to do at the monastery. Since she left, I don't think she's ever known the inner peace she experienced there, and she's always trying different things — like going to workshops and retreats, for example — in order to get that back. Her latest interest is in biofeedback, but I wonder whether it's going to give her what she's looking for."

The retreatant sighed. "You know, she never called what she experienced in the monastery 'God,' but I think that's what she meant. It just doesn't seem fair. There has to be a way for people like us to be able to experience the inner peace you monastics always talk about, without sacrificing an ordinary life in the world. I mean, I'm not a person who's cut out for monastic life. Yet the impression I get is that's the only place I'll ever be able to attain inner peace. Isn't there some secret, some series of exercises you're not telling us about?"

Sister Rebecca's face revealed a trace of a smile. "No, I'm afraid not, but in any case, living in the world needn't prevent you from coming to true inner peace. Look, I'm certain a lot of monastics from different religions know the inner silence you speak of — after all, that's an effect of the type of life we live. But just because we generate loads of alpha brain waves doesn't mean that we're experiencing God, or even that we're living as we should. Spiritual life and the contemplative path is much more than just brain waves and peaceful feelings. It's meant to lead to an entire transformation in the way we think about and act toward everything.

"When we feel total relaxation and inner peace, for example, as a result of breathing exercises or stretching (especially if it's for the first time in our lives), we might very easily take this for an experience of God. Obviously it's a 'divine' feeling, but let's not go overboard; that's *all* that it is. God is beyond anything we experience. You and your friend both have to learn to know God beyond the changing state of your emotions. That requires thoughtfulness and persistence, not magical techniques. And it's really no different for us."

The retreatant may have left disappointed. But Sister Rebecca's wisdom bears repeating: unlike popular, no-nonsense, just-give-me-the-facts pragmatism that promises "sure-fire" results, authentic spiritual practice involves every single aspect of our life. There is no magical shortcut that will give us what we desire. Attaining spiritual maturity and inner peace will take us the rest of our lives. There is no limit to how far we can go on this journey and the amount of virtue and virtuosity in living we can acquire. A technique can help us take any particular step in the spiritual journey, and we shall discuss those, but they are not the way, the path, nor the goal.

When Sister Rebecca brought up her conversation with the retreatant in a Saturday evening class, she noted, "I've been thinking about that talk all afternoon. Maybe it was because of the experience of her friend, but I sensed in her a reluctance to believe that spirituality could be lived without being in the right spot, knowing that perfect position, using the best technique. I think she wanted me to tell her precisely what to do and how to do it, and she was clearly disappointed when I didn't provide her with that. Why do so many people get stuck on techniques?"

Father Laurence drew his fingers together and raised them to his lips for a brief moment. "Isn't that the basic premise, the mythology of our technologically driven culture, after all? All we have to do is install the right software, so to speak, and we're set. Yet nothing in the spiritual life works automatically, no matter how technically sophisticated we might be in practicing it.

"The only way to advance spiritually is to advance in consciousness and understanding, and spiritual techniques alone can never provide us with that. No amount of technical proficiency can replace the seeing and knowing that springs from the deepest recesses of your heart. No tool is of any use unless we know what we're building with it. Once we see where we're going, we have a concrete basis for choosing the methods that are most effective to help us move toward our goal."

Brother David raised his hand. "Would you say that another aspect of this problem is today's self-help mentality, especially when it avoids any connection to community?" When Father Laurence nodded for him to continue, Brother David filled out his thought. "I mean that the techniques are everywhere, promising all sorts of things. All anyone has to do is go to a bookstore and choose from thousands of books describing any number of different spiritualities or methods of practice, but they're abstracted from the living communities, the cultures and the faith, of the people who gave birth to them. 'Do this technique and you don't have to bother getting involved with everything else that goes with it' is often the implicit subtext. People these days just don't seem interested in getting involved with a community that's going to make demands on them."

"It certainly seems that way," replied Father Laurence. "People are taking up spirituality solely for the sake of an individualistic agenda. We try to use it as a tonic for the high stress and chronic mood swings that are the results of our way of living, instead of attacking the root of the problem, searching for a means to find, live out, and deepen our true beliefs and aspirations. As a result, 'spirituality' becomes our latest drug. Actually, by emphasizing this talismanic character of would-be spiritual techniques, we simply reinforce the exaggerated and ultimately harmful individualism prevalent in American society."

Only when our own practice is linked to community, nourished by the bonds of a shared religious culture — faith, ideas, and struggle — does it have the potential for safely unleashing the spiritual energies in us all that can revitalize and even transform our parched society. This is not to deny the value and necessity of making use of insights from various spiritual traditions, but when we do so without a solid grounding in some kind of stable community, a circle of people with whom we can and do share our life and deepest concerns, our spirituality all too easily succumbs to the dominating tendencies of our own egos and personalities. We then feed on spirituality for ourselves exclusively, dining at a table set for one. Instead of tasting the true freedom of self-transcendence intended by a spiritual life, a healing from our own alienation, we end up insidiously narcissistic and self-preoccupied at the expense of maturity and balance.

It was not for nothing that Jesus said to his disciples,

> "I am the vine, you are the branches. Those who remain in me and I in them bear much fruit, for cut off from me you can do nothing." (John 15:5; translation New Skete)

Christian tradition has always understood this to mean that we truly abide in Jesus together, as a community. This is why the kingdom of God is likened to a great banquet, and why we place so much importance on eucharistic celebrations, where this experience is realized and manifested in a unique way.

JESUS' WAY OF BEING was just as obvious when he sat at weddings and festal meals as it was when he carried his cross. His focus was one of all-embracing wholeness. His life was not constricted by technique, but rather consumed by the infinitely more important thrust of interest and concern for others. It is not that he dismisses technique outright — our human reality requires that we somehow flesh out our intentions, and doubtless we will find some ways of doing this more helpful than others. But he criticized the misuse of technique, refusing to get entangled in debates promoting specific spiritual methods, and he deliberately looked beyond all techniques and rules. For him, it is artificial and harmful to separate spirituality from common sense and a compassionate heart.

Here, when we speak about the heart, we do not mean the physical organ; we are referring to the unique core of a person, where mind and will, body and emotions unite, where the person is who he is. True spirituality always flows from the heart. Throughout his life, Jesus did not hesitate to emphasize the priority of the heart, of loving with one's whole self, over any and all practices.

Then one of the scribes, who had been listening to the discussion and who appreciated how well Jesus had answered, put this question to him:

"Which is the first commandment of all?"

Jesus replied, "This is the first: 'Hear O Israel! The Lord our God is the one Lord, and you shall love the Lord your God with all your heart, with all your soul, with all your mind, and with all your strength.' The second is this: 'You must love your neighbor as yourself.' No other commandment is greater than these." (Mark 12:28–31; translation New Skete)

Later, when his disciples asked him to teach them to pray, Jesus did not discourse on different prayer techniques or teach them a method to relate to God. He merely said,

> "When you pray . . . you should say,
> Father, may your name be honored —
> may your kingdom come.
> Give us the bread we need for each day,
> and forgive us our failures,
> for we forgive everyone who fails us,
> and keep us clear of temptation."
>
> (Luke 11:2–4)

The Seeker remembered one of the first times he talked to Father Laurence about prayer, how careful Father was to emphasize the non-mechanistic use of any authentic formula of prayer. "Even traditional prayers that we learned as kids have to be interiorized," Father stressed, "made our own. For example, what's come down to us as the Our Father, or the Lord's Prayer, isn't just a formula of prayer we recite simply because Jesus uttered it: it's actually a powerful teaching; it expresses the depth of our relationship to God in terms of a loving Father; it reflects an attitude that should suffuse the way we think and behave, if we allow it to."

"But you couldn't attain that just by praying nothing but the Our Father over and over again, could you?" asked the Seeker.

"It depends on the individual," replied Father, "but that's not the point. What is to the point is making whatever words we use in prayer real and sincere. For example, people have been praying the Psalms for thousands of years, presumably because they express so

profoundly how people really feel before God. Just because they were composed by someone else doesn't make it impossible to use them as our own. So long as we pray them sincerely and from the heart, allowing them to express our deepest *sentiments, they'll do what they're supposed to do. Obviously, this demands some courage and creativity on our part . . . same with the Our Father. In fact, here's a very worthwhile question to meditate on: How are we,* in our own way, *going to express and live out the meaning contained in the prayer? Simply by rote recitation? It'll be nothing more than an exercise in futility and hypocrisy unless we seek to understand it and make it real in our lives."*

To one who wants to know exactly how to proceed in prayer, such a response can be maddeningly elusive. Would that Jesus had said, "When you pray, kneel this way, breathe deeply, keep your back straight, and prepare to meet your God!" At least then we would have some certitude about how to pray! But Jesus did no such thing. In fact, he criticized the misuse of prayer for less noble ends. Instead, he said,

> "But when you pray, go into your own room, shut your door
> and pray to your Father privately." (Matthew 6:6)

This is less a technique than a new way of looking at things, in which we come before God naked, without veneers, and without fanfare!

I'D LIKE TO GO BACK to what I was saying earlier," Sister Rebecca said during the same Saturday night meeting. "So what *do* we say to people who are genuinely serious about growing in the spiritual life, like my friend this afternoon? When they ask us, 'What, then, should I do?' it seems to me we ought to be able to give them something to help them out, but my question is, how?"

"I think your first instincts were right," Father Laurence replied. "Before getting into any specific methods or techniques, people need to be led beyond the notion that the techniques are anything except means, or that any particular technique is infallibly superior to another. They also need to recognize the importance of being connected to some sort of community of faith. You just can't practice alone out in left field.

"Once someone understands these points, then you can say, 'This is what I've found helpful,' and there will be less chance of their misunderstanding your suggestions. Now the perspective is entirely different; the focus isn't solely on the technique itself. Approaching it this way reflects a certain flexibility toward any method." Father paused a moment. "You see, people today as always have to get out of their heads the idea that adopting a particular position of meditation, uttering a favorite prayer, participating in any sort of devotion — are anything more than simply aids. They're not ends in themselves. Yes, at various times we will find one or another method attractive or useful. But the real value of a technique lies in leading us to open up authentically to God from our hearts, in helping us to be increasingly mindful of the presence of God, which is constant whether we are aware of it or not."

"But how do we stress the valuable role of community in the spiritual life without coming across as trying to convert people?" said Brother Gregory.

"I think it's important to be honest in articulating the principle, and then let people make of it what they will," replied Father. "The fact is that the best traditions of interiority and spiritual practice in Christianity have always emphasized interpersonal communion and community. Genuine Christian practice takes us beyond ourselves into the realm of love. From the material I'm acquainted with, this clearly differs from much of the popular New Age religious philosophy and mentality today, which is almost solely oriented toward the self.

"I think that despite the profound loneliness in our culture, the extreme individualism glorified in American life makes us shy away from being dependent upon anything outside of ourselves. We long for self-sufficiency, and we feel much more comfortable with 'spiritual take-out' that can be eaten in the privacy of our home — spirituality without the hassle of having to get mixed up with other people, teaching, learning, and relating to authority.

"But Christianity is not supposed to be a do-it-yourself, pick-and-choose, have it your own way, religion. At every point it requires us to give of ourselves to our 'neighbor' as well as to enter into ourselves in reflection and prayer. Both aspects are necessary in order to unleash its dynamism. By emphasizing the goal of connecting with every aspect of reality, of working with others in faith and service, we minimize the danger of obsession with technique, not to mention self-deception. We also give ourselves firm ground to stand on to keep us wise, a place to sink roots, to keep us sane."

It is no secret that there are abundant methods that can help open us up to spiritual growth. For twenty centuries countless Christian writers have helped their readers grow spiritually by suggesting innumerable spiritual techniques. If we are really serious about developing our spiritual life, especially our Christian life, we will have to learn how to practice some form of inner stillness, meditation, and prayer. But more important, we will have to examine over and over why we are doing this. The tools are many; what is helpful for one person might not be for another, but our intentions and the reasons for using any specific technique must be right and clear.

We should be alert to whatever will help us break through to the deepest motives of our hearts. With this goal in mind, when obstacles arise, we won't go flitting around to every new technique on the market. We will practice in an honest and persistent way, laying the foundation for our own better life. Specific techniques do not in any sense comprise the whole of the spiritual life, but they can be a valuable part, particularly today when an ocean of noise, distraction, and contrary voices surrounds us.

THE REAL QUESTION, then, is what is the connection between our becoming genuinely loving and our practice and prayer. Saint Paul said it perfectly:

> You should set your hearts on the best spiritual gifts, but I will show you a way which surpasses them all.
>
> If I speak with the eloquence of men and of angels, but have no love, I become no more than blaring brass or crashing cymbal. If I have the gift of foretelling the future and hold in my mind not only all human knowledge but the very secrets of God, and if I also have that absolute faith which can move mountains, but have no love, I amount to nothing at all. If I dispose of all that I possess, yes, even if I give my own body to be burned, but have no love, I achieve precisely nothing. (1 Corinthians 13)

We can sit in the lotus position for hours on end, we can chant Psalms all night, we can read Scripture daily, we can do this, we can do that . . . but if we are lacking in love, real love — the kind that spends itself unreservedly on another —

we accomplish nothing. Love, not technical proficiency, is the gauge of the effectiveness of our spiritual practice.

Before falling into the rut of technique in the ways of the spirit, we would be wise to take heed of the words of Abba Macarius, who, when asked, "How should one pray?" said,

> There is no need at all to make long discourses; it is enough to stretch out one's hands and say, "Lord, as you will, and as you know, have mercy." And if the conflict grows fiercer say, "Lord, help!" God knows very well what we need and he shows us his mercy.

Such faith and integrity puts any talk of technique into the proper perspective.

The Beginnings of Christian Monasticism

Ennobling the ethics and morals of men.

Hymn to Saint Basil the Great

During the first three centuries after Christ, the age of martyrdom, followers of Christ throughout the Roman Empire often had to forfeit their lives for their faith. At the same time, some Christians fled into the wilderness to live out their faith without imperial interference, free of the corruption of society. These became the first monks.

Then, as Christianity became increasingly popular and accepted throughout the Roman Empire (particularly after the conversion of the Emperor Constantine in 313 and Christianity's subsequent legalization), the persecutions ceased and the fervor which characterized earlier Christians seemed to wane. Christianity had more adherents, but these were perhaps less single-minded in following the Gospel. At the same time the western half of the empire was on the verge of collapse in the face of the barbarian invasions. Thousands eventually fled the cities to find solitude in the deserts, to rekindle their spiritual dedication and fervor, and to rediscover the simple way of life of the Gospels.

The sanctity and personal authenticity of Saint Antony the Great (c. 252–356) in Egypt, traditionally called the first monk, was written of by Saint Athanasius, archbishop of Alexandria.

Antony's heroic way of life caught the imagination of the age and drew many more into the desert.

Several loosely connected colonies of monks soon formed in three principal locations in Egypt: the Cells, Nitria, and Skete. Pilgrims from all over the empire traveled to these poor yet prestigious desert retreats seeking advice or healing and prayers — or simply to see the famous and holy. The most well known and experienced of these desert fathers and mothers were Macarius, Arsenius, Amoun, Ammonas, Agathon, Hilarion, Epiphanius, Evagrius, John the Dwarf, Moses, Pimen, Pambo, and Sarah. Out of respect they were called Abba or Amma — Father or Mother — and they inspired and nurtured a new life in their followers with their compassion, honesty, and insight.

Collections of their wise and colorful sayings and stories were recorded by their disciples and are known as the *Apophthégmata tôn Patérôn* ("Sayings of the Fathers"). They deal with every aspect of solitary and monastic life, and they display a rich variety of attitudes and personalities.

A second crucial figure in the history of monasticism was Saint Pachomius. In early fourth-century Egypt he established the cenobitic (from the Greek *koínos bíos,* common life) form of monasticism, in which many lived the monastic life together in communities that were self-supporting and united under the rule of life he developed. Pachomius's spirituality differed significantly from that of the hermits. Whereas the hermits sought to know God alone and in solitude, the monks and nuns in Pachomius's monasteries sought to know and serve God while living and working together in a community of service and support for one another.

We have become the slaves of our brutal thoughts and desires, O Lord,
and they drag us farther and farther away from you.
We have failed to live by your commandments,
preferring to follow our own whims rather than your divine will,
always looking for pleasure and satisfaction.
Therefore, come, now, and dwell in us through your mercy,
and teach us how to do your will in all things,
for you alone abound in loving kindness toward all.

Sunday evening sticheron, Tone Four

SIX

Self-Knowledge

EARLIER, WE TOLD A STORY about Pachomius — how the older monk Palamon hesitated to allow him to become a monk. As we saw, Palamon confronted Pachomius with the hard facts of monastic life. When it became obvious that Pachomius was resolute in his desire to be a monk, Palamon finally relented. "Try yourself in every area to find out whether you can be steadfast. When you come back I'll be ready, insofar as my own weakness allows, to work with you *until you get to know yourself.*"

Know yourself. The wise Palamon maintains that the first fruit of *áskesis,* of spiritual discipline, is self-knowledge. "That takes us by surprise," observed Brother Christopher, responding to a question Tom, a journalist, had asked him about the nature of the spiritual journey. They were taking a break from a story Tom was writing on New Skete's dog program, and the conversation had drifted away from dogs and onto spirituality. "From the very beginnings of Christian monasticism, monks and nuns have always described their motivation for entering monastic life as 'the search for God.' Now obviously we don't believe that monasticism has an exclusive claim to such a search — that's the point in a genuine life anywhere — but we do explicitly make this our primary value, and we commit ourselves to helping one another toward that goal. The irony is that once we actually enter the monastery, instead of finding God in the manner we had hoped, what we gradually discover is ourselves as we really are." The monk's eyes sparkled as he laughed in self-mockery. "That's a real shock because we weren't really prepared for it at all! What attracted us to monasticism was the prospect of living in communion with God, not getting to the bottom of who we are. But the fact is, you can't have one without the other."

"How do you mean?" asked Tom. "Surely you can't be saying that you didn't know who you were before you actually became a monk?"

"Well, of course not," replied Brother Christopher, "All of us have self-knowledge to some degree. But not nearly as much as we'd like to think. That's what the ancient philosopher Socrates saw so clearly when he made self-knowledge the very foundation of the examined life. He quoted the inscription on the Delphic oracle approvingly — 'Know yourself' — fully understanding what a daunting task that really was. For Socrates, self-knowledge wasn't simply being informed about things and having a sense of what one's about. Even more, it meant realizing how much one *didn't* know — informed ignorance. That's the real starting point in the spiritual journey: having enough self-knowledge to notice what one's lacking, that we haven't yet discovered who we really are, who we're meant to be."

"But I'm still not clear how that relates directly to your search for God," Tom said. "When you say we can't find God without first knowing ourselves, that intrigues me. Do we really go to God by first going into ourselves?"

"Absolutely, because the God who sees into our depths, who knows us as we really are, isn't interested in some sort of phony fantasy of what we think we are. He's interested in us *as we really are*. It's only when we try to own ourselves in our totality, when we respond to life as it truly is, that we can truly relate to God. That's the work of the spiritual journey.

"Unless we discover — and actually develop — who we truly are, which is the basis of our relationship with God, we'll continue to be like kids playing in a psychic sandbox. This might evoke God's compassion, but it's not really much of a relationship with him." Brother Christopher paused for a moment. "I remember a story the Jewish philosopher Martin Buber liked to tell, about Rabbi Zusya, an eighteenth-century Hasidic rabbi. Shortly before his death the rabbi said to his disciples, 'In the world to come I shall not be asked, 'Why were you not Moses?' I shall be asked, 'Why were you not Zusya?'"

Tom laughed heartily, grew pensive, then confided: "You know, I never considered myself a religious person, mostly because I didn't relate to the religious attitudes and beliefs of my friends when I was growing up — which was fine, I guess — they had their way of looking at things and I had mine. But in recent years, particularly through my work as a writer, I've come to see that I've always had a kind of religious dimension. It's just that I never put that label on it. I called it 'trying to find myself,' or something along those lines, and it's still going on. Yet more and more I see that God has always been in the background of my questioning, sort of as a silent observer. I've heard tell that the Russians say you're either for God or against him, but you're never without him. Listening to you talk about self-knowledge makes me wonder if he hasn't actually been present more than I ever suspected."

"Let me tell you a secret," Brother Christopher replied. "Contrary to what many people believe, the most important questions in life aren't the ones we've been conditioned to think of: 'Is there a God?' or 'Is there life after death?' This might sound odd coming from a monk, but I think 'Who am I?' is far more important. It's not that belief in God or in an afterlife can be ignored, but they've become increasingly disconnected from the way we live." The monk looked away, trying to recall something, and then turned back. "By any chance, did you see that recent nationwide poll asserting that ninety percent of Americans believe in God?"

"As a matter of fact I did."

"Well, if those results are really accurate, it leaves one hard-pressed to see what connection such belief has with our widespread social and personal problems. For me, this reflects a cultural climate that trivializes belief and minimizes the cost involved. Can't you just hear a typical respondent: 'Sure, I believe in God. And why not?' That's the sort of attitude that uses belief to cover its bases — 'just in case' — or even as a tool to try to manipulate God into fulfilling our desires." Brother Christopher shook his head. "C'mon, what do we really make God out to be? Do we ever ask ourselves who is this 'I' who says he or she believes in God? And if we do, how often do we allow that knowledge to really penetrate and change how we live? Without this kind of self-knowledge, our knowledge of God will remain shallow and superficial, just another fact in the vast assortment of information we catalogue in our heads."

The monastic, contemplative approach to the spiritual journey asks us deliberately to develop our own awareness of ourselves and the moral stamina we need to carry out the implications of this knowledge. This is crucial whether we are believer or unbeliever, for it is hard to imagine how anyone can live successfully, much less find lasting happiness, without these. And yet, it is not unusual for a spiritual seeker to be surprised at this. Self-knowledge? He understood the guiding principle of our journey to be centering on God, not what he naïvely presumes would be narcissistically dwelling on himself.

Tom brought up a related question. "Not too long ago I interviewed a pastor who was decidedly antagonistic toward any type of spirituality that emphasized the 'inner' as opposed to the 'outer.' He told me, 'I've heard more crap from so-called mystics than I can stand. How does any of that help my people?' I guess he was particularly sensitive to the issue because he worked in the inner city with the poor and homeless."

"Please don't misunderstand: pursuing self-knowledge is very different from narcissism," replied Brother Christopher, "and it certainly doesn't imply disengaging from society or from other people's needs. In fact, the more we really know ourselves, the more we'll be able to reach out compassionately and effectively to our fellow human beings. This is because our new self-understanding will go much deeper in perceiving our common humanity. The more realistically we understand ourselves, the more we bring to light the thoughts and impulses within us that are the sources of injustice and suffering throughout society. This challenges each of us to do what we can to overcome these tendencies beginning with ourselves. Striving for self-knowledge is quite the opposite of excessive, inordinate self-preoccupation.

"This is a way that is open to everyone, regardless of one's social status. Whether in a monastery or on the streets of Harlem, we can come to know God only by getting to know ourselves, our whole person . . . body and mind, heart and psyche, and then in turn, by coming to know him in one another. I suspect the minister himself, were he to consider the matter carefully, would concede that this paradox underlies all spiritual growth. Still, achieving it isn't so simple. Gen-

uine self-knowledge is a costly journey requiring c
questioning, reflecting, and assessing."

The monk reached over and plucked an enticing st..k of
timothy grass. While chewing on it, he thought for a few seconds before continuing. "The clues to our own identity are
usually based on opinions and presuppositions that we haven't
really examined; invariably they don't bring us any lasting
peace because they're far too simplistic. We have to go much
deeper. But just when we're really serious about getting to the
bottom of ourselves, it's like suddenly discovering that we're
wearing hundreds of layers of garish clothes. As we undress,
we keep finding more and more layers. The question now
begins to pierce through to our consciousness: who's hiding
underneath all the layers . . . all these veneers? Contrary to
what we might have supposed, knowing who we are isn't at
all self-evident."

Tom nodded in agreement. "I see this all the time in my
writing, particularly in my personal journals. One of the reasons writing's so damned difficult is because when it's honest,
it becomes a mirror showing you yourself, warts and all.
Once it's there, in print, you can't deny it. I can't count the
number of times I've gone over my writing from months
back and shuddered in astonishment. God, it's painful! I get so
sick of hearing my own voice that for a moment I feel like
throwing the computer out the window and taking up a job
washing dishes."

Brother Christopher's eyes brightened conspiratorially.
"Ever think about becoming a monk?"

"Yeah, but it's amazing how a wife puts a crimp in one's
plans!" They had a good laugh before Tom returned to his
previous thought. "Seriously, a large part of the challenge of
writing is not allowing the embarrassment and humiliation
of seeing yourself as you are to derail the momentum of

writing. When the words fly from your fingertips onto the screen, you begin to see yourself in a new way; you discover what's been hiding inside yourself; parts of yourself you've never before been introduced to become as plain as day. Maybe that's one of the reasons some writers are tempted to drink too much. The reality's sometimes hard to bear."

"Ah yes, Tom," said the monk, "but the reality's so much richer than the fiction, even if it needs to be worked on."

PERHAPS THE BIGGEST impediment to self-knowledge is the presumption that my familiar self — the self I usually take myself to be — is in fact my true self: "Who am I? Who else would I be! I am my name, the collective result of my personal accomplishments. I am the labels I affix to myself: doctor, mother, wife, Christian." Out of dozens of these fragments, I piece together an ideal image of myself, a mental facade that reassures me of my identity. Doing this year after year, I come to believe that this fantasy is really who I am, and I find myself beaming over the achievement. "So, this is who I am!" My self-image becomes a monument erected in my honor.

Naturally all of us do this! The problem is that our facade rarely goes deeper than our skin. It becomes an idol, conforming more to what we might wish ourselves to be than to what we actually are. We see only a highly censored version of ourselves, without being aware of the consequences. Anything that would mar or threaten our established self-image has been stealthily edited out. Thus, instead of truly seeing ourselves as a multifaceted personality, we cast ourselves solely as the *leading* man or woman in a stage production. In actuality, we are all sorts of characters — hero and villain, simpleton and clown, chorus member and extra. We have limited our self-image to only one idealized, yet ultimate cramped mask, and we end up disowning and denying everything else that is not favorable to our self-made facade.

The result of this is worse than simply living an illusion. Self-deception is destructive. By not acknowledging the reality of all that is inside of us, especially the emotions we are most ashamed of or embarrassed by, we allow them to metastasize into a vast army of personal demons with an astonishing power to control us. They drain our energy and constrict our freedom. Since our self-idol denies the very presence of these emotions, we have no way of effectively dealing with them when they unexpectedly erupt. We mistakenly interpret them as invading alien marauders. The threat of attack keeps us anxiously awaiting their next assault.

We are like a paranoid sentry guarding the fortress of our person, but we are looking in the wrong direction: this enemy is within. The source of these impulses, emotions, and feelings is ourselves. They are the children of our own inner country. Yet once we get an inkling that these manifestations are reactions to a secret part of ourselves, a part that we have ignored and don't want to admit is there, then instead of repeatedly being dominated by them, we can begin gradually to gain control over them. We can finally see them for what they are.

What else is there that so consistently prevents us from actually acquiring this realistic self-knowledge? Our own lack of interior silence, often compounded by distractions via job, television, radio, and an increasingly hectic pace of life, keeps us from really *facing ourselves*. Often our own foolish and hurried choices reinforce this. Facing our own shortcomings can be distasteful, and there are so many other things pressing for our attention. Earlier we discussed the problems of engaging with a competent, discerning teacher to give us a hand. Yet all of these difficulties are no excuse for not working on ourselves in solitude on a continuing basis. Our work, responsibilities, and even our relaxation and entertainment will be enhanced once we begin regular daily examination of, and reflection on, ourselves — if it is done correctly.

The Seeker was going through some of his personal journals when he came across this passage:

"Tonight at dinner, Brother Peter told us about a customer he had today, a fellow named Joe, who came to pick up his puppy. As he held the pup in his arms, he looked nervously at the surrounding hills with its dense forest of pine, maple, and birch trees and, with a tinge of tenseness in his voice, said, 'I don't like this much silence. It's too quiet here.'

"Later in the evening, I find that I'm still thinking about that remark. 'Too quiet?' Despite the fact that monasteries are supposed to be havens of tranquillity, many people have the same reaction. Perhaps the absence of familiar sounds is disquieting, and the silence precipitates reflections that are all too frequently smothered in everyday life. When the noise of the city becomes a tonic to make us breathe easier, beware! That's when we should ask ourselves what we're hiding from, what we're trying to snuff out.

"The truth is, silence is the real friend here, as any monk or nun will tell you. It enables us to see our wounds, and helps us face them. There's no sense ignoring them; they'll only grow bigger. The gash will get wider — a deep pit, draining our life, our joy, our happiness. In contrast, silence leads us to confront the reality, or come to terms with it; this gradually leads us to forgiveness and mending, if we're humble enough to accept it. It's only when I've used silence correctly that I have anything of substance to discuss with Father Laurence. But when I do this, how the inner murkiness becomes clearer!

"If living in the monastery has taught me anything, it's that silence is an inner phenomenon, transcending the simple absence of noise

around us. All it takes is several months of external silence to teach a monk what noise really is. Once the initial flush of peacefulness and tranquillity fades, a deeper, more disconcerting noise awakens, rudely showcasing a world previously hidden from you and living inside yourself. It is precisely the external silence, not absolute but something quite natural, that allows this to awaken by teaching us to listen. And when it does, we become aware of the extent of our self-centeredness. The monastery didn't create this: it's been with me all along, though I was never really conscious of it. It can be alarming, but there's no need to despair! As Father Laurence told me the other day, 'A monastery worth its salt deliberately fosters this, and anyone who refuses to deal with it can't possibly be a monk.' Only by owning it, facing the exterior silence *directly and honestly, will we ever move in the direction of* inner *silence, and the peace that allows us true freedom. The reason for silence is not to be an end in itself, but to be the means whereby we can listen to ourselves, and to everything around us."*

Let's be honest: anger, jealousy, envy, lust, cynicism, greed — are these not all present within every one of us? They are involuntary emotions, what the Orthodox Catholic tradition calls passions, that come and go. They arise from a normal, natural part of our personal landscape, energies that are neither good nor bad in themselves, but which certainly give color and texture to life. What a relief it would be to discover not only that we are not responsible for their presence, but that we need not dance to their drumbeat! Our moral stature depends not on their presence or absence, but on whether we let them affect our behavior. This is why being aware of them in ourselves is so crucial.

In fact, it is not sufficient simply to be aware of them. If we really want to be free, able to act right in spite of our emotional reactions, then we must also come to understand them — what they arise from, what triggers them, what kind of thinking feeds them. To become self-possessed individuals, we will use this awareness and perception to control our reactions and channel our emotional energy correctly. Once we are familiar with the length and breadth of our inner landscape, "the good, the bad, and the ugly," we can realistically work on becoming whole, free, and creative — who and what we are supposed to be.

This demands intense inner work, and it is hardly surprising that many people try to avoid it with any number of clever distractions. A psychiatrist friend who visits the monastery periodically told us recently, "With many of the people I deal with today, there's such a temptation to clutch for 'magical' techniques that can keep them busy externally — yoga, vegetarianism, channeling, even esoteric techniques of prayer, for example — which can actually get in the way of really getting to know ourselves. We'll do anything, no matter how outlandish, to avoid facing our own souls. And yet everything we need to grow in self-knowledge is right here inside us, if only we'd stop and take a look."

SAINT PAUL GIVES US an illustration of this process of self-knowledge. Throughout his letters in the New Testament, Paul reveals himself as dedicated, passionate, and outspoken. Never one to mince words, he called things as he saw them, bluntly pointing out ignorance, malice, and confusion in the early Christian community. His zeal for the Gospel helped guide and form the early church, and it is no mystery why he was one of the first to be considered a saint.

Yet Paul's emotions were a constant challenge to him. In his letters, we see a highly volatile personality who suffered from the same sort of proclivities, tendencies, and personality quirks we all have. We see him going through the same spiritual changes we do, struggling to come to terms with himself, to understand himself, so that he could better do his work.

He himself was among the first to confess his own limitations and imperfections. In one of the most illuminating passages in Scripture about self-knowledge, Paul faces the negativities of his own inner life:

> For we know that the Law itself is concerned with the spiritual — it is I who am carnal, and have sold my soul to sin. My own behavior baffles me. For I find myself doing what I really loathe but not doing what I really want to do. Yet surely if I do things that I really don't want to do, I am admitting that I really agree that the Law is good. But it cannot be said that "I" am doing them at all — it must be sin that has made its home in my nature. And, indeed, I know from experience that the carnal side of my being can scarcely be called the home of the good! I often find that I have the will to do good, but not the power. That is, I don't accomplish the good I set out to do, and the evil I don't really want to do I find I am always doing. Yet if I do things that I don't really want to do then it is not, I repeat, "I" who do them, but the sin which has made its home within me. (Romans 7:14–20)

This is an exceedingly remarkable passage. Its difficulty and complexity are a challenge to any attempt at exegesis. Yet it seems that a careful consideration will point up that whether he was really speaking of himself or not, Paul illustrates the exact dynamic that human beings so often manifest when considering themselves. With sharp perception, he bemoans doing the very things that he knows he should not. He sees himself imprisoned by something within him — and this is the crux of the matter — he experiences his interior fragmentation and looks for some reasonable explanation for his behavior.

The solution Paul comes to at this stage of his life is as ingenious as it is fallacious: it is not the "I" that does these things, but sin residing in the "I." Like an alien parasite growing within, sin feeds on our moral weakness and inclines us away from all that is good. For all practical purposes, in the face of sin's assault, the human being is virtually helpless. It is solely the grace of Christ (here understood as an extraneous, *Deus ex machina* phenomenon) that can rescue us.

With all due respect, here is a classic, all-too-familiar example of passing the buck. If we follow Paul's words too literally, instead of honestly facing up to the whole of who we are, we could easily conclude, "Of course! It is not 'I' that feel and do these things. How could that be so? After all, I believe in God, I follow Christ. I couldn't possibly have these feelings. Yes, it is sin [or whatever else] within me!"

Even if it were not Paul's intent to minimize our freedom, his words come perilously close to giving that impression. Human nature has been given the gift of freedom by God precisely so that we can deal with both our positive and sordid inclinations correctly. It is entirely up to us to take the steps to deal with all this, to desire to grow and to change, to ask for help, to train ourselves.

What Paul did not seem to understand here is that our own often hidden emotions and desires are what lead us not only to good actions, but also to those which we would rather refrain from. The more intense the emotion or need, the more our thinking is blinded and our free will shackled. This can cause excruciating conflict and erroneous rationalizing within us. Attributing negative feelings and the behavior that stems from them to "sin living in us" disregards our nature as emotional as well as rational creatures. The whole spectrum of emotions are a part of what we are. They are intrinsic to our humanness. They will always be present, reacting to everything positively or negatively. Sin, on the other hand, is a product of our free will. It does not exist in us until we actually intend to behave incorrectly.

Paul's gift was in illustrating the conflict between ideals and actions, but for us today his explanation of the emotional life leaves much to be desired, especially since he did not have the same psychological tools we do to understand fully and deal with internal conflicts or erratic behavior. Attributing these to "sin living in him" (something we all try to do at one time or another) did not help him overcome their force. He had to overcome them by realistically coming to terms with them. Later in his life he seems to have come to a healthier state of psychospiritual integration, more in harmony with the ongoing development and understanding characteristic of spiritual growth. Writing from the stark reality of a prison cell he notes:

> Not that I claim to have achieved all this, nor to have reached perfection already. But I keep going on, trying to grasp that purpose for which Christ Jesus grasped me. My brothers, I do not consider myself to have grasped it fully even now. But I do concentrate on this: I forget all that lies behind me and with hands outstretched to whatever lies ahead, I go straight for the goal — my reward the honor of my high calling by God in Christ Jesus. All of us who are spiritually adult should think like this. . . . (Philippians 3:12–15)

WHAT ROLE SHOULD contemporary psychology play in spiritual life? Admittedly, this is vigorously debated in contemporary religious thinking. To be sure, there are those who think that modern psychology has nothing to contribute to spirituality, that everything we need to climb to the heights of spiritual perfection can be found exclusively in the Scriptures or in the writings of the church fathers. For them, any incorporation of modern psychology is at best a polluting influence, distorting a religious worldview that can only be understood from within the tradition itself.

At the opposite end of the spectrum are those who reduce spiritual life entirely to psychology, who turn their noses up at anything written about the inner life prior to the modern era, and who view the spiritual life as a convenient invention of human beings terrified of accepting reality as it is, without dependence on a divine being. Both positions seem extreme.

When a visiting priest asked Brother Marc about using psychological principles in spiritual direction, he prefaced his question by explaining that his professor in the seminary was very suspicious of modern psychology and discouraged his students from becoming involved with it. "The only problem," said the priest, "is that a number of the people coming to me are seriously lacking in basic psychological health. It isn't only that their interpersonal skills are poor, but their basic self-understanding also seems sadly deficient. That always gets in the way of any specific spiritual guidance I might be able to give them. It's almost as if they need to reach a certain level of basic psychological integration before they can even comprehend, much less respond, to the deeper challenges of the spiritual life."

"I agree. That's a common problem these days," Brother Marc replied. "People looking for spiritual help usually come with a lot of other unresolved issues. Those issues undoubtedly affect their overall spiritual growth and don't disappear just because they're looking for God. In fact, the spiritual search itself should actually lead the individual to face these issues honestly; in some cases the person will require the help of a professional, when the severity of the problem goes beyond the level of our training. But in general, most people end up facing these unresolved issues more peripherally, in the context of spiritual direction. Those of us who have the responsibility for helping people in such a setting will have to be informed about, and sensitive to, basic human psychology. We have to be aware of the games people play and the pitfalls of the journey. If not, all sorts of problems arise."

Brother Marc paused. "Not too long ago we heard of something that happened in an ultrareactionary monastery here in the States. It seems that one of the young monks there got it into his head to practice 'the asceticism of filth,' that is, to live without washing himself, because he'd read a story of an early desert monk who'd done the same. Anyway, he had this practice approved by one of the older monks living with him." The priest rolled his eyes. Brother Marc went on, "I kid you not. Well, when his parents came to visit, you can only imagine what they thought! Eventually they were able to get the young monk removed from the monastery and into therapy. Obviously the poor guy was really mixed up. But the greater sin lies with whoever allowed such lunacy. Such extremism is a far cry from real self-knowledge or dedication to a loving God. Yet no doubt the older monk is the sort who scorns psychology or feels it has nothing to say to spirituality.

"This kind of nonsense goes on all the time, and makes it all the more obvious that basic psychological health is intimately related to spiritual health, and even to healthy religion." Brother Marc looked the priest in the eye. "You tell me, Father: isn't part of what you have to do simply teaching people how to think, how to live sanely, how to deal with each other effectively, because that's part of what spiritual growth is about?" The priest nodded. Brother Marc continued, "It seems to be the height of folly not to use sound psychological principles and the wisdom of experience and observation gathered over the centuries to help both ourselves and others live more in harmony with our possibilities and with what's right.

"Psychological and spiritual health — and physical health, too — are inseparably linked in the necessity that we learn how to deal with our emotions. Strong positive or negative emotions need not threaten us, blind us, or compel us to act wrongly. Yet so often we let them. People get angry and presume that they've got to act on that anger, or that they have a right to, instead of deliberately controlling it and getting past it. We have to empower our free will by striving to see what's really going on within and why, and by refusing to act on the feelings alone. By identifying our reactions and emotions, we enable ourselves to see them for what they are instead of either giving in to them or arbitrarily denying them. If we mindlessly repress it, it will bite us ever more strongly next time."

Brother Marc smiled. "Have you ever heard the story about the monk who was sitting in his desert cell and discovered a scorpion crawling on his toe?"

"No."

"Well, obviously when he saw it he was terrified, so he shook his foot frantically, trying to flick the beast away. Yet the scorpion held on all the more and ended up stinging him repeatedly." Brother Marc now broke into a broad grin. "The abba who first told the story remarked that the monk would have done better simply to take a sting and let the scorpion leave of its own accord."

The priest laughed. "See the emotion for what it is and then move on to the next bit of reality, eh?"

"There's a lot to be said for that," replied Brother Marc.

WHEN WE CONSIDER our feelings as only one part of us, instead of identifying ourselves completely with them, we can more easily avoid being blinded by their intensity. We can catch ourselves before we act inappropriately or sinfully. By being more and more conscious of what we are made of, we can act more and more wisely and with discretion. This is the only sensible and effective course for achieving a dynamic self-understanding and healthy self-control.

As a familiar saying has it, the difference between a hero and a coward is that cowards act because of their fear; heroes act in spite of their fear. When we acknowledge the wide spectrum of our emotions, how strongly we are influenced by them, and that our behavior does not have to be determined by them, we open for ourselves an opportunity to grow in virtue and mature in character that we cannot afford to pass up. Our self-understanding and our happiness depend on it.

Nevertheless, as essential as such interior work is, it does not constitute the end of our search for self-knowledge. We are not simply the sum total of every thought, feeling, virtue, and vice that we have ever had. Even if we were completely aware of them all, we must go further, because we still sense a deeper ocean of mystery within us. As we learn to channel our energies in positive and creative ways, this awakens in us the recognition that here also is where we meet a fountain of energies much greater than our own. Paradoxically, this is so only because we truly meet ourselves as we really are.

Without coming to know this mysterious reality at the center of our person, we will remain ignorant of what we can be. *We will not fully know ourselves.* Yet here we can also work with that overwhelming power and goodness beyond ourselves. Here, too, our inner and outer worlds come together as we bring this rich unity into all our relationships and deeds. Herein, finally, lies the basis and goal for all spiritual discipline. Once we taste the truth of this, we will understand that we can never truly be ourselves without these intimate ties to the very ground of our being. Without such connections, we would be like trees growing in midair. This is why Palamon considers self-knowledge crucial in the spiritual life.

The practices of the spiritual life are concrete means for advancing this process of self-knowledge, of self-understanding. They are efficacious when they help awaken us to what we are really like, who we really are. This in turn brings us ever more closely in touch with the mystery that is God, even if we come only to a better comprehension of what God is not. By training ourselves to listen attentively to what life says to us (and this means not only during meditation), we have an unparalleled opportunity to transcend self-deception, to break through our own facades, to become more deeply rooted in reality, and to come to know ever more clearly how we must change.

O only Son and deathless word of God!
For our salvation you took flesh of the holy Theotokos
And ever-virgin Mary.
Without change, you became man; you were crucified,
 O Christ, our God;
You conquered death by death;
You are one of the Holy Trinity,
Glorified with the Father and the Holy Spirit:
O save us!

Hymn from the eucharistic liturgy

SEVEN

Sacred Reading and the Word

T OWARD SUNSET, our community gathers for vespers, the traditional Christian evening prayer. It is a time of compelling beauty, when the weariness and fatigue brought on by the day's work are assuaged by harmonious chants, the soft brilliance of the candle-lit icons, and fragrant incense. All this combines to create an offering that elevates and reenergizes the community. The effort we bring to worship actually revivifies and restores us, making us more conscious of the deeper things of our life, and of a sacred presence that mysteriously fills the gathering.

And it is not just the monks and nuns who experience this, but also the guests who quietly join us for prayer. They listen to the chanting and choral renditions of Scripture, hymnody, and prayer that are the hallmark of Byzantine liturgical worship, and they leave reassured and revitalized by the experience.

The Seeker remembered when his best friend from college, Jack, first visited the monastery. They had not seen each other for a number of years when the Seeker invited Jack to attend his profession of life vows as a monk of New Skete. As it turned out, Jack was able to come several days early, giving them the chance to visit and catch up on old times. However, the night before the actual ceremony, while they took a walk on the road after dinner, Jack suddenly grew reflective. "You know, when you first decided to become a monk, none of your friends could understand what you were doing. It took all of us completely by surprise. I was perplexed by it, perhaps even a bit threatened, which is probably why it's taken me this long to visit." He smiled, somewhat embarrassed. "I know that seems immature now, but that's the way I felt. It just seemed like you were running away from all you had worked so hard to achieve."

"I know," the Seeker agreed. "No one was able to understand. I suppose part of that was because I couldn't talk to any of you about it beforehand. It was just too private, an attraction I was almost ashamed of."

Jack nodded. "But I don't think that way at all, now. Being here these past days has given me a very different perspective, one that almost makes me envious of you. It hasn't just been getting the chance to visit. While it's been great and we've had a lot of laughs, I expected that. That's not what I'm talking about. What's really made an impression on me has been more the atmosphere in which you live here, the peacefulness of it, especially the way that comes out in the services." Jack shook his head wistfully. "It's a different world from what I'm used to at home."

The Seeker's eyes expressed surprise. "I'm not sure exactly how you mean that."

"Oh, I think you are. I don't suppose it would surprise you to learn how few churches even remotely exemplify what one experiences here, even for a person like me. Just to give you an example: my wife and I go to Mass on Sundays, and when we enter the church there's all sorts of noise — kids crying, people whispering. I mean, I'm not particularly pious, but the atmosphere inevitably deadens things. I end up sort of tuning out, and I'm more relieved than refreshed when it's over. Here, however, just walking into the silent church focuses one's attention."

"At least in theory," added the Seeker. "But it still requires a constant, deliberate effort, an attitude of listening that we're continually trying to deepen. It certainly isn't automatic, and it's not at all impossible to be unconscious in the most silent of settings."

"But at least you have the constant reminder to refocus your attention. From the general atmosphere of peace one finds here, to the services themselves — the alternating of silence and chanting, the vibrancy of the hymns — it's as if they continuously prod you to make sure you're awake. The pace of everything seems relaxed, yet reverent, and I can't imagine that a lot of people who visit here aren't struck by that. There's a tone that's different from what I normally encounter. It's an invitation to become more reflective."

"You're really saying this?" The Seeker laughed.

Jack blushed. "I know, worldly people aren't supposed to talk like this." He paused. "But that's the way I see it. And I find that I'm asking myself, how can I take some of this away with me when I leave? Any ideas?"

The Seeker raised his eyebrows, then reflected on Jack's words for a few seconds before responding. "That's just it, what you've been describing, the prayer you've experienced here, isn't just for monks. It's for everyone, and it can be found anywhere, because it's the most natural of human activities. 'As natural as breathing,' one of the older monks used to tell me. It may take quite a while to grasp this, but what helped me most to get a sense of it was meditating on the Psalms."

"What, you mean like what happened at the beginning of vespers, when everyone sat and listened to the Psalms being read?" asked Jack. "Incidentally, that was the first time I've ever seen anything like that."

"That's one way of doing it — a very ancient way," the Seeker replied, "but you can easily use the Psalms for prayer and meditation by yourself. That's because of the way the Psalms teach us, the response that they trigger in our hearts. More than any other kind of

*literature I know, the Psalms hit on the whole gamut of human expe-
rience, illuminating it and turning it toward God. They're remarkably
honest, especially about feelings of anger, injustice, and resentment.
On a practical level, they're a perfect way to give structure to meditation
when you're starting out."*

Traditionally, monks have always had a deep love for the
Psalms. Novices are encouraged to spend some time every day
meditating on them. What Jack was referring to was one of
the ways our community uses the Psalms liturgically. The
Seeker explained that at certain times of the year we begin
vespers with a slow, meditative reading of a *káthisma,* the traditional term for a section of Psalms, by one of the community.

*The Seeker went on, "That's why the reading was done slowly, Jack.
Whoever is assigned to read recites each verse aloud so that everyone
can hear and savor it. It's not a question of being theatrical or artificial
about this. The slow, thoughtful pace allows the words to enter our
psyche and work on the hidden depths of our person."*

Supporting each other here by our silent presence together,
the members of the community listen attentively, as verse after
verse, like waves breaking on the shore of the ocean, washes
over and progressively smooths away the rocky crags of our
being. It is precisely the same experience Abba Pimen spoke
of in the desert over a millennium and a half ago when a
monk asked him how to come to single-heartedness. Abba
Pimen replied,

> "The nature of water is soft, that of stone is hard; but if a
> bottle is hung above the stone, allowing the water to fall drop
> by drop, it wears away the stone. So it is with the word of

God; it is soft and our hearts are hard, but those who hear the word of God often, open their hearts to revere the Lord."

The Seeker's response surprised Jack. "So you're actually suggesting that I use the Psalms for daily meditation?"

"That's one very good way. Look, why not try using them by yourself at home, first thing in the morning, before you go to work? Just take a couple at a time, and then listen quietly to what's stirred up inside. Don't try to analyze them, just pay attention to the thoughts that occur to you. Then follow up on that. If you faithfully work at doing this each day, you'll see the value for yourself soon enough. That's a realistic and time-honored way of beginning a regular practice of meditation."

Jack hesitated. "You know, one thing that did strike me the other night was that while several of the Psalms we listened to were beautiful hymns of praise and were easy to pray, there was another one, very different, that made me feel very uncomfortable. I'm not sure which one it was, but I remember some of the imagery vividly: 'Oh God, smash the teeth in their mouths, tear out their fangs,' *and something similar,* 'The just will rejoice at the sight of vengeance, they will wash the blood of the wicked from their feet.' *Isn't it kind of tough trying to pray with those ideas, with that sort of thinking?"*

"Sure it's tough, but it's not hard to understand those feelings, is it?" the Seeker replied.

"No, not at all, but that's just the problem. I'm not particularly proud of those sentiments; in fact, frankly, they're unchristian. They typify all that I want to get away from in myself."

"And that's precisely why the Psalms are such a valuable point of departure. Their earthy honesty refuses to let us off the hook. I'm sure you see, Jack, how most of us prefer keeping a nice image of ourselves, spotless, sanitary — and superficial. We don't really want to know

ourselves at all. We're so far into denial of what's possibly lurk inside of us that we can't afford to let the truth reveal itself. As a resu our conflicting attitudes and feelings never do get resolved.

"The Psalms challenge all this. Sure, most of us have no trouble praying the 'beautiful' Psalms, those that extol the glory of God and the wonders of nature." The Seeker lifted his hands slightly and glanced around. "'The heavens declare God's glory and the work of his hands, the firmament proclaims!' That's easy! But what about the others: the laments, for example, those that kick and curse our lot in life, whose venom spews forth feelings that are just as much a part of us?" The Seeker cocked his head quizzically before continuing. "What about them?" When Jack remained silent, the Seeker continued, "Well, by entering into their world, one which at times is wild and frightening, we encounter a darker side of ourselves, where hypocrisy, anger, jealousy, resentment, hatred, and grudge-bearing fester. That's a side of ourselves that must be healed by the light of consciousness if we are ever to come to spiritual maturity. That can happen only by descending in prayer with Christ into those depths. The Psalms are able to do this, without leaving us to despair about it. Once we're there, then we can truly pray with our whole reality, praying that these emotions somehow will be transformed."

Jack was quiet for several minutes before he finally said, "I never thought about it that way. Actually, that does make a lot of sense. The way you describe it seems to mean we're not actually praying for whatever the Psalm might be praying for, or even some modern-day equivalent, but instead, we're using the words to better understand ourselves. Once that begins to happen, then we can truly pray from the heart. Is that right?"

The Seeker nodded. "And if not for ourselves alone, then also for all those who can't put these uncensored complaints into words. Yes, I'd say that sums it up pretty well."

THE PSALMS WORK on us progressively, subtly, sometimes without our even being aware how. Here at New Skete, for example, as we listen to them consecutively, *káthisma* after *káthisma*, vespers after vespers, year after year, different verses inevitably strike us differently. The verse that inspires us today may not speak to us tomorrow. Another takes its place. Each reading is fresh, because we who listen to the Psalms today are different from the way we were the day before. Through our response or reaction to them, the Psalms portray in vivid relief our inner state at this very moment. As a result, they are perfect for meditation.

As a monk, the Seeker had experienced this for himself, getting beneath the civility of pat theological thinking and comfortable religiosity. The Psalms look for God in the vast drama of everyday life, amidst the highs and the lows. Until we experience this reality for ourselves, no amount of words will ever suffice to describe it for us. It will all remain on the level of theory.

Nevertheless, we can provide the reader with something of a running start by sketching out the way such a meditation may occur based on our own monastic experience. Let us imagine the interplay of listening and prayer in the heart and mind of the Seeker during a vespers service. In doing so, however, the reader should understand that if we attempt to describe this — the innermost goings-on in the depths of the heart — such a description can easily sound like talking to oneself, like stream of consciousness, perhaps even like day-dreaming. It is anything but. It is, in fact, more than words or reflection; it is turning oneself toward another, deliberately stretching out to meet God. Naturally, the language each of us uses will be our own most personal, private language. At times it may come more from the heart than from the head, in the stark earthiness of what we really think and feel. And even though our description uses words, the reality, at times, may frequently be wordless.

A FTER THE BELLS announcing the beginning of the service have stopped, and the peaceful silence gives way to the priest's opening intonation, the community sits down in wooden chairs lining the nave of the church, to listen to the Psalms. After some initial silence, the reader begins, "I will extol the Lord with all my heart, in the council of the upright and in the great gathering of the people." (Psalm 111[110]:1) This evokes the Seeker's response:

"God, let these words touch my heart! Let me desire to praise you honestly, thoughtfully. Yes, I extol you, I praise you, I give myself over to you with my whole being. Help me do this because it is right, because this is what you want of me . . . not because I want to feel good. . . . Yet, is this really the way it is? Do I really know what this means? . . . So why do I allow petty, smart-ass remarks to spew forth from my mouth? I did it again today. . . . I'm looking for commendation or approval from others, instead of only from you. You know this is so, O God . . . God, my back is killing me . . . , there I go again, worrying about my aches and pains. Please, help me to let go! . . ."

"His handiwork is truth and justice; trustworthy are all his precepts, ordained to last for all eternity." (v.7)

"How blind I am to this at times, my God! Why don't I see that you are inseparable from what is right and good? Why don't I see that the slightest stitch of reality bears your presence? . . .

"Yet — given the way I do things — how can I really say I respect truth and justice, or trust in your presence? It is so easy to find you only in pious truths, but isn't your majesty present everywhere I

might look? That's where I have to go . . . for the rest of my life. . . .
Who was that trying to clear his throat . . . On and on . . . God,
can't he cut it out at least during the reading? . . . Dammit, there I
go again! . . . C'mon, bring your mind back. . . . What was that
verse? . . ."

"Reverence for the Lord is the beginning of wisdom."
(v. 10)

"Okay, point taken. I've been careless again today, unmindful of
your word for long stretches. Is this laziness? Instead of being reverent
in everything, I've let my forgetfulness excuse me from any thought of
you. Why did I give in to complaining at work? I was getting royally
pissed off at Brother ———— , I lashed out at him like a spoiled kid.
I let my irritability spoil everything I touched today . . . seems like a
long way from wisdom! . . ."

One does not have to be a wizard to see how human even
monastics are. Obviously, with such meditative listening, each
Psalm can provoke a variety of responses. This is precisely
what the Seeker told Jack to expect in such a routine practice.

"The genius of the Psalms," explained the Seeker, "is that their
diversity touches each person uniquely, as he or she is at this particu-
lar time of prayer. That's what's so beautiful about them. As each of
us listens, the verse that strikes me or triggers a vivid recognition of
myself may have no effect on the monk next to me. Who knows? He
might still be mulling over a verse that came up in the previous
Psalm. In both cases, however, each of us savors it, gleaning whatever
insight it has to offer. And the same goes for the other monks and
nuns. The point of this type of meditation is not that we get some-
thing 'specific' out of the Psalms, but that we let them reflect us back
to ourselves."

*The Seeker's expression revealed a sudden recollection. '
that's how one of the better-known figures of the early Chur
Athanasius, described them in the fourth century. He said
Psalms 'become like mirrors to the person singing them.' They reveal
us as we are, blemishes and all, including attitudes, thoughts, and
emotions which we are largely blind to. When we engage with the
Psalms through this meditative process, we are increasingly confronted
with how we are in the raw. Then maybe we can begin to work realis-
tically and profitably for our betterment."*

Simplicity characterizes this way of meditating, whether done together or in private. This "reading and listening" is the basis of an ancient monastic practice, what Western monks traditionally call *lectio divina,* sacred reading, which also has its equivalent in the Christian East. To hear the Psalms read this way (and for that matter, the rest of the Bible, particularly the Gospels) enables us to move beyond a purely academic approach to the Scriptures. Instead, it becomes an arena for wrestling with our own conflicts and for developing an abiding and expanding prayerfulness and consciousness of God. Although an individual monk may in fact be a biblical scholar, at *lectio divina* he does not read the Bible on the level of scholarship. When studying Scripture, he engages with the scientific and theological world and uses their tools to learn, analyze, compare, and discover. This is especially important to realize today when the study of Scripture has become such a highly academic pursuit. But when he reads it personally, in his own struggle for self-knowledge and self-understanding, he allows the moral challenge of the Psalms or Gospels to shake him up, plow up his self-image, plant seeds of a new spirit, exercise and test him heart and mind. In study we aim to master the word; in *lectio divina,* we let the word master us.

Without in any sense surrendering to the blinders of an anti-intellectual piety or demagogic fundamentalism, monastic tradition has always given primacy of place to the word as it addresses each of us personally. The words confront us as we are existentially — somewhat different from what we like to think we are — and eventually reveal the darkest areas of our heart. We must respond. For now, we listen and watch this within ourselves, patiently, expectantly.

"God in his goodness will give understanding to all who strive for it." (v.10b)

Does understanding really come from you, God? Or do we come to greater understanding by striving after it with the whole of our being? Isn't this what the mind craves? Seems like laziness is the real obstacle to my understanding, to my real growth in wisdom. . . . I see I need some honest reflection — and regularly. To a great extent, Lord, aren't wisdom and understanding really mine for the taking? But getting them requires more initiative and effort than I usually want to make. I'll never grow wiser by just waiting for you to inject wisdom into me. I must work for it. Yes, I see that. . . . Yes, I really do see it. . . . But help me to do it. . . .

By following the trail of the living Word, anyone can enter into an ever-expanding conversation with the ultimate source of that Word, and the relationship gives birth in us to a growing awareness of the underlying and all-pervasive love that sustains the universe. In the face of such love we feel inadequate, humble, and we long to bring ourselves to ever closer conformity with this infinite goodness. We become listeners.

For the monk as well as for any human being, the fundamental question at the core of our existence is not whether

God exists (in fact, a reasonable case for this can be made purely natural grounds); the real issue is whether or not God has spoken — indeed, speaks — and if so, what does he say? If God does communicate, then the most pressing issue in our lives is to learn how to hear and to respond to this. Silence is no less a part of this than speech. As in any language, we have to learn to understand what the silence means. This is what happens in *lectio divina*.

Christian prayer and meditation on the Scriptures develops out of the persistent conviction that we come progressively to a deeper realization of who God is, not only in the marvels of creation around us and in our written traditions of spiritual wisdom and insight, but also in a more unique way through Jesus Christ. Christians believe Christ is the fullest incarnation of God's Word, his very self-expression. Every other word must therefore be interpreted in the light of him. Above all, Jesus revealed God as a compassionate Father whose Holy Spirit we are called to acquire. By engaging with the Word (as a person) we can come to the fullest relationship possible with God our Father. All of God's words, including the person of Christ, confront us both as individuals and as the race of human beings in expectation of a response. Only insofar as we see them as addressed to us will we respond and grow in the relationship. Only by training ourselves to calm down and listen can we begin to recognize the word of God in everything, even the most mundane utterances of life.

I 'VE HEARD religious people talk about the existence of God and how they know God," a young mother remarked to Sister Helen in the nuns' gift shop. "But I have trouble understanding what it all means. Doesn't it seem like God is more silent than anything else?"

Sister Helen nodded toward the woman's young child sitting on the floor nearby. The girl was quietly absorbed in petting Nattie, Sister Helen's handsome German shepherd. "Oh, I don't know," she mused. "I suspect that if you think about it, God's speaking a lot more than he's keeping silent."

The woman, seeing the connection, smiled, a bit embarrassed. Sister Helen went on. "It's all in how we think about it, I guess. If we limit 'God speaking' to his actually making physical sounds, then for sure God is silent. But it seems that communication is much more than speech. Communication flows from presence, and we can become aware of the wonder of it all in the most ordinary of circumstances."

The woman was listening intently, so Sister Helen went on. "Let me give you an example that a friend told me about recently. He was on a business trip, driving to his hotel in an unfamiliar city. As he parked at the hotel and got out of his car, his wallet accidentally slipped out of his pocket by the curb. It wasn't until he was finishing his dinner in the hotel restaurant that he realized he'd lost his wallet. Well, he explained to the restaurant manager what had happened and then anxiously began searching for the wallet, retracing all his steps. He scoured his hotel room, but turned up nothing, nor did a careful inspection of his car. Finally, running out of options and fearing the worst, he asked the hotel clerk whether by chance anyone had happened to turn in a wallet within the past several hours. When the clerk checked with lost and found, she relayed the news that the hotel doorman had indeed found a wallet by the curb and turned it in. The clerk handed him his wallet. Well, you can imagine the flood of relief he experienced, how grateful he was for the doorman's honesty. Yet when my friend found the man to thank him, he realized just how easy it would have been for him to pretend that he had never found the wallet at all. 'No ___ would have known,' he told me.

"Now were we to have experienced this, we might have been tempted to think God was really looking out for us, leading us to thank him that we recovered the wallet. But is that what's really going on here?" Sister Helen shook her head dubiously. "No, I don't think so. Think about it for a minute. Beyond the literal facts, 'between the lines of the event,' *what word do we hear?* Was it God who gave my friend his wallet back? If we're awake, such an experience communicates a more down-to-earth word, one that speaks of goodness and thoughtfulness, of the reality of another's concern. This word speaks of God indirectly, through the concrete circumstance of an everyday happening." The nun smiled warmly. "When we listen to the meaning, to the truth of the event, we can receive that word of God whether it *pleases* us or not. For it's absolutely the case here that had my friend never recovered his wallet, there would have been no less a word present for him to hear, to understand."

Life is rife with these *words* that have the power to transform us. When we finally listen, we learn that human events overflow with words that connect us with a deeper meaning, which speaks ultimately of God's multifaceted presence. A thoughtful response to these events depends on the reality of our faith, on seeing the word of God revealed in the changing circumstances of everyday life.

Throughout the warp and woof of life's tapestry, in becoming more observant, we quickly discover that God is not peddling dogmas of belief. Our faith is in a person, not in some thing, and we must be careful not to be too arrogant in our presumptions of what we know. Authentic faith recognizes the provisional nature of my own understanding, of trying to express in human terms what ultimately cannot be expressed. Ours is a God of mystery.

This is not some sort of intellectual copout; on the contrary, "mystery" is a word charged with deep significance within our tradition. Coming from the Greek *mystérion,* it is related to the verb *myéin,* which means "to contemplate." It is also the word we traditionally use for the sacraments of the Church. A mystery in our sense is a reality we truly encounter yet which is of such profound depth and meaning that it is, finally, beyond the comprehension of the human mind. Would God be God if he could be entirely understood? As Saint Gregory of Nyssa cautions,

> Every concept formed by the intellect to comprehend and circumscribe the divine nature can succeed only in fashioning an idol, not in making God known. (*Life of Moses*)

A number of years ago Father Laurence wrote an article called "Semantic Bankruptcy" in *Gleanings,* the monastic journal once published by New Skete. In it, he discussed the notion of mystery, showing that though it can never be fully understood, nevertheless, we can grow in understanding certain aspects of it:

> We might more clearly portray the nature of mystery with an example. For a man born blind, a two-dimensional representation is a mystery. He does not have what it takes — sight — to comprehend this reality. Sight is required for a person to understand how a two-dimensional representation actually does represent something that is three-dimensional. Since he does not have the means to see, it is a mystery how this flat something is a likeness, let us say, of his brother. In fact, that it is a likeness of his brother is something that he must be told, and then he must take it on faith. He may have some idea of

what his brother "looks like" since he has, for example, felt the features of his brother's face with his hands. Yet, the photo remains a mystery for him. It is beyond the power of a man born blind to understand this.

However, we note that not every aspect of the photo is a mystery. Even the man born blind can feel its flatness. Even the man born blind can feel the smoothness of the glossy print or the lesser smoothness of another kind of photo paper. He can even perceive it is paper, not wood. Even the man born blind can smell the photo, comparing it with other papers, with other flatnesses he has experienced this way. Thus, it is possible for some aspects of even the greatest mysteries to be understood, at least in a limited way.

Though we cannot fully understand the mystery in itself, we can nonetheless come to know and value it in certain ways through contemplation, to meet it through our own ever-deepening awareness and love of the world around us, of our fellow human beings, and of the universe itself. Though our knowledge and understanding of the mystery will always be imperfect and provisional, we will know more and more the experience of loving and being loved by God.

To become more authentically human as we are meant to be, regardless of one's creed, involves becoming a listener, a hearer of the word that comes to us continuously through the changing complexion and complexity of everyday life. For the Christian, however, this means listening to and contemplating the mystery that is Jesus Christ, and ourselves especially in relationship to him. This is what the full flowering of the tradition of *lectio divina* ultimately involves.

The Growth of Christian Monasticism

Pray and work!
Rule of Saint Benedict

Cenobitic monasticism spread rapidly throughout the Empire from its beginnings in Egypt, first to Palestine through Saints Hilarion and Epiphanius and later Jerome and Melanie of Rome in Judea and Dorotheus in Gaza, then on to Sinai, Syria, Asia Minor, Greece, and Western Europe. Saint Basil the Great, archbishop in Cappadocia (a part of modern-day Turkey), visited the deserts of Egypt in the middle of the fourth century, but he returned home a staunch critic of the solitary life, teaching that the cenobitic form of monasticism is more closely allied with the Gospel. To stabilize monasticism in his communities, Basil composed the *Long Rules,* a question-and-answer document that provided a basic foundation and perspective for both Eastern and Western monasticism. He stressed the importance of sharing life and worship, manual work for self-sufficiency, moderation in asceticism, love of neighbor, generosity and service to the poor, care for the sick, and the foundation of monasteries closer to urban centers.

By the fifth century a more austere form of monasticism began to flourish in Syria and Palestine that lacked Saint Basil's creativity and flexibility and strove instead to emulate earlier Egyptian austerity. Saint Sabas founded the largest and most influential of this kind of monastery in Palestine. At the same time Saints Theodosius and Euthymius founded cenobitic monasteries there, as well.

Monasticism at Mount Sinai, where Moses traditionally had received the Ten Commandments, was at first only a cluster of hermits living around the side of the mountain in individual caves. In the sixth century, however, the Emperor Justinian established a monastery at the site (now known as Saint Catherine's) where Saint John Climacus (author of *The Ladder of Divine Ascent*) later resided. Monks from Armenia, Georgia, Persia, Arabia, and Ethiopia were trained here and took back to their native lands its liturgical and spiritual traditions.

In the western half of the Roman Empire, Saint John Cassian (c. 365–435), who traveled to Egypt and lived with the desert fathers for a time, founded a monastic community in southern Gaul. His *Institutes* and *Conferences* gave solid direction to a thriving monasticism that soon extended from Italy to Ireland, with self-governing monasteries formed by the work of such saints as Ambrose of Milan, Augustine, Martin of Tours, Hilary of Poitiers, Aidan of Lindisfarne, Columban at Leinster and Bangor, and David of Wales.

In sixth-century Italy, the creative genius of Saint Benedict adapted an earlier monastic rule of life (the anonymous *Rule of the Master*) in such a way that its ascetic excesses were tempered and all the elements of monastic life were brought into harmony and balance. This classic rule eventually inspired many autonomous monasteries in Italy, Gaul, Germany, and Britain to adopt it, thus creating something of a federation of monasteries. The vast reforms of Saint Gregory the Great in Rome further helped Benedictine monasteries to become the main centers of culture and learning throughout the West, and Saint Benedict was eventually called the father of Western civilization.

Hearing the words of the holy gospels
you left your earthly father to serve
    your father in heaven,
showing us the riches of poverty and
    the perfect joy of the cross.
And in opposing the pride of the
    mighty with the humility of
    the simple,
and breaking down the walls of hatred
    with the power of your love,
you became yourself an image of
    the crucified Christ,
who is everywhere present and fills
    all things

        Kondakion for Saint Francis, Tone Six

EIGHT

Practicing Sacred Reading

THE BASIC SIMPLICITY of sacred reading makes it more accessible than other, more exotic ways of meditation. Though *lectio divina* is a central ingredient of monastic spirituality, there is nothing exclusively monastic about it. Neither is it some sort of pious technique whose value and relevance would be lost in the rush of everyday worldly life. It can be experienced and used with profit today by anyone who is sincerely searching for the truth.

"I first tried meditation when I was in college," a retreatant who was seriously thinking about entering the monastic life at New Skete explained recently. "In fact I went through an introduction to transcendental meditation and actually practiced it for a while. Initially, it seemed to give me a sense of peace and well-being, but it wasn't long before those feelings leveled off. After a couple of months I grew bored with it, so eventually I stopped."

"What did you find boring?" asked Brother James.

"I guess reciting a mantra that I didn't understand proved the biggest difficulty for me. Over time, my mind rebelled against it. The more I thought about it, the more the whole effort seemed to be a waste of time, so finally I stopped doing it. But later on, I gradually came to realize once more that something definitely was missing from my life, and that it was out of this need that I had gone in the direction of TM in the first place."

Brother James listened thoughtfully and then responded. "Over the years more than a few people have visited the monastery who tried not only TM, but a number of other esoteric types of meditation. Often they've been individuals who felt a deep attraction to the inner life but received little encouragement or practical guidance in their own church communities. The way most of them describe it, after poking around a bit they were left with the general impression that if you were really serious about meditation and prayer, you'd have to look elsewhere than Christianity, most likely to Far Eastern religions.

"We just had a guest like this. She became a Buddhist after she graduated from college, and is now practicing a type of meditation known as *vipassana*. She had grown up in a strict Southern Baptist family, but she gradually fell away from her faith in college. I remember her telling me how shocked she was to discover that Christianity had a long and venerable tradition of meditation and prayer, as well. She grew up totally unaware of that."

Brother James looked out toward the horizon. "It's sad, though it's our own fault, really. We've done a poor job of making people aware of this contemplative tradition within Christianity, and so they look for it in other places. It would seem to be more in harmony with a person's roots to be able to search for and find this wisdom within the framework of the tradition in which they were raised."

The retreatant agreed. "I know I've come to think that for myself, but I also know several people who more or less fit the pattern you just described, who ended up joining a Far Eastern religion. Invariably, what led them in that direction was the belief that they'd finally be able to learn a viable way of meditation." The retreatant shrugged his shoulders and said, "I'm not really sure what to think about it." He paused a moment and then asked, "So tell me, when a person comes here looking for guidance in prayer, what do you tell them?"

"That depends largely on where they happen to be in their spiritual journey," the monk replied. "Prayer isn't something you can approach by formula. Different people will be attracted to different ways of praying, depending on their personality, temperament, and social circumstances. Nevertheless, since most of the people who visit the monastery are from some sort of Christian background, we believe that the tradition of sacred reading — *lectio divina* — is an approach to meditation that *anyone* can benefit from, whether they're just beginning or whether they've been on the spiritual journey for some time."

"You mean reading the Bible?"

"It's not *just* reading the Bible — lots of people do that. It's reading it in a very particular way, a way that fosters a contemplative orientation to your life. We can use *lectio* to learn and experience a type of inner listening that, as it becomes more and more characteristic of our lives, makes us more fully human. With *lectio,* the focus is on developing an underlying attitude of prayerfulness rather than on saying prayers, and this thoughtful, perceptive prayerfulness has a powerful impact on our daily life. The practice of *lectio* fosters a certain interior silence that makes us more alert and able to listen, so that we can respond to life as correctly as possible."

Brother James continued, "Of course, this is nothing new. Monks and nuns have practiced this way of meditation since the very beginning, because they discovered how truly helpful it is. They see the concrete and profound effects in their own lives. And since practically everyone respects the Bible, it's an especially nonthreatening type of meditation for people outside the monastery. Even non-Christians can make positive use of it. That's because in *lectio* we're not memorizing dogmas or espousing the tenets of a particular church. Rather, we're engaging with the text in the depths of the heart, listening intently to what it provokes in us. The fact that a Christian may interpret this differently from a non-Christian really doesn't matter here. Both will profit greatly from doing it."

Brother James went on to underscore the simplicity and naturalness of the practice of *lectio*. All that is required is the ability to read and a place of silence to let words sink into your heart and be heard. Although it is a good idea also to have a general understanding of the Bible and the many literary forms it uses (we recommend several excellent introductions to the Bible at the end of this book), we also reiterate once again that in *lectio* itself the emphasis is not on intellectual study or even "Bible study" but on the individual's own gut reaction. As our tradition puts it, the primary purpose of *lectio* is to lead us into genuine dialogue with the Spirit of God, which occurs when we hear the Spirit, who is present everywhere, addressing us through the scriptural text in front of us.

This led the retreatant to ask, "So the mind still does play an important role in this?"

"Absolutely," replied Brother James. "Contrary to what some schools of meditation seem to say, the mind is necessarily always thinking about something, even if we're not aware of it." Brother James tapped his head. "The mind is made for thinking. And in *lectio,* we're directing that activity in a very specific way. By listening and reflecting upon the text, rereading it slowly and attentively until an aspect of it strikes us personally, we'll find ourselves standing before God and conversing inwardly with him, honestly searching for his truth and ours, questioning, listening, becoming ever more absorbed in this inner dialogue. As with any relationship, it's an ongoing process. Yet when this is sustained over a period of time, then we go from mere acquaintance to deeper and deeper levels of discovery, familiarity, friendship, and love."

The retreatant was listening carefully, and feeling somewhat relaxed, finally brought up a question that was nagging at him. "I've read a number of books on meditation, but most of them recommend some form of 'single-pointed' meditation, which is different from what you're describing. They seem to say that if a person really wants to learn how to meditate, they'll do meditation that focuses only on a single thing. At least, that's the impression I get from them as well as from some of the friends I told you about. Would you say that your approach to meditation brings better results than those others?"

Brother James shook his head slightly. "I don't think it's a good idea to put the question that way. Meditation really isn't about getting results, and when you make that your focus, you tend to get into trouble. Besides, there are forms of single-pointed meditation in Christianity, and other forms as well, which certainly all have their value. And God alone can judge results. Instead, I think it's better simply to speak from our own experience. We find that when any of us allows the words and meaning of these texts to confront us personally and in turn to evoke an authentic response, then this kind of reading stirs up a spiritual awakening in us that impacts our whole life. *Lectio* acts like a rototiller, plowing up the soil in our hearts if we are at all open. It's an eminently realistic approach that most people can easily learn, and since it is so personal, it fans the fires of interest, growth, and change; so used over time, it becomes a powerful and effective means of transforming ourselves."

THIS PROCESS of transformation initiated by *lectio* can happen in an infinite variety of ways, from the dramatic to the pedestrian. A well-known example from our tradition is the story of Saint Antony the Great, the first and probably most famous of all the desert fathers, who lived in the late third and early fourth century. The Seeker remembered being given Saint Athanasius's *The Life of Antony* to read shortly after he entered monastic life, and the impression it made on him when he read it. He learned that Antony was inspired to embrace monastic life on the force of a scriptural passage he heard read in church one day, something which struck the Seeker as hard to imagine. Already for some time Antony had been pondering how he could best respond to the Gospel call, and on that particular day he heard the text *"If you would be perfect, go, sell what you possess and give to the poor, and you will have treasure in heaven. Then come, follow me."* (Matthew 19:21) He did so by becoming a monk.

The Seeker asked Father Laurence about this. "Isn't it a little risky to give that much credence to an arbitrary passage from Scripture? I mean, couldn't a person easily go off the deep end this way? I can just imagine someone hearing, 'If your right eye should be your downfall, tear it out and throw it away, for it will do you less harm to lose part of yourself than to have your whole body thrown into hell.'"

Father Laurence smiled. "I think we're a long way from that sort of literalistic thinking here. No, I suspect something much more vital is taking place, which you'll see if you think about it for a moment. No doubt Antony, like all Christians, had heard this text many times before, but on this particular occasion something different happened. The text pierced him to the heart. It was as if he had heard it for the first time. It wasn't a question of his misunderstanding it and letting it impel him to do something foolish. No, the text penetrated all his defenses and illuminated his deepest desire, and gave him a clear and radical way to live the Gospel ideals. 'Come, follow me.' I'll bet that text echoed in his mind and heart for a long time, so that he allowed it to really inspire him. The results proved this to be an extraordinary moment of personal enlightenment that changed Antony forever. Upon hearing those words and meditating upon them intently, he experienced the truth of those words as it related to his own life, and he responded to it in a positive and decisive way."

Father was looking right at the Seeker as he went on without a break. "Do you really think Antony was being reckless, acting foolishly simply on a literalistic interpretation of the Scriptures without considering the consequences? When you look at the rest of his life, it sure doesn't seem so. On this particular occasion, the text only pointed out to him his own inner truth in the depths of his soul, and he had to respond to it. Others have responded to the same passage just as genuinely, but often in very different ways."

The Seeker replied, "Well, all I can say is that I've never had a text affect me quite that strongly."

"That doesn't matter in the least," Father observed. "Lectio doesn't have to be dramatic. In fact, more often than not, the turnabout it starts is unassuming and gradual, changing its practitioners steadily day by day — year by year — as it works in conjunction with all the rest of their life. What matters is that you do it faithfully, instead of making a lot of excuses not to. Daily practice of lectio isn't complicated, nor is it an end in itself. But it has to be regular if it's to deepen our self-awareness and relationship with God and help us respond to the prodding of the Spirit throughout our lives. The slow, reflective pondering of the text, repeated inwardly with our fullest attention — savoring it over and over again — in time empowers the words and images to awaken connections and insights we might otherwise pass by in the haste of our daily life."

H OW DOES SUCH a meditation happen? Simply by doing it, without a lot of fuss. Look for a regular time and place where you can anticipate being undisturbed, a nearby church or library, for example, or a bedroom, study, or even the back porch of your home. Any time of day can be adapted for meditation, but early in the morning, when most activity is at a minimum, seems to be the most natural. Even in the busiest of households such time can be found by rising a half hour earlier than normal. Wash your face briskly, drink your coffee, then sit attentively with the Bible while the rest of the world sleeps. You will need to focus on your meditation for twenty minutes to a half-hour, so use a chair with firm back support to keep your spine straight. This will help you breathe deeply and keep your attention sharp. Be conscious of the presence of God. Get comfortable enough not to be thinking how uncomfortable you are, but not so relaxed as to nod off to sleep.

An advantage of using sacred reading for our meditation is the endless wealth of material Scripture provides for our use. So we need a translation that speaks directly to us, not one that forces us on the spot to translate the translation, so to speak. It makes little sense to use an archaic translation whose hieratic language obfuscates the text's meaning. Your Bible for *lectio* should be a modern one, but not a "paraphrase." Some excellent translations also contain helpful introductions and notes for use outside your time of meditation. Since the Bible is a vast compilation of stories, poetry, prophetic exhortations, letters, and wisdom teaching, chronicling and illustrating the countless ways in which human beings both encounter and resist God, whatever we can do to promote our own fuller understanding should be encouraged.

A sharp caution: one of the most misdirected and destructive tendencies in modern Christian life is to focus on the Bible so narrowly that we inadvertently make it into an idol. The Bible is not divine. God alone deserves our worship. Bibliolatry, worshipping the words of Scripture instead of the God they manifest, absolutizing them and using them out of context, is a most insidious vice that parades itself as a virtue. It "reveres" the Scriptures by suffocating them in a prison of literalism and inerrancy they could not possibly survive undistorted. This fails to do justice to the vast cultural and religious context in which they were written and the dynamic character of all human expression and understanding.

For example, how often do we hear misguided enthusiasts quote the Bible, authoritatively saying, "An eye for an eye . . . ," completely oblivious to Christ's Gospel teaching that condemns that? The Scriptures were never written to circumscribe the limits of truth and human morality once and for all, like some easy-answer textbook that resolves all our doubts. Expecting them to do this drains them of their very lifeblood. Rather, like Jacob wrestling with the angel in the dark of night (as recounted in the book of Genesis), we simply have to struggle with the many problems and layers of meaning in the Bible, if necessary revising the way we understand things so that we hear its word correctly. Only then will it confer its blessing of life on us. But be forewarned, the effort may leave us, like Jacob, limping away from the encounter, purged of the arrogance that believes one possesses all the answers.

This is what believers have always done, which is why we see change and development take place within the Bible itself on attitudes as diverse as monogamy, Sabbath observance, dietary laws, and slavery. Such development underscores the danger of misusing the Bible by taking it solely at face value. The Bible is not a static text, and its moral teaching often seems to change at the precise moment when we come to a more mature understanding of reality.

Our purpose here is not to get into the intricacies of biblical exegesis and interpretation, but we feel impelled to sound this warning to anyone using the Bible as a means of growth in the spiritual life. Read it correctly; read it as a whole. Don't fall into the trap of using the Scriptures to self-righteously condemn everything from homosexuality and abortion to people of non-Christian faiths. To do this simply because we can find texts that seem to say as much is a regression to a fundamentalistic mind-set that does violence to the very nature of the Bible. Furthermore, it is utterly foreign to the spirit of *lectio divina.* The Bible is meant to change and convert *us, continuously,* not to become a weapon of hatred that we use to attack those with whom we disagree. People who do this may protest that they are only standing up for the timeless truth of the Bible, but it does far more harm than good. Not only does it manifest a glaring lack of charity, but the self-righteous attitude driving these denunciations actually immunizes its proponents from the transforming power of the Word itself. It cannot touch them. After all, they believe that they have already heard the Word: they are *already* saved, once and for all.

Taking the Bible literally and simplistically without regard to its literary forms, historical context, and even its use by the living tradition of the Church, ultimately is a sterile exercise. It transforms what is meant to be a contemplative practice into a shortsighted grasping for certitude and security, in which we wield the word of God like a bludgeon to mask our own fears and insecurity. This is hardly the way of faith. Faith calls us to renounce the security of certitude and easy, established answers for a demanding journey into the unknown. Thus, while the Bible possesses strong historical value, it is not a work of history but of faith, and therefore it deserves to be encountered on that level.

Considering the fact that the Bible was written over a period between eighteen hundred and three thousand years ago, it is not surprising that contemporary conceptions of truth and historicity cannot be applied to the biblical writers in the same way as to later authors. The authors of the biblical books lived at a time when various dimensions of insight and truth were expressed through literary forms as diverse as story, myth, symbol, poetry, law, prophetic exhortation, and hyperbole. To insist, then, that truth exists only within the narrow confines of a modern understanding of empirical science and history is either to dismiss the Bible as irrelevant, or to live in denial of the numerous contradictions, mistakes, and cultural biases present within its pages. To say which is worse is a toss-up.

Though the Scriptures are invaluable in mediating God's word to us, they are by no means our only source, nor is the manner in which they do so always self-evident. It is quite possible to think we are hearing Christ while actually we are only listening to our own projections. It is only too easy to fall into a futile swamp of subjectivism, especially when it comes to the Bible. However, we can dramatically reduce the odds of falling victim to this through the safeguards of patience, intellectual honesty, and a healthy self-doubt. These can ensure that our reading of Scripture is not simply a solo or group exercise in delusion. Our parish, our connections with church tradition, provide a context and perspective that may help guide our understanding and interpretation. For example, if we understand a text in a manner that is utterly foreign to the general understanding of it within the Church, chances are good that we are reading into the text something that just is not there, and that we are not hearing the Lord correctly.

I F WE LOOK TO the wisdom of our monastic tradition, there is a more honest and realistic approach to utilizing the spiritual riches of the Bible that need not compromise our intellectual integrity. *Lectio divina* is a way of absorbing the word so that it may bear fruit for us in wisdom and insight. Without discounting its original meaning, we home in on how the text might apply to us, to me, today. What is God, and our own conscience, saying to us now? By allowing these questions to work on us, by making those connections in our own life that reveal our blindness and stubbornness, the practice cleans away the stains of ignorance and deception.

Above all, the point in *lectio divina* is to let the words penetrate into the core of our lives so as to effect change, instead of passing superficially over the surface. A tale from our community clarifies the nature of this process. It happened once that a monk who was especially enamored of reading books left his dog alone in his room while he went out on an errand. While he was away, the dog chewed up half of his favorite theology book, a priceless volume the monk had obtained during his university days. When he returned and found the book destroyed, the monk, in utter frustration, took the damaged book and tied it to the dog's mouth, thereby thinking to teach her never to chew again. When the abba saw the dog with the book in its mouth, he said to the monk, "You see? Your dog has accomplished something that you, for all your reading, have never been able to do. She has digested its words!"

Sometimes, the results of *lectio* are immediate, bringing clarity to our confusion before we even fully realize it. Then we find it easy to explore our thoughts and feelings silently in God's presence. At other times we may find ourselves struggling in uncertainty or emptiness, unable to perceive anything for ourselves in the text. We search, but cannot see a thing. We should not let this upset us. The discipline of trying to meditate on the meaning of the text, even if it seems to result in little of substance, nonetheless focuses our mind in a way that will affect how we live. Through a continual return to the text, we learn to ignore and banish distracting or unwanted thoughts, acquire concentration, and foster within ourselves patience and attentiveness.

This way of reading, what we might describe as contemplative reading, differs fundamentally from the way most people read today. In *lectio divina* it is quality, not quantity that counts, and it is meant to engender real, personal changes in us. In contrast, contemporary attitudes toward reading seem less oriented to personal transformation than to entertainment and accumulating information. This is even true of many self-help books. How many do we return to again to help us grow? Few indeed. Their numbers alone demand that they be sped through, frisked for what they can give, and then shelved. Before we realize it, we begin to choke on this vast flood of knowledge, never having time to digest much of it at all. Most reading does not change us; it ends up as food for our boredom.

Precisely because it is not entertainment, the active exercise of contemplative reading takes a bit of time to get used to. The Bible, too, has never been an easy book to read, and the novice in its use can easily be overwhelmed without some practical guidance. Monks know this better than anyone. Rather than tackling it at random, playing some variation of Bible roulette, they often use the Church's cycle of daily Scripture readings as a starting point for meditation.

For example, some Bibles (for example, *The New American Bible*) list daily liturgical readings in an appendix at the back of the book. Others contain a daily reading list that takes the reader through the Bible in a year. There also exists a common ecumenical lectionary worked on jointly by theologians of the different Christian churches. Orthodox churches often list their readings on calendars. Or try the liturgical lectionary of the particular church you attend, since this will put you in sync with the services and the sermon. If you do not belong to any church and are unfamiliar with the Bible, read through the Gospels several times in their entirety, then take one episode daily for your meditation.

A good preparation for daily *lectio divina* is to read the following day's Gospel selection the night before, just before going to bed. Your subconscious chews on it as you sleep, becoming material for your dreams, and preparing you for your morning meditation.

One more thing to note: When you meditate, do not be alarmed or discouraged if you initially experience a high degree of inner noise — fragments of conversations, TV shows, loud music, recollections of the previous day's events — seemingly making a travesty of your desire to sit quietly. Given the amplitude of ambient noise that surrounds us, it is little wonder that an interior riot breaks out once we settle ourselves in a quiet spot. We are so unaccustomed to silence that its strangeness provokes a protective reaction of noise in our heads, to compensate for the threatening absence of sound. Stay calm, be patient, and persevere. Simply focus on your chosen text, read it aloud softly if necessary, and go over it slowly several times. You will notice the inner noise begins to fade.

In the Gospel of John, when Jesus cleared the Temple area of money changers and pigeon sellers, he made a whip to drive them out, overturned their tables, and cried, "Get this out of here! Stop using my Father's house as a marketplace!" This is more than a colorful historical vignette. The event was a living word, able to work personal change in listening

hearts. If we allow such a word to simmer in us
stock, we will find it displacing our chaotic though
vie incessantly for our attention like desperate stockbrokers.
Then we can be drawn deeper into the story and its meaning.
Focus, clear away distractions, remind yourself of God's presence, and listen.

TOO MANY in our society are unfamiliar with the experience of meditating, and so we usually lack a climate of
support and encouragement for our own efforts. By making
a "sample" meditation together, inviting you, our reader, into
a session of *lectio* as it might be done by a monk, we can
help you begin without too much embarrassment or self-
consciousness. Obviously, the purpose of doing this is not to
meditate for you, even less to script an "acceptable" session; it
is intended solely to encourage new practitioners, by giving
you a concrete sense of what such a meditation can be, based
on monastic experience. We hope this will give you the confidence to start practicing on your own.

Before we begin, however, keep in mind that it is impossible to recreate a period of sacred reading exactly the way it
occurs. The uniqueness of each individual and the fact that
each of experiences everything in our own particular way,
should make us wary of defining too rigidly the shape of a
meditation. Each session will be different and unrepeatable.
No one has a relationship with God that is exactly like anyone else's, and no one really thinks about God in exactly the
same way. Therefore, we each will respond in our own way to
the experience of *lectio divina*. Do it your way, but do it!

So in a spirit of faith — and adventure — let us begin!

It is a good idea first to spend a few moments settling
down. Open the Bible to the passage you intend to use, and

calm yourself with several deep breaths. Remember that God is present everywhere. Invite God's Spirit to lead you to deeper understanding and a willingness to show it in the way you act. Or say a favorite prayer. Then begin reading your chosen passage, very slowly. No need to race through it. Reading it by moving your lips can help slow you down, but don't make it dramatic, don't exaggerate it. Repeat things. Listen to what it says to you.

> On that day, when evening had come, Jesus said to his disciples, "Let us cross over to the other side of the lake." So, leaving behind the crowd, they took him with them in the boat from which he had been teaching. Other boats went with him. And a violent gale arose, and the waves crashed against the boat, so that it started taking in water. But Jesus was in the stern, asleep on a cushion; and they roused him, saying, "Master, don't you care that we are sinking?" He woke up and rebuked the wind, and said to the sea, "Quiet! Be still!" Immediately the wind ceased, and there was a great calm. He said to them, "Why are you so terrified? Have you still no faith?" They were struck with awe, and said to one another, "Who could this be, that even wind and sea obey him?" (Mark 4:35–41; translation New Skete)

Read the passage through several times slowly, meditatively. Just as we cannot speed-read poetry, so it is with sacred reading. We need time to savor the text, allowing it to make connections beneath the surface of our consciousness. If extraneous thoughts assail you, simply refocus your attention on the text and continue reading, slowly. What lights up for you? What strikes you? Is it the image of Jesus beckoning the disciples to cross over to the other side of the lake? Or is it the image of him asleep in the stern, seemingly oblivious to the storm? Perhaps it is his ordering the wind to be still; or

perhaps it is the wind being still. Is it the sense of gre
following the storm, or the disciples wondering aloud ...
Jesus really is that even the wind and sea obey him? There is
no right answer here. *What part of the text strikes you?* At this
point, do not interrupt your reading to reflect on it yet, just
take note of it for now.

After you have read through the passage several times,
focus in on the particular phrase or sentence that you connect
with, the one charged with meaning and interest or feeling at
that very moment. *"Why are you so terrified? Have you still no
faith? . . ."*

So here it is; this is the line that catches you, the thought
that you're going to spend time with. Begin ruminating on
this segment, repeating the text again and again in your heart.
This is precisely what the Latin word *meditatio* (from which
comes our word meditation) means: learning the text by
heart by repeating it over and over. Greek had a similar word
for this process, *meletán,* which means to be concerned for
something. In its traditional sense, meditation means turning
the text over in your mind again and again, being preoccupied with it, learning it by heart. *"Why are you so terrified?
Have you still no faith? . . ."*

This is not simply rote memorization. Repeating the
phrase again and again in our heart makes it a part of us; we
begin to imbibe the words in a more intuitive way. *"Why are
you so terrified? Have you still no faith? . . ."* At this point, we
should be less concerned with "figuring out the meaning of
the text," than with letting ourselves be absorbed by it. The
words wash over us, again and again, penetrating ever more
deeply, and we begin to realize how they apply to us. *"Why
are you so terrified? Have you still no faith? . . ."*

Suddenly, a spontaneous burst of prayer pierces our awareness like an arrow: "There it is, God . . . I'm always scared . . .

scared, scared, scared . . . terrified. And why? Why can't I
trust you? . . . Why can't I let go of my fear and simply meet
life as it comes? . . . When anything unexpected happens,
anything bad, I always fear you're not present, that you've
abandoned me . . . I actually doubt your presence . . . I panic.
. . . Why do I keep doing this? . . . that must be it . . . it's
because you refuse to be my pawn . . . because you choose to
be yourself, totally other, totally free . . . God, what a jerk I
am . . . I want you to act as I see fit . . .

"Yet after such moments, calm does return. I'm okay. . . .
You weren't really asleep after all. . . . So why do I demand
that you prove yourself again and again? . . .

". . . I know what the problem is — I don't have enough
faith . . . but I want to believe . . . I do believe . . . help my
unbelief! . . . You said, 'Why are you so terrified?' . . . Why
am I so terrified? . . . I don't know. . . . You're not out to
condemn or mock me, but to reassure me. No matter how
frightening, disturbing, or dry life gets, your love doesn't
change . . . it's as simple as that. . . . We're all in the same
boat. You were in the boat with your disciples, you're also
with me . . . even in pain. . . . Help me to accept this and see,
help me really to know it . . ."

Normally it happens that at some point in our prayer we
run out of words. Don't get anxious about this. Just sit there,
quietly, and relax with your uncertainty. Linger for a while,
keeping your mind and your heart open. Forget about time,
words; simply be still in the experience of the moment.

There is no need to worry about flying away in some sort
of ecstatic trance or even falling asleep! Soon enough other
thoughts and feelings will return, bringing us back to ourselves. If time remains, you may wish to return to the text and
continue in the same vein, ruminating on it further. Otherwise, conclude with a brief prayer of thanksgiving.

THE FORMAL *lectio* session has ended, but the spir
ing it will lead you over time into an increasing
fulness and openness. This might not be so obv
one or two times . . . or even a dozen. Sacred reading will
not bear any fruit if we practice it in a helter-skelter way.
You have to make it into a daily habit, and this can be challenging.

When the retreatant whom Brother James was speaking to
earlier in the chapter asked him what problems he could
expect once he began practicing *lectio* at home, Brother James
replied, "If your experience is anything like mine, initially
it'll be difficult to get up for your sacred reading regularly.
That extra half hour or so of sleep early in the morning can
be really tempting. Doing *lectio* once or twice is easy, but further it gets tougher. It will no longer be novel. Most likely
you'll find yourself skipping a day — maybe even several
days — and with that will come a certain natural discouragement that will have you wondering whether this practice
is really feasible. Don't let yourself off the hook! The first
insight you can glean from this experience is how clever we
can be in making excuses. Keep to your original intention,
and make a mental or written note of thoughts and questions
you struggle with. We can talk about those when you come
back to the monastery for visits."

When we have begun, really begun, to be faithful to this
highly disciplined (and creative) routine, "to present yourself
daily before the Lord" — then the morning's prayer will
gradually remain with us throughout each day. Its quiet encounters will help us to stay serenely down-to-earth. *"Why
are you so terrified? Have you still no faith? . . ."* Our frequent
recollection of the passage will immediately put us in touch
with the spirit of the meditation. We will find an inner
strength and peacefulness, a spiritual continuity to our day.

The practice of sacred reading is entirely straightforward. There are no gimmicks, and the change that occurs in us, while powerful, does not happen overnight. Real transformation of character is gradual, occurring over a lifetime. Just as Abba Pimen used the image of water dripping on the stone to illustrate how the word of God changes us, so let us approach our practice of *lectio divina* with faith and confidence, persevering in it despite occasional bouts with dryness, boredom, discouragement, or other forms of spiritual adversity. We can expect to go through these valleys along our journey.

We are not without guides. The wisdom accumulated from the teachings of hundreds of spiritual masters reassures us that ups and downs are inevitable parts of the trek, not ominous signs of a spiritual impasse. When we persevere day after day, we will soon enough come to a different elevation, another vista. We will hear yet another word. More and more we will recognize that life itself is an exciting text, vibrant with meaning, for us to read and respond to from moment to moment. Then our practice will embrace all the words of God without exception, and we will steadily realize a new level of insight and integrity in our spiritual journey.

What can we offer you, O Christ, for coming to earth as a
    man because of us?
The creatures you fashioned offer you their grateful thanks:
the angels bring their hymns of praise, while the heavens
    offer you a star;
the magi present gifts and the shepherds, amazement;
the earth offers a cave, and the wilderness, a manger,
while we present you with your virgin mother.
O God who are before the ages, have mercy on us.

Sticheron for Christmas, Tone Two

NINE

Pray Without Ceasing?

A MIDST THE TURBULENCE of the bustling Tuscan city of Florence stands the peaceful sanctuary of Saint Mark's, a thirteenth-century Dominican monastery that was once led by the fiery and controversial ascetic and preacher Savonarola. Visiting the monastery today, you would never suspect that its history was so deeply intertwined with the precarious and violent politics of medieval Florence. Saint Mark's tranquil cloisters are much more reflective of its real legacy, the unique culture of beauty and serenity created by its early monks, particularly the most famous one, Fra Angelico.

A monk at Saint Mark's in the mid-fifteenth century, Fra Angelico was given the chance to utilize his artistic talents by illuminating the monastery with brilliant frescoes of various scenes from Scripture and church tradition, the most famous being the stunning Annunciation, in which the archangel Gabriel is depicted telling Mary that she will bring the Christ into the world; in fact, each of the forty-four monastic cells contains a wall-sized fresco taken from the life of Christ, to be a source of inspiration and meditation for the monks. The collective result of his work was an utterly distinctive monastic environment that even today has a powerful effect on the sensitive visitor. It makes clear the function of beauty in our striving for contemplation.

Monastic custom has always cautioned monks against holding on to sentimental nicknacks and memorabilia, yet even the most austere monk will dignify his cell with a well-chosen reminder of what his vocation implies: a cross, an icon perhaps, a beautiful photograph. For us who are made of flesh and blood, works of art, even when not explicitly religious, can help us to focus our attention, gently directing our thought toward our priorities, reminding us of the dedication of our life.

In this spirit, the Seeker keeps a hand-carved Mexican angel sitting on his desk, a solitary relic from Christmas celebrations long past, when the angel stood atop his family's tree. When as a novice he happened to show it to Father Laurence, he explained, "Of all the ornaments that decorated my family's Christmas tree, my favorite was this angel." The Seeker looked off and mused. "I clearly remember when I was still a kid, lying on our living room floor and staring up at it. In a very real way, I'd say that was perhaps my first taste of contemplation. Though then I could never have expressed it so, I think the angel symbolized for me, just as it does now, the very natural and basic human capacity for wonderment and awe. Just gazing up at it, I think I sensed a heartfelt need to thank God for the gift of life." The Seeker's face reddened as he looked at the ground.

Father Laurence quickly observed, "Yes, I'm sure it did. With that angel you sensed something remarkable. The angel wasn't simply a messenger of glad tidings; it is pointing to God by its gesture of praise. Remember in the Gospel of Luke a full chorus of angels breaks into song at Christ's birth. How did that go . . . 'And in a flash there appeared with the angel a vast host of the armies of heaven, praising God, saying, "Glory to God in the heights! And on earth peace, to those of good will!"' Angels are creatures of praise."

"Well, anyway, with all of the way-out stuff being written about angels these days," replied the Seeker, "I just didn't want you getting

the wrong impression." He grinned. "I'm not in touch with the angel Gabriel."

Father chuckled, then replied, "You'd better not be! But there's a valuable truth here, too. We should take a look at these angels in Scripture, not in a literal, historical sense, but metaphorically, as symbols of something much deeper. As pure spirits of course, angels aren't bound by time or space or any physicality; they were obviously created to expend their knowledge, energy, and service for God forever."

The Seeker raised his eyebrows and said, "Yeah, but are they real?"

"At least we can say that the reality they portray is for real," replied Father. "Look, the name of the thing is not the thing. We catch a glimpse of the thing itself through our poetic and artistic images. That's what the Book of Revelation does, for instance, when it describes a heavenly vision reminiscent of some elaborate Byzantine court, with angels and elders prostrate before God's throne praising and blessing him." Father challenged the Seeker. "How are we supposed to understand that?"

The Seeker thought for a moment and then shrugged saying, "I'm not sure I really know how to answer that."

Father pointed to the angel on the desk. "Oh no? . . . I'd say that image describes it pretty well." He considered the angel, with its eyes modestly downcast and its mouth open wide in song and said, "Its beauty expresses the passion for prayer and dedication, and the drive to move outward and away from ourselves towards a greater reality, that should characterize all our lives, too. It's a poignant metaphor of life's true focus and meaning. The angels keep nothing for themselves: they give themselves completely to their work, which is nothing but the glorification of God. That constitutes and defines what they are. And that's what we need to notice. Even though they're bodiless, their very nature asks us about who we really are and how we live."

No doubt it is in the spirit of this ideal that monastic life can be called "the angelic life," an intriguing metaphor that unfortunately has become oddly distorted throughout history.

"How did that expression come to be applied to monastic life anyway?" asked Jim, a young student visiting the monastery from a nearby college. He had come to New Skete in hopes of getting background for a paper he was doing, and now he was taking a walk with Brother Stavros.

"The phrase goes back to the beginnings of monasticism in the fourth century," the monk explained, "a life in the desert of single-minded dedication to God, of constant prayer, and the search for genuine spiritual values. Unfortunately, however, monks themselves haven't always understood this in the correct way. There's plenty of evidence to suggest that monks and nuns felt that the monastic life was angelic because it enabled them to repudiate material existence, to the extent that this is possible for human beings. By stubbornly trying to eliminate our fundamental human needs, they naïvely sought to arrive at the same nonphysical condition that characterized angels."

Brother Stavros pointed to the left, and they proceeded along a trail knifing through the woods. "Ironically, instead of using the life of Christ as their model, they did one better — or so they thought — by imitating the angels! Celibacy, fasting, poverty, silence, isolation, and sleepless vigils — in short, anything that went against the natural instincts of the body — came to be misused as tools of a disembodied 'angelic' ideal."

Jim shook his head. "That pretty much coincides with what I read in a couple of scholarly treatments on early Christian asceticism. In this, the early monks and nuns suffered severely from the influence of Neoplatonism and Manichaeanism, the predominant philosophical schools of that time. Both were characterized by a hatred of the material world."

Brother Stavros nodded, "I'm sure that's true. Many of the early monastics were well educated and familiar with those systems of thought. It would be only natural to expect that the intellectual climate of the day would have had a definite influence on how they viewed their relationship with God, as well as the world. But it wasn't only that. The monks looked for confirmation and support of these ideas in the Bible, as well." He stopped and took a small pocket New Testament from his shirt pocket and flipped through several pages. "For example, listen to this passage from the Gospel of Matthew:

> On the same day some Sadducees [who deny that there is any resurrection] approached Jesus with this question: "Master, Moses said if a man should die without any children, his brother should marry his widow and raise up a family for him. Now, we have a case of seven brothers. The first one married and died, and since he had no family he left his wife to his brother. The same thing happened with the second and the third, right up to the seventh. Last of all the woman herself died. Now in this "resurrection," whose wife will she be of these seven men — for she belonged to all of them?"
>
> "You are very wide of the mark," replied Jesus to them, "for you are ignorant of both the scriptures and the power of God. For in the resurrection there is no such thing as marrying or being given in marriage, *men live like the angels in Heaven*." (Matthew 22:23–30)

Brother Stavros went on, "This is a perfect example of what I mean. In other words (they deduced), our physical appetites will be totally abolished. That sort of thinking is very problematic. Human life, after all, involves appetites; they're part and parcel of being human. Granted, if we let them run amok they'll destroy us; that's one of the right reasons for ascetic discipline. But instead of using ascetical practices simply to counter the undisciplined and distorted direction we've taken with our lives, they went overboard, allying them with an unjustified worldview characterized by a horror of anything sexual, indeed with a condemnation of everything physical or material. The whole of creation, if not evil, had been, in the minds of many, totally corrupted. I mean, do you realize that there are people even today who think that earthquakes and other natural disasters are actually the result of original sin?"

He stopped suddenly and pointed up the trail toward a pair of wild turkeys that were waddling across the path. Jim's face lit up at the sight, and they waited silently for a few moments to let the turkeys saunter off.

"In any event," Brother Stavros continued, "for many of our religious forebears, living an angelic life meant at all costs ignoring and despising our physical nature. And any voices to the contrary were few and far between. If you could do it, it meant you could be like an angel." Brother Stavros pushed an overhanging branch to the side as Jim followed up behind him. "If you've been reading up on the literature, then no doubt you're aware that monastic history is littered with examples of extreme physical asceticism. Not only did that often result in serious illness and early death, but it also fostered personalities crippled by a lack of human integration."

Jim agreed. "You know, I just finished reading *The Ladder of Divine Ascent* by Saint John Climacus, and while there was a lot in it that I found very perceptive, I was actually alarmed by the section called 'the prison.' To me, it read more like a psychiatric ward than a monastery."

"That's exactly what I'm talking about," said Brother Stavros. "We can't afford to be naïve and uncritical when we read about the ascetic exploits of the early monks. Not everything they did is to be emulated, and we can get into real trouble if we try. Even the early monks themselves were aware of this temptation to ascetic excess. For example, one of their best sayings is, 'If you see a young monk climbing to heaven in an effort to flee his human nature, grab him by the foot and pull him back down, for what he's doing will ruin him entirely.'"

Brother Stavros motioned for Jim to watch out for some thick roots along the path and then continued. "Instead of facing the challenges inherent in being human, things like sexuality and the whole host of human appetites, learning to control and live with them in a balanced way, they often turned ascetic practice into an ill-conceived attempt at escaping the human condition. They sought to become beings of an entirely different nature. Well, that's simply impossible. There were wrong turns in their experimenting, and a failure to be guided by the wisdom of a broader understanding and to recognize the essential unity and dignity of human nature as a whole."

"If that's true, maybe the whole idea of referring to monasticism as 'the angelic life' is mistaken. I mean, if there's been so much misunderstanding about it, wouldn't it be better just to chuck the concept?"

"Yes, as far as we're concerned," replied Brother Stavros. "Such thinking, however well intended, is an insult to God's goodness and creativity. We have to face the fact that we can only live in God's presence through our own nature, in the realm of time, amidst the material world around us. That's what we have to wrestle with in all the various contexts of everyday life."

The two came up to an overlook that beautifully showcased the hills of southern Vermont, whose trees were slowly coming to life now that spring had arrived. They rested for a few minutes, silently drinking in the beauty of the scene, then headed back to the trail to return to the monastery.

As they walked along, Jim finally said, "You know, it seems what we're really talking about here is the true nature of sanctity, how a human being becomes like God. One thing that I've found noteworthy with the reading I've done for this course at school is the similar sorts of excesses you find in most other religions. By no means does Christianity seem to be alone when it manifests tendencies to extremism. I wonder if this inclination to repudiate humanness is something that is endemic to all religions."

"Oh, no doubt," Brother Stavros agreed, "but I don't think that's because religion is of its nature antihuman. Freud may have had profound insights into the human condition, but his understanding of religion was pretty impoverished. The religious quest by its nature takes us into vast areas of mystery on all sorts of levels, so it's not surprising that throughout history we've taken some bad turns.

"What's important is to learn from our mistakes. True religion is really about ultimate sanity and health! If you ask me, understanding and pursuing sanctity in a very down-to-earth way — and wisely — is a daunting task, largely because we're so often scared stiff of our bodiliness." For emphasis, he pinched the skin around his own arm pointedly. "You know, as human beings we find it hard to be convinced of the basic goodness of everything, except for ignorance and malice, in God's eyes. In single-minded desire for angelic goodness and purity, we deny our own humanness. We live in terror of confronting the pain of struggle and ambiguity involved in being human. It's easier to throw up our hands in despair and simply resign ourselves to the fact that since this package of flesh and bones is a magnet for misery, it must be unredeemably 'bad.'"

Brother Stavros stopped walking for a moment to finish his thought. "That might seem realistic to those who blame our flesh for always getting us into trouble, but it seems more like cynicism, a repudiation of grace, goodness, and our basic freedom. I guess it's safe to say that there's no human being who isn't crippled by this thinking to some degree, but it's still a copout; we have to work hard to get beyond this sort of mentality. And we must get beyond it!"

Jim remarked, "I suppose it's not hard to figure out how our experience of the human condition helps foster this thinking. I mean, when our appetites unleash a flood of temptation and desire, isn't it only natural to feel as if our bodies are hopelessly enslaved to these passions?"

Brother Stavros continued the thought, "Or when we become ill and infirm, isn't it our bodies that eventually die and decay, leaving the spirit, we hope, to ascend to the next world? From this point of view, being incarnate is clearly a burden, in fact a punishment for the original disobedience of our first ancestors. And how easy it is to rationalize this — after all, didn't Jesus himself say, 'Flesh gives birth to flesh, and Spirit gives birth to spirit' [John 4:6], and 'It's the Spirit which gives life; the flesh won't help you. . . . The things which I've told you about are spirit and life' [John 6:63]. Can't you just imagine the erroneous conclusions that could be drawn from this: 'Oh, if only we could be free of our bodies, then we could be free of suffering and temptation and be as God wishes us to be!'"

"You almost sound as if you believe that," Jim teased.

The monk smiled. "Then you'd better have me committed! Seriously, that's the seduction of a foolish, reckless asceticism, and the misunderstanding of God's will that many people throughout the ages have succumbed to. The thought process is hopelessly illogical. Really, what sense would it have made for God to give us bodies if our sanctification couldn't be realized through the blossoming of our physical humanity? Denying this is to divide off an essential part of ourselves and demonize it.

"It doesn't make much sense. No, God made us incarnate beings out of love, because he valued such a life as good, because he knew that we were capable of attaining our end by living in an integrated way. In our haste to disown our own flesh, we often fail to understand that true holiness is fully human, that grace works in a manner entirely in harmony with our nature as spirited flesh. Holiness is in no sense bloodless, passionless, nor can it be aloof from the tempestuous character of fleshly life. Were that the case, it would be utterly unachievable. Nor does denying that we have a body solve anything either. Human nature, of its very essence, expresses itself through matter, and true holiness can only be realized by accepting, training, and using our bodies. Incidentally, Jim, this is precisely why the liturgy, our worship of God, is so important for an enlightened and well-grounded pursuit of wisdom: it sacramentalizes the whole of life through a conscious offering of ourselves in our very physicality, *along with the material world in which we exist.*"

They emerged from the trail behind the puppy kennels and were greeted with a cacophony of barking from the dogs in their kennel runs. Brother Stavros told the dogs to quiet down, which they did immediately upon recognizing him. As the two parted to prepare for vespers, Jim shook the monk's hand, saying, "Thanks for taking the time to talk with me, Brother. You've given me a lot to think about, and I'm sure it will affect the substance of my paper. I hope I can come back again in the future."

W<small>E CAN SEE</small> a concrete example of what Brother Stavros was discussing with Jim, the importance of the material world in Christian worship, in the rite of baptism, the "mystery" of formal initiation into the Church. All too often, the many layers of meaning in this rite have been reduced to superstition. Baptism is not some quaint, legalistic ceremony that magically washes away the stain of an original sinfulness. This idea robs it of any real power to challenge and change the tired status quo of the human condition. It also colossally misses the point. Baptism is much more profound than a simple purification ceremony; it vividly symbolizes each person's death and resurrection by joining them with Christ's. It is an ancient, dramatic sign of radical change that initiates the baptized into the believing community, a public pledge of a new and deeper life. It is a rite of personal passage, a passover and entry into this new "way." The words of the service make this clear.

When a priest blesses the baptismal water at the beginning of the service, he affirms the original purpose of the world. Creation is good, and is to be used for the glory of God, which creation proclaims by its very existence. When he breathes on the water, invoking the Spirit of God that hovered over the original waters of creation, the priest draws our attention back to what "water" was in the beginning: grace-filled and blessed by God, to be valued and used by us wisely in order to grow and prosper in body, mind, and spirit.

Water, the primal element of creation, along with the entire physical world, is meant to be the very support, context, and even vehicle of our communion with God. Throughout history, however, many have overlooked this. They have seen creation as an obstacle to God, an impediment, rather than the way to learn about him more deeply. This has resulted not only in a split within us, but also in an estrangement from the external physical environment.

Such a view and the way of life that flows from it is a dead end. Wise Christian teaching correctly sees nature as the primary means through which we come to know God, and through which we express our love of God. Those who recklessly indict the Bible and Church teaching for the rape and abuse of the environment are entirely ignorant of the true ethic that proceeds directly from baptism, and sorely miss the point. Through baptism a renewed reverence for creation places enlightened stewardship and spiritual awareness over the expediency of politics and greed.

The symbolism of the sacrament goes even deeper. When the candidate for baptism is initiated, he ritually enacts the death or dissolution of his old ways of thinking and behaving through immersion in the primal waters of chaos and regeneration, and subsequently he emerges as a new person, healed, modeled after Christ. He is born into a new worldview, which recognizes that the body and soul are essentially a unity — they are the temple of the Holy Spirit — and which will continue to utilize the elements of nature sacramentally (for example, oil, bread and wine, ritual, clothing, touch, and word). The rite thus graphically affirms and restores the integrity and dynamism of human life.

To cling to an ideal of holiness that is rooted in dualism leads to several options, all of which are problematic: (1) either to deny or ignore what is intrinsic to us, (2) to make war on the body with all our might, or (3) eventually, in despair, to dismiss spirituality as irrelevant. True holiness can only mean facing and accepting the challenges to personal wholeness, balancing, integrating, and appreciating the value of everything life presents us. This struggle is an ordeal, at once a dying and rising to new life, but it is also the essence of any genuine spiritual and religious life and the core of true sanctity. A model of holiness fit only for nonmaterial beings amounts to no holiness at all, and ultimately leaves us less than human.

Unfortunately, such a life-denying agenda often found in Christian and monastic — in fact all religious — thought throughout the ages has negated, skewed, and defused the revolutionary character of the Gospel. It has frustrated any truly human — and bodily — holiness, both in monastic and secular life. It has marginalized the sacral value, the possibility, of finding redemption by living in the world and of raising a family, for example, while still belonging totally to God.

T HE FALLACY of the so-called angelic life image manifests itself most clearly in the realm of prayer, specifically with the biblical admonition to pray unceasingly. The nature of the angel is a continuously prayerful being, directly and completely oriented to God. Biblical imagery intended this as a meaningful inspiration for all believers. Monks, too, have sought to emulate this, through their own dramatic attempts at ceaseless prayer. Inspired especially by the classic text from Saint Paul's first letter to the Thessalonians, *"Pray without ceasing . . ."* (5:17), monasticism maintains long-standing and widespread customs devoted to trying to realize this to the maximum degree possible. Serious problems have occurred, though, when the admonition has been taken in a narrow, literal way, quantitatively instead of qualitatively. In fact, seasoned monks have learned that genuine unceasing prayer has little to do with saying prayers unceasingly, and can even be hindered by such a practice. Saying prayers at the same time as we attend to our other responsibilities results in doing two things at once; usually we end up doing both poorly.

The Seeker remembered Brother Christopher once telling him a story about this that made a deep impression on him. "When I first entered monastic life, I, too, was captivated by the idea of unceasing prayer. I earnestly sought to achieve this ideal by piling prayer upon prayer, invocation upon invocation, atop the already practice-filled contents of my daily life. The trouble was, I didn't recognize my life that way at all. Instead of listening attentively to God's presence and word in all the events of my own life, I 'said' prayers. It was a brave attempt, I guess, one made by most aspiring monks at one time or another, but it actually introduced a split into my consciousness that left me less aware of my surroundings and less aware of the presence of God. My ill-conceived efforts at unceasing prayer only distanced me from the reality I was trying to embrace.

"Fortunately one day, my folly was brought home to me in a very convincing manner, as I was doing chores in the kennel. I was busy repeating my prayer over and over as I worked. I was so wrapped up in my prayer that I neglected to lock one of the gates after I had cleaned. When I opened the hatch and let the dogs into their pens from the outside runs, an aggressive dog was able to flip the latch and bound out into the room. It lost no time in giving me a sharp bite in my ass — a rather painful experience of enlightenment."

True prayer is loving and serving the God of prayer, not the prayer of God. The call to unceasing prayer is not an invitation to divided consciousness; it does not imply that we pay any less attention to daily realities or retreat from life's responsibilities. Rather: *It is a call to learn to live always in the presence of God in a manner appropriate to changing circumstances, through these very circumstances,* none of which are an end in themselves, but which lead us to God. For this reason we do everything to the best of our ability, with the utmost attention, as each thing deserves. We never make an end out of the means. Whatever we think, whatever we do, should always be permeated by this intention and awareness, this fragrance of prayer. It also means cultivating a sound way of thinking and acting, an awake and expansive state of mind that is habitually present in us regardless of external circumstances or our own momentary feelings. True prayer is never an obstacle to living life correctly, fully.

U NCEASING PRAYER, then, is not a technique. To isolate Saint Paul's admonition, to take it out of its context, does violence to his intent. Surrounding the admonition are two other exhortations that express how he conceived unceasing prayer:

Be happy always*:*   Greet everyone and everything openly and cheerfully, even in adversity. Sing together joyfully.

Pray without ceasing*:*   Don't forget to pray; be open to God's presence. Don't stop praying together just because difficulties arise, or when everything's fine. Pay attention and avoid distractions.

Be grateful in all circumstances*:*   Be generous and appreciative, find something positive, even during reversals and setbacks. Display your unity and heal your divisions by giving thanks in prayer and eucharist.

for this is the will of God for you in Christ Jesus.

(1 Thessalonians 5:16–18; translation New Skete)

Reflecting on this in class one day with the whole community, Father Laurence observed, "Every Jew was expected to
pray three times a day, but if we leave it at that, we've missed
the point entirely. Saint Paul isn't just recommending that
basic prescription; much more profoundly, he's exhorting his
readers to an *attitude,* a frame of mind, a way of being that's
outgoing no matter how discouraged they might happen to
be, a habitual, unfailing spirit of joyful openness and largesse.
In other words, he's reminding his listeners of their recent
baptism and liberation from the law, and of the more profound spirit of Christ that should prevail in their new life
together. This means being *consciously constantly conscious* of
the presence of God amidst the changing complexion of
everyday life. This is what unceasing prayer means, not saying
prayers continually. As we grow up, as we learn to respond
creatively with faithful trust in the presence of God in the
most difficult of human circumstances — tragedies, disagreements, even moments of ennui — we'll manifest the constant
prayerful direction that doesn't flinch in the face of doubt,
darkness, despair, and even death."

A CONSTANT, PERSISTENT, and pervasive attitude of prayer
is precisely what the Psalms demonstrate for us. The
Book of Psalms is the principal source of both Jewish and
Christian liturgical prayer, and for centuries its 150 Psalms
have inspired believers as seemingly diverse as devout Hasidic
Jews, fervent Methodist believers, and silent Trappist monks.
The Psalms can do this, in part, because of their simple
humanity, their direct response to every human situation
imaginable. Believers as well as unbelievers instinctively relate
to the concrete situations these hymns describe and interpret:

celebration at deliverance, despair in the face of tragedy, patriotism, plaintive cries from the throes of suffering, shouts of praise in a moment of clarity and insight, or incredulous lamentation and anger at unjust persecution. Even the most cynical can recognize the humanness of an individual trying to own up to powerful emotions, to make sense of outrageous fortune:

> Why, Lord, do you stand aloof? Why do you hide when times are hard? In the wicked man's pride the lowly man is consumed; he is trapped by the schemes of the other.
>
> For the wicked man crows about his unbridled lusts; the covetous man reviles and scorns the Lord. In his arrogant scheming he thinks to himself: He will never demand an accounting; God does not care! His plans evolve successfully, step by step; your decrees are far from him, and for all his foes he has nothing but contempt. He assures himself: I will make out well; harm shall never touch me! Cursing, deceit, and violence fill his mouth; under his tongue lurk mischief and evil. He lies in wait in the bushes; in secret he murders the innocent; his eyes are on the watch for the helpless. He lurks in hiding, like a lion in his lair, ready to pounce on the hapless; he seizes the afflicted to drag him away in his net. He is ever on the watch, crouching, ready to jump, and some luckless wretch falls prey to his might. He says to himself: God pays no attention; he turns the other way; he never looks.
>
> Arise, then, Lord! Lift up your hand! O God, do not forget the poor! (Psalm 10[9]:1–12, as in the *New Skete Psalter*)

Such uninhibited sentiments show a freedom in relating to God that is straightforward and blunt. Who would dare approach the creator of the universe this way save one who knows that love impels this honesty, that honesty undergirds all genuine love? He can speak this way *because* of his prayerfulness, because of his intense dedication, his being conscious of the presence of God. For he knows that he is already a friend of God, that he has been placed in a relationship with God by God himself. Certainly such prayer is devoid of any sort of phony obsequiousness. Whatever we believe about God, such a Psalm should at least command our respect: if God does exist, it is of some comfort to know we can be so honest with him.

In fact, such frankness toward God has a long history. The Psalms were written and compiled over the course of more than seven hundred years, for use at times of crisis, great gatherings, worship, and prayer. They were part of the innumerable compositions used to convey to God the concerns of the kings, prophets, and priests for the Hebrew nation in wildly varying circumstances. Most likely, the Psalms in the Bible finally became part of the scriptural canon because they were the most universal and relevant, the most unreservedly expressive of their kind.

If we read them with an open and attentive mind, their striking and colorful words can help us to understand the essence of Scripture, what loving God actually means. Before all else, it means offering the whole of our experience to him: joy, sadness, anger, suffering, desires, frustrations — hiding nothing from him, even our deepest thoughts. *This is what prayer is.* The Psalms reveal the inner disposition, drama, and dynamism of prayer in those who live in communion with God through the turbulence of everyday life, who in spite of this turbulence, strive to do everything in a manner that pleases God. Because they bring God into every nook and cranny of human existence — even the most disturbing — the Psalms educate our hearts, converting us, teaching us how to live, experience after experience, in a perennial climate of prayerfulness.

This is unceasing prayer that is in accord with the mind of the Scriptures and with the realities of our lives.

JESUS HIMSELF, as a first-century Jew, was raised in this same spirit of prayer, as the Gospels show us. His life opens up for us the meaning of unceasing prayer. Jesus knew the value of both liturgical prayer and private prayer, but he hardly walked around mumbling prayers all the time. Like the prophets, he openly criticizes those who multiply their prayers instead of fostering the requisite interior attitude.

> "And then, when you pray, don't be like the play-actors. They love to stand and pray in the synagogues and at street corners so that people may see them at it. Believe me, they have had all the reward they are going to get. But when you pray, go into your own room, shut your door and pray to your Father privately. Your Father who sees all private things will reward you. And when you pray, don't rattle off long prayers like the pagans who think they will be heard because they use so many words. Don't be like them. After all, God, who is your Father, knows your needs before you ask him." (Matthew 6:5–8)

Jesus is one in whom we see the integration of the inner and the outer, the sacred and the secular. While teaching the importance of both formal liturgical participation and prayer in solitude, he demonstrates that the scope of his spirit of prayer extends far beyond these, to embrace the whole of his daily experience. Amidst the demands of his public ministry, Jesus is perpetually prayerful, in a manner appropriate to whatever life brings before him. His whole life is a prayer, because he is always conscious of the heavenly Father, in

whose presence he lives; he is never "not praying," yet mo
people observing him might never have suspected this.
Through the contents of his everyday life he becomes prayer,
though in a manner entirely in harmony with his human
nature. Every act and gesture, no matter how seemingly
insignificant, is a movement of adoration, an offering of
prayer.

Our human reality is what we bring to God, our very
means to God — and this finds its clearest, richest expression
in a regular liturgical life. For those with eyes to see, liturgy
nurtures the whole of life, as incense pervades the church. It
integrates and offers to God, all at once, our interior life, our
need for support from the presence of others of like mind,
and our own witness, service, and support of others.

If there is any truth at all to the "angelic life" image, it is
simply this: just as the angels are true to their nature by praising and glorifying God according to their own modality, so
too must we be equally true to praising God in the modality
of our humanness. When applied to the human condition,
the angelic ideal is not a recipe but an invitation to healing,
wholeness, and awareness, and we human beings can be justly
said to be living in that expansive spirit to the extent that we
are in touch with all of reality.

If, like Jesus, we are to become a living prayer, it cannot be
in a purely quantitative way, by futilely multiplying prayer
upon prayer for the rest of our life. We can only be faithful to
the mandate to unceasing prayer when we seek it qualitatively, by reverently listening and discerning the presence of
God in every situation in life; by conforming our hearts and
minds and behavior with the words and attitudes we articulate in prayer; and by embracing our whole life and present-
ing it as a gift to God.

The Seeker remembered asking Father Laurence one day, "Abba, when we last talked, we were talking about Saint Paul's injunction to pray without ceasing. But to be honest, I'm stymied. How's one supposed to do that? When I try to pray always, I'm doing the very thing you say we shouldn't do, which is attempting to repeat verbal prayers. Then when I don't say prayers, I feel I'm not praying at all! What can I do about this?"

Father nodded in understanding, "There's a paradox all right, but it's really not the impossibility you're suggesting. What we're really looking for is to live in a state of prayer."

The Seeker seemed perplexed. "A state of prayer?"

"That's right. Being in a state of prayer involves living in such a manner that regardless of what we might be doing, we're always praying."

"Yes, but what do you mean by that; how do I get to that?" said the Seeker.

Father Laurence continued, "The question is, what does this involve?" The Seeker remained silent, waiting for Father's answer. "Well, for starters, wouldn't it seem to require that we strive to become conscious of being in God's presence, because prayer is above all a relationship? And this has nothing to do with feelings — it's a question of awareness, something that's present regardless of what we're feeling. But it would also seem to require more than that. We could imagine, for example, how the 'Evil One' could be aware of being in the presence of God, yet we'd hardly say that he was living in a state of prayer. What makes all the difference, I believe, is the intention to please God. In addition to the consciousness of being in God's presence, were we to have the constant willingness always and everywhere to do what is pleasing to God, then such an attitude would then constitute a state of prayerfulness."

"Yeah, but I still don't see how that translates in actual practice. I mean, my problem is that when I'm busy living, I seem to forget

God's presence. Then when I try to change that, it seems to take me in the direction of saying prayers all the time, like repeating the Jesus prayer."

"You have to remember that the state of being I'm talking about has nothing directly to do with an act," Father Laurence replied. *"For example, simply uttering a series of prayers doesn't constitute a state of prayerfulness. Your mind could be a million miles away! Prayerfulness is a condition we bring about in ourselves that is the correct climate for any individual acts of prayer . . . and, in fact, for everything else we do. This can seem subtle, but it's not just word games. It means recognizing that we're not always thinking about everything that we're conscious of. Take yourself right now: you know you have two feet, but you weren't actually thinking about them before I mentioned them. In a similar way, we can become increasingly conscious of being in God's presence in spite of the fact that we're not always thinking thoughts about him. But we will think of him often, nevertheless, and the more we do think of him the more likely we'll also become aware of how we should better conduct our living."*

"But that still doesn't answer how we're supposed to bring the presence of God to mind when we're not thinking about it," complained the Seeker.

Father went on. "A very good way to do this is by consciously associating elements of our daily experience with the presence of God, allowing them to remind us of it. When we do this over time, they not only sustain our consciousness of being in God's presence, but actually strengthen our determination to live in a way that pleases him.

"For example, this is one of the intentions behind the custom of making the sign of the cross before a meal, or before some other activity: we do this to call to mind God's presence. But such an idea can be creatively adapted in any number of ways. Let's say a secretary works in an office where phone calls come in rapidly, one after another.

What if she were to associate each ring of the phone with being conscious of being in God's presence? Now initially, this will obviously require deliberate *work on her part, but as she perseveres in doing it, the practice will become more and more a* habit. *Eventually every time the phone rings (or any bell for that matter) she'll be reminded of being in God's presence. In the context of a busy office where phones ring frequently, being and remaining in God's presence will gradually become the habitual state that the secretary lives in and which spurs her to always give her best and which in no way interferes with her work."*

The Seeker raised his eyebrows and stroked his beard thoughtfully.

Father continued. "In a way, the process can be likened to repeatedly placing a drop of red ink into a pail of clear water. At first, the red color won't be perceptible. But over time, should the process continue, the steady addition of drops will change the color of the clear water to red. In fact, the point will come in which there won't be a perceptible distinction between the water in the pail and the ink in its container.

"The way in which we mindfully and deliberately form the habit of being conscious of being in the presence of God, the way it gradually begins to color our whole life, is a process very much like that.

"And so, if in the course of consciously building this habit of being in the presence of God," Father went on, "we add as well the habitual intention of pleasing God in all things, then no matter what we might be doing or thinking about, it becomes an act of prayer simply because we're performing these acts in a prayerful state. For example, a doctor performing surgery is hardly able to give his attention directly to God. He's totally immersed in what he's doing. Yet if he's developed the habit of being conscious of being in the presence of God and has the intention of praising God, his surgery is indeed a prayer, and when he's finished with the surgery his mind will go back naturally to thoughts of God."

Father summed it up. "So take heart: as human beings we can't think much more than one thought at a time. But if we train ourselves, we can think about whatever we have to think about without it interfering in any way with our dedication to God, because of the prayerful climate of our interior reality, of our consciousness."

Later Developments in Monasticism

A new heaven and earth.

Hymn to Saint Francis

Even though monasteries have usually existed on the boundaries of society, they have been extremely successful because of the inspired balance in their great "rules of life." These reflected a firm but enlightened organization and respect of members for one another, a profound dedication to the highest spiritual goals, and the practice of virtue and love of God, which included honest self-appraisal and change for the better.

Each day was mapped out to include not only simple meals and adequate rest, but instruction, work for both sustenance and social good, prayer alone and together, study, communal recreation, and hospitality for travelers. The day was divided usually into seven or eight parts, punctuated by the call to church for the dedication of that "hour" to God. The division was based on Jewish reckoning of time and the "watches" of imperial Roman time, with vespers beginning the new liturgical day at sunset. Sometime after vespers would be the final hour before sleep, in the West called compline (from "complete"), in the East called the "after dinner" service because it was taken after the evening meal. The middle-of-the-night office (or vigils) came around 2 A.M. (with the change of the night watch), and matins with lauds (the final psalms of praise) at dawn. Then followed the first hour at about 7 A.M., the third hour around 10 A.M., the sixth hour about noon, and the ninth hour toward 3 P.M. Eucharist was usually celebrated after the first hour. The exact times of the services changed with the seasons of the year. All the offices were structured with specified psalms, prayers, hymns, canticles, and reading from Scripture, especially the Gospels, and explanations of church feasts and lives of the saints. Vespers and matins were more elaborate, with incense, candlelight, vestments, processions, and more hymnology. These two main hours were standard also in cathedrals and parish churches throughout the Christian world.

Because Saint Benedict insisted that all his monks should be sufficiently literate to sing in choir and to be able to read the Bible, the writings of the apostolic church fathers, and the ancient philosophers, monks were known for their scholarly pursuits, particularly copying and preserving the classical texts of Western civilization. Manual labor increasingly became the responsibility of a special class of monks who were not ordained clerics, the lay brothers, who farmed and cared for the expanding lands of their communities. Monasteries like Cluny in France and its affiliates became extremely wealthy and influential in church and state matters.

In the eleventh century, some sought to return to more primitive and rigorous ascetic ideals. These eventually developed into unified orders, the Camaldolese, the Carthusians, and the Cistercians. The most famous representative of the last was Saint Bernard of Clairvaux, who because of his vast theological and spiritual writings, his tireless travels, and his political and organizational skills, has been called "the founder of modern Europe."

In the twelfth and thirteenth centuries, Saint Dominic and Saint Francis founded new kinds of religious orders, with their members more mobile and less monastic in many respects, dedicated to the evangelization of Europe. These were the mendicants, the friars, who also vowed themselves to live lives of poverty, chastity, and obedience to a religious superior and who supported themselves largely by begging. They experienced phenomenal growth and fame, and have provided the Church with large numbers of teachers, preachers, and theologians down to the present. Both Saint Thomas Aquinas and Meister Eckhardt held the chair of theology at the University of Paris and were Dominicans.

In the Christian East monks wielded great social and religious influence also, as exemplified by their successful struggle in defense of icons in the eighth century. Unlike Western monasticism, that of the East never split into separate orders. Each monastery was autonomous. For example, there were over seventy monasteries just in Constantinople. Each was a unique though similar foundation with its own rule. From the ninth century, the rule of life of Saint Theodore's monastery at Studios in Constantinople has been the major pattern of Eastern Orthodox monastic life. In the tenth century, Saint Symeon the New Theologian, who was trained at Studios, wrote the famous "Hymns of Divine Love" on his experience of living the sacramental life with intensity and devotion.

In the late tenth century, Saint Athanasius began his monastery on the Greek peninsula of Athos, which eventually developed into a semiautonomous republic of monks, with dozens of other monasteries, sketes, and hermitages, at times with thousands of monks. Athonite monks such as Saint Gregory Palamas, who successfully defended the practice of prayer known as *hesychasm* (from a Greek word meaning "quiet"), have had a strong influence on Orthodox theology, and Mount Athos itself maintains a high profile in Orthodox church life to this day.

Soon after the conversion of the Slavs in Kievan Rus to Christianity in 988, Saint Anthony introduced monastic life to Rus, and his disciple Saint Theodore went on to found the famous Kiev Monastery of the Caves, which provided a prophetic example of social awareness through his work in the city during famines and epidemics. Since then, monasticism has continued to exert a profound influence throughout the Balkans, Ukraine, and Russia.

After two centuries of Mongol Tartar subjection of the country, Saint Sergius in the fourteenth century sparked a renewal of monastic and national life in Russia, followed by Saint Nil of Sora and Saint Joseph of Volokolamsk and a host of pioneer monk saints in the far northern "deserts." In the nineteenth century, the spiritual fathers or "elders" at Optina Poustínia hermitage spurred another renewal of monastic and church life. Some of these places were centers of church and civil administration and defense in war; all are centers of pilgrimage and piety today.

In the evening, in the morning, and at midday, we praise and bless you,
we give thanks to you, and we entreat you, master of all things,
Lord and lover of all mankind: Let our prayer rise like incense before you
and let not our hearts be taken up with evil words and thoughts,
but rescue us from all those who hunt after our souls.
Our eyes are firmly fixed on you, O Lord, and on you do we count:
Do not disappoint us.

Prayer of the incense Psalms at vespers

TEN

One Mind, One Heart

I F YOU LIVE IN a rural setting, as we do here at the monastery, you know how much deeper and darker night is in the country than in the city. On evenings of the new moon, when low cloud cover blocks out the stars, if a monk forgets to take a flashlight with him for night chores, he can easily become disoriented. Pitch-black night enfolds him. The easy, short walk to the kennels quickly becomes an unnerving adventure into darkness. It is all too easy to stumble into trees and ditches, and his embarrassment at this is exceeded only by the pervasive fear elicited by the darkness. It is raw, primal, deep in the imagination. Perhaps it reminds us of times when nature was not so easily subdued, when night was really something to be feared.

Premodern cultures were constantly confronted by the terror of darkness, and when they celebrated the gift of light (or of any primal force), it was natural and easy to use ritual and symbols to portray those realities. Think of the early cave painters of Lascaux, with their stunning images of nature, of wild animals, and of hunting. However superstitious these people of earlier times may have been, they were in closer touch than we with elemental powers and innate needs. Their social interaction was suffused with repetitive ritual, in song, dance, and gesture. They had no doubts about how important it was to gather together to confront the great mysteries of life through these rituals. They considered themselves anchored anew in reality by doing this.

In the ancient world, the daily return of light was as wonderful as it was mysterious — and in their minds by no means guaranteed — as ancient prayers attest. What fears and hopes the daily and seasonal cycles brought with them! It seems only natural that dawn and evening became earnest occasions of prayer, when clan, village, or city would gather ritually to rejoice in the advent of light from sun, moon, or fire. Such occasions portrayed these primal forces as manifestations of the sacred, not graspable by sheer reason alone. These ritual events gave ancient peoples the tools of symbol, myth, and poetry to understand and communicate their experience of ultimate reality. But performing ritual also helped sustain and transmit knowledge of the regularity of natural cosmic rhythms. This same impulse led to the development of art, language, literature, mathematics — all systems of symbol and communication.

Many people today mistakenly believe that symbols are not real but are poor substitutes for "the really real." "If you ask me," said a feisty neighbor of ours as she talked with Brother Barnabas, "when I need to talk to God, I just talk to him. Candles, pictures, all that other stuff — it's all a lot of superstition."

"Well, Jean," replied Brother Barnabas, mildly amused, "you mean to tell me that you don't keep any souvenirs or sentimental photographs of those you love?" He eyed the locket hanging around her neck. The flustered woman blushed and shooed the monk away playfully, saying, "Oh, you monks!"

Fact is, symbols are exceedingly real, for their power puts

us in touch with realities that are not tangible. They help us become aware of that which is beyond words, what is ineffable, but often deeply felt.

The word "symbol" comes from the Greek *symbolein*, which means to throw or bring together. Symbols allowed the ancients to *bring together* the power of nature and the realm of the gods — the abstract or unapproachable, the terrifyingly distant or uncontrollable — into the realm of the everyday. Symbols in the form of ritual, festival, and worship gave meaning to their lives. Through symbols they established a relationship to the natural world and control in their lives, to ensure survival and prosperity. Symbols provide meaning and order to the cosmos, allowing mere humans to know and experience in a relative way the inexhaustible and unfathomable depths of reality.

In ancient Babylonian times, we would have celebrated the miracle of light by chanting hymns in which the sun and moon appear as conquering heroes in a two-pronged assault upon darkness. In the very singing of these hymns, we would have evoked and supported the coming of light, thus pointing to its deeper significance — the victory of the divine realm of light. Thus we would have provided stability, security, and peace for our people.

A similar idea is present in the Vedas, the Hindu sacred writings, and in the Hebrew Psalms. In their hymns on the dawn and the sun, these Scriptures personalize their subject, allowing the symbol to dramatize deeper truths:

> Glorious to behold, she awakens the world of men
> Riding ahead, opening the way
> In her lofty car, majestic, delighting all,
> Spreading light at the break of day.

As though proud of the loveliness of her body,
Freshly bathed, the young Dawn stands upright,
To be seen. Darkness, the enemy, is expelled
When Heaven's Child appears, spreading light.

Rg Veda V. 80, verses 2, 5

The heavens declare God's glory,
and the work of his hands, the firmament proclaims!
. . . There, he pitches a tent for the sun
that comes forth like a bridegroom from his chamber,
bursting with joy, like a champion in running his course.

Psalm 19(18):1, 4c–5

In one civilization after another, the translation of certain realities into representations — symbolic images — of other realities, originates from something deep and inherent in human nature, a sense of awe and wonder, a perception demanding expression. Symbols may differ, as well as our understanding, interpretation, and use of rituals, but the impulse to use them itself is a universal drive in human life. We are oriented toward meaning, and to the celebration of it, and ultimately our individual taste for the "really real" will be satisfied only when we join our fellow human beings in recognition of our common search for the essential truths of human life.

We may scoff at primitive man's need for symbolism and ritual, dismissing it as nothing more than superstitious mumbo jumbo that our scientific era has made obsolete. But a closer look at our own lives reveals that we, too, are inescapably creatures of symbols. From language to dance, wedding rings to diplomas, military medals to flags, in art and music, in secular culture as well as religious practice, symbols not only represent and express deeper, often more elusive thoughts and feelings, but actually stimulate and refine our experience of these realities.

A LL THIS IS THE BASIS for what we call *liturgy* — a term ordinarily used only in a religious context. But even in the secular realm it is a dramatic and powerful reality. "We human beings by nature seek to gather together," Father Laurence explained, addressing a small interfaith group on retreat at New Skete to discuss the place of liturgy in spiritual life. "Even in the distant past they did this as more than a survival strategy. They obviously felt a powerful drive and need *to celebrate* in common what is most meaningful in life, *to reinforce* the bonds that make us a society and a culture under divine protection, and *to pass* that wisdom on to the next generation."

"If you're speaking of tribal societies in primitive cultures, weren't their rituals often based on fear and superstition?" asked Rob, a middle-aged teacher.

"Sometimes, but that's not what matters here. *Why* they did it is not as important as the fact *that* they did it. Their coming together reveals something essential for human life, even for all of us today. It comes from here," he said, tapping his heart, "from the guts. When you study history and human nature, when you look at how we human beings have always lived together, you see this need for familiar and recurring rituals, regular ceremonial and formal commemoration, which express, strengthen, and define the state of our relationships, our common ideals, our shared triumphs and griefs. That's something we can't afford to forget, for it's just as true for us."

We really cannot celebrate alone. For all our individuality, we are social beings; each member of either clan or community needs to be aware of and participate in the shared expressions that define the group mentality, that delineate the greater context of our lives, that clarify our individual roles in society and with regard to each other. What happens in such gatherings is something that cannot happen to us when we are alone: we joyfully experience ourselves as part of a bigger reality whose richness gives our lives broader dimension, shared purpose, and renewed energy.

Cultivating a communal sense of ritual celebration is the very basis of civilization and the origin of culture. This is the authentic "work of the people" in any society, as the word "liturgy" shows us in its Greek origins. From this perspective, we can see why a presidential inauguration or funeral, for example, is so important. Because of the powerful impact of these events, we celebrate them with formalities and ceremonials that express and bear witness to what we feel and believe as a society, our common excitement or grief. They also serve to reinforce our beliefs and deepen our sense of belonging, of working together.

A dignified-looking gentleman named Peter raised his hand. "So even when formal religion is absent, you're saying that society will naturally create *civic* ceremonies, *civic* liturgy to give meaning to the events of life?"

Father nodded, "Even an atheistic society such as the former Soviet Union. After the revolution, it categorically and ruthlessly repudiated any and all religion; but it soon discovered that it had to provide its people with public rituals of national and patriotic celebration. May Day parades and the cult of Lenin's tomb are obvious examples. The pageantry of Nazi and fascist political rallies was also liturgy divorced from its religious moorings. Whatever we may think of those secular substitutes and their message, they point out the absolute necessity of some sorts of celebrations to enhance, enrich, inspire a society. They add real spice to life." Father shrugged. "Without some form of liturgy, civil life can be pretty barren, a wasteland, and the fire of its spirit soon goes out."

Ritualized social activity in fact pervades most facets of life — eating, drinking, mating, greeting, war, sports, business, entertainment, and holidays. Though much of this "work of the people" is deadly serious and helps hold society together by enriching individual cultures and civilizations, it often follows the patterns of play, courtesy, and mutual consideration that ease the starkness of living by the sweat of our brow. Father smiled. "All work and no play makes Jack a dull boy."

I T IS NOT OUR INTENTION or desire to proselytize or convert the reader to a particular religion. Our intention throughout has been to offer a vision of human life that can be of benefit to anyone. We firmly believe that the principles enunciated in this work are universal, transcendent realities all human beings must connect with if they are to know true happiness. Nevertheless, we ourselves can truly witness to these principles only by speaking out of our own experience and understanding as Christian monks. When we talk about liturgy and worship, it is because we see them as central to human life, as something more and more neglected, disdained, and even corrupted, but which we passionately believe are required for the benefit of all human beings.

If you have no experience of this yourself, or if church experiences in the past have been negative, or if you never even knew what these experiences were supposed to be about, our emphasis on them may seem incomprehensible or threatening, and may even provoke some strong defensive reactions. Yet to tiptoe around the issue of liturgy simply because it may be threatening or distasteful to you would be doing you a gross disservice. Our own experience and study have convinced us of its crucial place in healthy spirituality.

Liturgy, as we Christians use the term, signifies *the official ritual worship of the Church.* "Strictly speaking," Father Laurence explained to the members of the interfaith retreat, "in the Orthodox Catholic, as well as the other Eastern Christian traditions, the word 'liturgy' refers only to the eucharist, while the Roman Catholic tradition, and by extension the traditions that flow from that, use the term 'liturgy' to include all the official services of the Church. Here, in our discussion, since we're from different Christian traditions, we want to concentrate on the principles that are universal to Christian liturgical practice, East or West.

"Liturgy is a living tradition that provides the means by which we actively unite in celebrating the sacred mysteries of life and our faith. Even more so, it's decisive for our happiness because it enables us consciously to enter into the mystery of our relationship with God in an utterly unique way, differently from what happens in private prayer or meditation, or even group gatherings such as reciting the rosary, or other prayers." Father Laurence paused to look at the various members sitting around the conference table. "It doesn't do this by magic or empty actions, but through self-forgetful, thoughtful, and wholehearted engagement with others, working to produce an offering of praise to the source, creator, enlightener, and savior of life. Doing this we come to understand and develop ourselves, both individually and as a society, in ways we can't achieve by ourselves. Imagine trying to put on a play alone! Life is lived with people, and liturgy is where we experience the truth of this in a preeminent way."

All things considered, this would seem to apply to non-Christian religions, as well. As Christian monks, we don't feel ourselves either qualified or inclined to delve into other religious traditions in this book. Yet doctrines, beliefs, and revelations aside, there is vital nourishment to be gained from participating in the traditions of worship, from congregating together for the religious practices, of any religious body. The *liturgical community* is the earth into which we sink our spiritual roots and which gives us a context for our struggles and maturation, support for a deepening of faith and dedication — even when we find within that community itself different degrees of spiritual understanding and insight.

SUCH AN ASSERTION goes against the cultural tide. "Traditional worship isn't easily understood these days," Father Laurence said to the retreatants. "Perhaps it's not so much that people are actively against liturgy, as that it tends to get lost amidst all sorts of other possibilities — from ignorance to the trendiness of personal spirituality. People nowadays especially are attracted by quick, convenient prayers or meditations tailored to the privacy of their own home, without the fuss of going to church. Personally, I wouldn't give you ten cents for most of it. Rather than challenging people with what they need, it caters to what they want and how they feel. We won't grow by catering to our immaturity. Believe me, something crucial is missing."

Rob replied, "I work with a fellow like that. It's not that he's uninterested in spirituality. In fact, we often talk at lunch about mutual spiritual concerns. But going to church — he sees it as a waste of his time. I remember him telling me, 'I gave up on church when I was young. Don't see much sense taking up time for something I don't think God gives a damn about.' This person thought William James had said it best: 'Religion is what happens to us in our solitude.'"

"Sure, this fosters a mentality that views liturgy as a crutch for the intellectually weak," added Tom from the other side of the conference table. "My wife and I talk about this all the time. Lots of people we know go to church primarily because they feel they're supposed to, not because they really want to. There's a lot of fear there. It's an obligation, a burden of some sort. Others consider themselves 'liberated' and attend only when they feel like it, when nothing else is going on. Then there's the 'twice a year' crowd. Our parish has lots of people who are listed as members but only show up once or twice a year for the big feasts, mostly for sentimental reasons. If you ask me, the people who really seem to understand and appreciate the importance of liturgy are in the minority. For most, liturgy just doesn't have the value and power it's supposed to have in our lives."

Father Laurence responded quickly, "Know what I'd say? If custom, law, and sentiment are all that liturgy is, then by all means let's ignore it and get on with life! But my money's on another explanation: People today — whether because they're too busy or haven't been taught properly — are simply unaware of what liturgy really means and therefore can't see what it accomplishes. It's like looking at a great work of art with no means of understanding it. At first you can't figure it out. Only when we catch a glimpse of what it is *really* all about, when we get in touch with the higher realities underlying the thing, then we actually break out of our own little worlds and unite in approaching and responding to a greater reality. This is how it is with understanding liturgy also, no matter who we are. It takes understanding to see that spirituality without liturgy and worship is like life without nourishment — something fundamental is missing."

"Yes, but what do we say to the person who asks us why he should bother at all with liturgy, that his spiritual life is fine without it?" cut in Tom.

"Such a person really doesn't understand what liturgy is about and probably sees it as just another thing for needy souls. For him, it's most likely just an irrelevancy. But he's also making a serious mistake in letting *how he feels* become the determinator of the quality of his spiritual life. A lot of people do this today, but theirs isn't a sound criterion at all. Doing what is right as best we can as an offering to God, whether we happen to feel good or not, is what's really to the point."

So the interior, spiritual life is not supposed to be an exercise in narcissism, in self-satisfaction. This would only further fragment our life. The goal of a healthy religious and spiritual development is the full integration of the adult personality. This includes the redemption of every aspect of our life, from negativities, backsliding, unconscious influences, ignorance, malice, and sin. No one, of course, can ever accomplish this as an isolated individual, though attaining a sense of individuality and autonomy is an important step in growing up. But a further aspect of development is the sharing, *the giving away of ourselves.* What we are and have is a gift and talent that will only corrode unless we eventually use it in the service of love for others.

Joining with the church community is a powerful stimulus for this. The liturgy is a richly human reality that leads us to recognize God's presence and activity in our midst. It is an inspired instrument for leading us, through our remembrance of Christ's love, to pursue our love for one another. Though we can never see God directly in any literal sense, he can be encountered in the liturgy nonetheless as we together commemorate these mysteries of Christ's life. By invoking the grace of God, we also evoke it; it becomes accessible. "Liturgy is the usual, primary way this occurs," Father continued. "At least, that's what our tradition says. But don't simply take my word for it . . . look at the religions of the world. Liturgy finds many different expressions in them, but its presence is universal. Liturgical experiences may vary according to the practice of a particular religion. But to try living a spiritual life without liturgy is like drilling for oil with a shovel."

WHAT IS DESERVING of worship? "Worshipping anything less than God alone is an exercise in alienation, a substitute that will never really fulfill the ultimate need and yearning we humans have," Father Laurence explained. He had been asked by a young dentist named Tim to clarify the importance of worship for spiritual health. "Worshipping some thing — money, for example — only leads to disappointment once we discover that no amount of it can make us happy. Or power. Inevitably, in time, it corrupts or destroys those who idolize it. Even beauty — which so easily reflects God. When we worship beauty rather than the one who created it, when we divorce it from its author, its true purpose is perverted. You can be sure that today's cover girl will one day look in the mirror and see how fleeting good looks really are. You work with teeth; what happens over time?" Tim smiled.

The history of religion shows us we cannot afford to worship nor make an idol of our own limited image of God; worship belongs only to the true, living God. Authentic liturgy and worship of God uses all of God's creation — including our own bodies and minds — to praise God, to reflect the transcendent, spiritual, nonmaterial, or divine aspects of reality for our awareness, to direct our consciousness beyond the immediately evident, superficial, and often blinding situations, thoughts, and requirements of daily life. We come to liturgy as flawed beings, never quite living up even to our own expectations, but needing edification and inspiration to keep struggling over a lifetime.

Monastic spirituality teaches nothing if not this. Yet its wise and tenacious insistence on an active liturgical engagement with God is often disdained or forgotten. Saint Benedict admonishes, "Let nothing be preferred to the work of God" (that is, the liturgy). He emphasizes the importance of liturgy not as some legal obligation, or to keep us busy and so out of trouble, but as the very foundation of our spiritual struggle for wholeness. It feeds the souls of the monks and the spirit of the monastery.

One of the classical Greek words for worship is *therapeía,* from which comes our word "therapy." "Liturgy is indeed therapy for the soul; it helps to make us whole — both the self and our relationships," Father insisted. "It's truly healing because only in and through right worship do we become who we are truly meant to be, adult sons and daughters of the Most High. As we come home to ourselves in this radical way, we become more peaceful, for we begin to taste lasting happiness. We cannot hide this, of course — it radiates from us."

I F THIS IS SO, why are liturgical worship and private prayer repeatedly pitted against each other today, when both are necessary? Why do people think they can dispense with liturgical practice so long as they pray in solitude? There are two reasons, when all is said and done. We have already mentioned the common misunderstanding of what place individualism should play in all this. But it is also true that worship can be hard and inconvenient. It eats into the free time we guard so jealously. Even when we correctly understand it and wholeheartedly participate, liturgy requires preparation, discipline, and the self-sacrifice involved in work.

This led Tim to observe, "I don't think that we can underestimate how demanding liturgy can be. I have to drag myself out of bed on a Sunday morning, and it's the only morning I might sleep in. Then we add excuses like, 'It's boring . . . the pastor can't preach . . . the congregation is elderly and conservative . . . the singing is atrocious . . . or (the ultimate reduction) I don't get anything out of it,' and pretty soon church becomes less and less attractive, easier to dismiss. Why *not* stay in bed an hour longer and then do my meditation in the privacy of my own home? After all, does God really care?"

Father smiled. "If you're asking whether or not God *needs* our worship, then the answer is obviously no. God doesn't need either our prayer or worship to feed his ego (were he even to have one) or to buoy up his self-confidence (were he to lack any). But I think God does care in the sense that he recognizes that *we need* church for our wholeness and growth. When Jesus said, *'The Sabbath was made for man, not man for the Sabbath,'* he was saying that God made everything, the worship of God included, for us — to lead us to himself.

"Part of the problem is that parishioners often don't have an understanding of where liturgy comes from or what it means, and so they never even suspect that what they 'get out of it' isn't the question." Father emphasized the point by tapping his finger on the table. "In liturgy, *we're* not the center of attention; *God* is, but we are the ones who benefit and are in need of it; and so it's of prime importance that we put our best into it." As elsewhere, it is in giving of ourselves that we receive. Gathering together in worship sends a profound message both to ourselves and to others that this is where our values are."

"But is this really different from what happens in private prayer?" asked Bill, an electrician who looked to be in his late fifties. "I mean, when we pray, we do the same thing, don't we, regardless of how we feel at the moment? Don't we worship in solitude, too?"

"The dynamics are quite different," replied Father. "We are unable to do alone, by ourselves, what is by nature social and a function of the community. Worship is that type of reality. We may pray in solitude, and we may even go to pray in church, and this is indeed part of the spiritual life, but solitary prayer isn't liturgy, it's not worship."

"Why not?"

"Because worship, that is, liturgy, is corporate by nature and by definition — just as a social movement signifies something more powerful than a lone advocate, and a parade more than the grand marshal. We aren't all loners when it comes to God. God isn't exclusively hidden in the depths of individual conscience; he is present where two or three are gathered in his name, in the actions of love; and that's why people desire and need to come together for this. Private prayer isn't the same thing, but it prepares us for this and, in turn, is enhanced by it. When each of us brings our offerings, prayers, and hymns, we join with those of the rest of the church, which includes those of the apostles and martyrs of long ago, as well as seekers of God always and everywhere.

"Actually, the greatest offering of praise and prayer, of liturgy, is our living together in harmony and service to one another. Everything in our church is tailored to facilitate this: instruction in the faith, preaching, spiritual counseling, eucharist, charitable works. Even our sacred Scriptures are community documents that show this. The Gospels and Epistles were written to and for specific congregations of early Christian times to make them grow in unity and love.

As the Acts of the Apostles points out, *'They shared everything in common, praising and singing together.'* The energy to sustain this comes from liturgy."

Because only the community can reflect or manifest the larger, universal, cosmic, reality that is implicit in belief, so it is that only a community truly worships, and it does this first and foremost in its liturgy. Liturgy is the symbol, the witness, and the festival of our fellowship.

As we said already, "liturgy" (from the Greek *leitourgía,* "people" plus "work") literally means "the work of the *people,*" as distinct from the isolated, private, personal work of an *individual.* It is a corporate action through which the faithful become something together that they were not as individuals. When people join together for the highest intentions that liturgy implies, the serene joyfulness and energy for good that results is much greater than that of the mere sum of those gathered. It is palpable! And infectious. Together in worshipping God they give communal witness to the word, the love, and the work of God on earth. *Liturgy, finally, makes them the church.*

M OST PEOPLE misunderstand this. Say "church" and they reflexively think "building" or "institution."

A guest once told the Seeker quite bluntly, "I don't have to go to church to worship God. Besides, you can't believe how uninspiring a place it is. 'McChurch' is what I call it, an all-purpose monstrosity. There's nothing beautiful about it in the least." From this perspective, going to church means attending some service in a particular building once a week, which people like our guest might feel they can easily do without. Unfortunately, they have "thrown out the baby with the bath water"!

*A better image (or symbol) to describe the reality of the church
would be a living organism, an integral body, which Christianity
understands to be the mystical body of Christ. Here the individual
members are fashioned into a unity, altogether a new creation, unique
and comprehensive. "What about the people you're there with,"
replied the Seeker to this guest, "the congregation? Aren't they actually part of your life, members of the same human family you belong
to? And isn't the one God the same creator and redeemer of us all?
Wasn't it Saint Paul who asked whether the eye would ever say to the
hand, 'I don't need you,' or the head say to the feet, 'You're of no
importance to me'? The church is part of who you are, too." The
guest seemed mystified, which is probably more an indictment of poor
Christian teaching than of ill will.*

The mystical body of Christ is the tangible symbol and
arena of God's presence in our midst. By virtue of our mem-
bership in Christ we are now intimately related to each other.
The very definition of church, *ekklesía* in Greek (*ek*, "out
of," plus *klesía* from *kaleín*, "to call" — those who have been
called out of their *old* place and summoned together into this
new reality) refers to persons, therefore, and not buildings.
This living church is the community of Christ's disciples
responding to the call to be the assembly of God in a specific
place. God calls us from out of the chaos and alienation of
everyday living to be a people, his people in our own day.

"For me, I'd say attending the eucharist each week is
where I most experience that sense of worship and belonging
you're speaking of," said Peter in response to Father Laurence's admonition.

"I think that's so for some Christians," replied Father, "but
not for all. Not by a long shot. The eucharistic liturgy should
be understood as the occasion par excellence that defines
Christians, but I get the impression many people — Orthodox,

Catholics, and Protestants alike — don't really grasp this. How many have a clear idea of what it's all about?"

The group seemed somewhat uncomfortable. Father continued, "When we gather together to celebrate the eucharist — to reconnect with the Last Supper, the crucifixion, the resurrection, and the kingdom to come — the actions in which Jesus gave himself body and soul for us (and for that matter, for the whole world), how many of us realize, not to mention experience, this re-presentation as God's eternal love reaching out to us here and now? The eucharist makes us truly one body — and equally united with those who came before and with those who continue after us. It both creates the church and reveals its meaning in the very act of our celebrating these realities. If we really understood and believed this, it would transform our attitude toward everything."

This is the Christian faith. When Jesus identified himself with the bread and wine of this assembly, with these elements symbolic of what is most characteristic of our bodily existence, he gave his followers an intimate memorial through which they would be vividly united with *his* very body and blood, that is, with his own presence and reality. Through this we are brought together in a new and powerful way; together we eat the same bread and drink the same wine, enlivened by our sharing of the same spirit; our life together as believers becomes the nourishing context and anchor for our individual growth and maturation.

Father Laurence added that we should not understand this in some magical, or superstitious, manner, but by acknowledging that what occurs is a mystery of faith, the sacramental transformation of our own situation. "We become his body the church here and now; we join our sacrifices and love, our 'blood, sweat, and tears,' with the deep compassion and sacrifice of Christ, celebrating this festival, this banquet of joy that manifests his victory over all evil. To get into polemical debates about when the elements actually change during the service, for example, is useless. It's the whole service, the entire celebration of liturgy by the clergy and people, that constitutes our worship. Our coming together, our celebration, calls down upon ourselves and upon the gifts of bread and wine the Holy Spirit that transforms the same bread and wine into the body and blood of Christ. This same Spirit transforms us, present at this service, into the living presence of Christ on earth. We set the stage, so to speak, but God fulfills the mystery."

By this dramatic and mystic enactment of the eucharist, believers come to see and know the risen, living Christ anew in themselves as the church. As Saint John Chrysostom, (d. 407), one of the most eloquent and authoritative of the early church fathers, wrote,

> Let us reflect on this wonderful mystery, its purpose and effects. The scriptures tell us we become a single body, members of his flesh and bone of his bones. This is brought about by the food he gives us. He blends himself with us so that we may all become one single entity as a body is joined to its head.

Liturgy is thus not only an epiphany wherein God is revealed, but a sacrament, a sacred encounter with him. Through the liturgy, it is God who brings us together into a unity of mind and heart. *Sýnaxis* was an early Christian term used for this gathering together for the eucharist (*syn,* "with," plus *ago,* "to lead" — a congress). At the *sýnaxis* we give praise to God for his incomparable gift of life to us and for the tangible mystery and sacrament of Christ's presence in our midst. We do this by celebrating the passion and death of Christ and the coming reality of his kingdom, that is, the final perfection, fullness, or completion of salvation history. In that kingdom, "Gone is the distinction between Jew and Greek, slave and free, male and female — you are all one in Christ Jesus." (Galatians 3:28)

WE CAN'T LIVE APART from each other for long. Our relationships mix us together in such a complex way that our individualities are inescapably intertwined. "Monks are especially aware of the social nature of reality," said Father Laurence after a coffee break. "Human beings were never meant to live alone. Just as an infant will die without constant physical handling and human contact, so, too, will we die spiritually if we attempt to live out our spiritual lives in isolation from a community of faith. Experience makes it absolutely clear that at every level we were made to live with others, to create ever greater ties of familiarity, support, and love."

"I've got to confess that I'm still a little stumped with what you're saying," Bill interjected. "I don't go to church to relate with others, I go to receive the sacrament. Receiving Christ feeds my prayer life, makes me feel closer to him. It helps me to keep up my devotions throughout the week."

"I think part of the reason you say this, Bill, is that you're missing a crucial dimension of what the eucharist is about," Father answered. "The liturgy is not a 'me and Jesus' phenomenon. The eucharist ushers in the kingdom of God and makes us its citizens. Here we willingly enter into a relationship with God and with each other through the command of Christ and his mediation. This transcends and supersedes every separation and division — a challenge for us all, for Christ says, 'Love one another as I have loved you.' Isn't it remarkable that we become most truly who we are by giving ourselves entirely to others! That's the only way we can become most fully ourselves. The sacraments feed our union and make it visible in the assembly where we partake of them. Many of us still don't understand that this worship is more than just 'me and Jesus'; after all, no one can 'muster up' the eucharist alone; it's interpersonal, 'we together' who are shown how expansive the mystery of Christ is. Again, it's beyond anything we could achieve alone."

"That's also why Orthodox Catholic theology has characterized the human being as liturgical," added Brother Marc, who had been listening attentively off to the side. "All liturgical worship, but especially the eucharist, is our very taking possession of this as our heritage. It's a dramatic, colorful, sacred language enriched and refined by hundreds of generations from diverse cultures. In fact it's a culture in itself, consisting of theology, spirituality, preaching, poetry, music and chant, art and architecture — our very living together as a community of believers.

"Liturgy isn't just an attempt to feel close to God. We struggle to assume the spirit of Christ, in communion with others, working this out with them. Together we're commissioned to carry this into all of our life in the world. If we don't fully share in this, an entire dimension of our life is missing."

By its nature liturgy initiates us into becoming full-fledged members of the church. In this process, there is a very crucial balance and interchange between the local and universal church, so that the universal church becomes authentically present in the local setting. This is because liturgy invites us to *listen and get a feel for life in a way consistent with the ideals and teachings of the church as a whole.* Through liturgy, we *act in and with the rest of the church,* because we *believe, hope, and love in and through the whole church,* just as we pray *in and for the whole church*. In order for our existence as members of this community to mature and flower, we need to participate in what the church does — beginning with the liturgy. We cannot afford to be mere spectators, much less loners.

The texts of the services, whether we can hear them clearly or have to read along with the priest or chanter or choir, tell us precisely what is going on, and explain the connections with Christ's life, leading us to a taste of the kingdom of God in our midst. In other words, Christ himself becomes the living sacrament for us of God's compassion and grace; by participating in the sacramental mysteries that portray this (baptism, confirmation, eucharist, confession or reconciliation, anointing during sickness or at the time of death, the daily cycle of services, and matrimony and ordination), the church is built up and strengthened.

"Keep in mind there's not only a vertical but a horizontal dimension here," said Father Laurence, as he stroked his gray beard. "Liturgy both symbolizes and enacts the lifting up and offering of our lives to God, but it also reveals here and now the presence of God in our lives. We're different from other species not least by our capacity to will and to love freely, and we can draw on this only in our relationship with other people, whom we depend on and who depend on us. The more we truly love, the more human we are, the more we strengthen the bonds of community, and the more we get on track in trying to fulfill our nature as members of the human race."

THE CHRISTIAN EXPERIENCE of liturgy can fire up our relationship with God, yet the hard truth is that for many people, liturgy itself is lifeless, fine in theory, perhaps, but not much help in everyday life. Tony, a young businessman, spoke up: "I have to confess that the only reason I came here this weekend was as a concession to my dad." He looked over at Pete. "Although I was raised Orthodox, I haven't gone to church since high school, mainly because I found it boring and irrelevant. I don't know, maybe that was my own fault, but the reality was that it just didn't mean anything to me. So I stopped going, though I never stopped believing in God. And I do pray now and then.

"Anyway, after graduate school, there was a time when I was having personal problems, and I did try a couple of churches, but nothing seemed to click; often the service was in Greek, which I don't understand, and the preaching didn't speak to me. I don't know, it just seems to me our Orthodox Church is living in another century. Now I admit, I don't know anything about liturgy, but still, when I did try to find something out about it, the two priests I talked to didn't seem to have the time to help me. Seeing the beauty of vespers last night and matins this morning, and listening to what you've been saying here, my inclination is to say, 'All this is fine when you live in a monastery, but what if you don't?' Can ordinary people really experience this?"

"Well, I for one think that I experience this very much, son," said Pete. "In fact, it helps my ordinary life a lot. Even though you live in New York now, and are far from home, you know no parish is perfect. But even with its limitations, I depend on parish life. Belonging to my parish and attending services there fills a gap in my life; it gives my faith a place to express itself, to grow."

"Still, you're bringing up a very important issue, Tony," said Father Laurence. "Liturgy is by no means only the province of monks or clergy, yet so often people find themselves just going through the motions. Sometimes this *is* the fault of the clergy, who do little to educate people in this regard and whose own appreciation of liturgical life may, surprisingly enough, be sadly deficient. Recently at a parish liturgy I was stunned with the way the priest presided. He looked disheveled, he raced through the service, didn't enunciate clearly when he spoke or sang, and was pretty much off-key in his singing. A disaster! Telling ourselves that liturgy is automatically effective regardless of how we carry it out is a copout and smacks of superstition; we fail to comprehend that religion and worship are at the apex of human endeavors, that our life *depends* on them. Look, if the clergy fail to invest the time, interest, and attention to serve the liturgy in a compelling and meaningful way, they can hardly expect their flocks to respond. Church is more than a theology or doctrine club. Somehow, priests and pastors have to be encouraged and supported in taking up their liturgical roles more effectively. At the same time, let's remember that the responsibilities that fall on pastors are not light — in fact they're extremely demanding and warrant our understanding — but nevertheless, these are still deficiencies that have to be addressed."

Tony nodded, listening attentively.

Father continued, "But the fault is our own also, as the faithful. Believe me, some people could be privy to the most beautiful and reverently celebrated liturgy possible, and it would still fail to move them. They're asleep!" Father shook his head. "It's bad; in some churches, you have those who are experimenting, foolishly trying to reinvent liturgy to make it relevant to the needs of a modern, increasingly dysfunctional society. Then you have our church — stuck with exaggerated baroque forms of worship that suffocate the pristine beauty of the liturgy. Both of these tendencies get in the way of our meeting the mystery of God.

"Who's seeking to understand liturgy nowadays? Not many people, I fear. Thus, the end result is worse than what we started with. Instead of being provided with an irresistible sense of divine mystery, the possibility of healing by getting in touch with God, people come away with a vague sense of confusion and disappointment.

"To be meaningful, liturgy needs the competent, skillful, and intelligent involvement of all the members of the congregation. You've got to be willing to enter into it, Tony, even if it means hunting around for a church where that's happening or where it can happen. Just because the services are abused, curtailed incorrectly, crippled in their execution, we can't allow ourselves to use this as an excuse to ignore their value or toss them out completely."

"I think another factor is that once you've found a church, you've got to be brave enough to get involved with it," said Tom. "For example, join the choir." Tony made a face, and the others laughed. "Seriously, you'll be surprised how your perceptions change when you become more active in this."

"This gets more to the heart of things," said Father. "What does each of us do? Only we can answer that for ourselves. Doesn't Christ say, 'Where your treasure is, there also is your heart'? If you remain passive or a spectator, you never experience the inspiration and challenge of liturgy. You remain locked within yourself. You rate the liturgy like a TV show and grade it on the basis of how it entertains — without it ever entering your mind that the purpose of liturgy is not entertainment."

Father's voice grew passionate. "Liturgy truly *is* 'work' in the sense that it requires us to move outside ourselves, to prepare, study, attend, sing, and listen together in faith and love. When liturgy is celebrated correctly and with care by everyone involved, its beauty and majesty does nourish and inspire us. These become the very vehicles that enable us to meet the mystery of God, giving us the strength to live life well and deal creatively with its problems. Only then does this 'work' bring us to Christ. Let's face it: Liturgy's also about energy and belief, life and death. It's not about comfort, amusement, entertainment, and distraction. Christian liturgy is about *dying,* leaving behind the old self and becoming a new person, *so that we may live more fully,* more abundantly."

I'M STILL NOT CLEAR on how practical all of this is," said Rob. "After all, not all of us can sing in the choir. I'm Roman Catholic. We were always taught that the Mass is the center of church life — and I go to Mass regularly — but I have to confess that something's missing. What can I do to change that?"

Father thought for a moment. "Today, we need knowledge and understanding of everything more than ever. That's no less true of our religious observances. First, you have to pursue further understanding by study and reflection, together with more attentive participation. We have to understand that a liturgical community is a must for a healthy spiritual life. We can start only by changing ourselves, but when we do, just watch what happens. Our attitude changes, and we're able to become involved more dynamically even when the external circumstances aren't ideal. We sense something deeper, almost intangible. When enough people begin to experience these dimensions of liturgy — and not just in an emotional, soppy way — a kind of chain reaction starts to happen. Healthy enthusiasm develops, and growth occurs."

"Yes," added Brother Marc. "Our belief isn't just a creed and being with people who support and affirm us, whom we happen to like. Real faith means looking ahead with trust, working at what the church community is all about, starting with worship, but also searching out how to go about doing that, using our creative powers. We're talking about a process here, but when it happens, as we said, incredible energy is released."

This is what we mean by the living tradition of the church. As we enter into it wholeheartedly, intelligently, and with persistence — we discover that liturgy nourishes us in mind as well as heart, feeding our hunger for meaning. The human spirit naturally responds to it like a fish to water. The result is an ever-greater consciousness, intuition, and ability to enter into and integrate our relationship with God, faith, spirituality, humanity, the world — all the values of life.

Tom, clearly excited, said, "For me, it's precisely the sense of mystery that liturgy awakens that I find so compelling. And that's true even at the little Episcopalian church I attend. We're lucky — our priest has a good voice and celebrates the liturgy beautifully — and I really feel it. Maybe it's because I'm a musician, but the music, Psalms, and prayers just sweep me up; it's almost as though I forget myself in the worship. I leave church refreshed and inspired. As a result I'm more open with people, more patient and tolerant, as well as more responsive, I hope, to God."

"That's what we're talking about," stressed Father, as he perceived that they were beginning to understand. "But I don't think it's just because you're a musician that this happens, Tom. All kinds of people have experienced this very thing from the start, whether or not they were musicians. The entire context of liturgy with its manifold beauty reaches out to different people in different ways.

"And speaking of beauty, it was the nineteenth-century Russian writer Dostoevsky who wrote that beauty will save the world. A dramatic illustration of this is the legend of the Russian emissaries sent over a millennium ago to Constantinople by Prince Vladimir to examine the Eastern Orthodox faith. They were overwhelmed by the liturgy there. *"We cannot forget that beauty. . . ."* How can it be said to save? By promoting in us a rebirth of integrity, innocence, and a visible, effective hope. Such dynamism can be transforming, and all of us need it, because it touches the very core of our being."

"Look at poorer neighborhoods," Brother Marc interjected, "and the effect beautification has upon them. Programs designed to clean up city blocks have had a profound impact when coordinated intelligently with local residents. Crime decreases, an active sense of community develops, people take greater pride in their lives and surroundings. Culture and care flourish. The light of beauty, like love, brightens everything it touches. Just as life needs light, for life cannot exist in darkness, so life needs beauty; without beauty we become like plants without sunlight and water and fresh air. When we can't perceive and appreciate beauty, our lives are threatened with degradation, with being reduced to inhumanness."

Father Laurence nodded, scanning the men sitting around the table. "He's right. Beauty, like truth and goodness, is essential to human growth, and liturgy brings all of this to us in a perceptible and really sensuous way. This is why we've worked so extensively with liturgy here at New Skete, that the treasures we've inherited might be more brilliantly manifested.

"Through its beauty of thought and imagery, poetry and symbol, ritual and sacrament, the liturgy elevates us and our life; it engages us heart, mind, and body, in union with everyone in contemplation of the kingdom of heaven. In saying this I'm not just talking about beautiful vestments, glorious singing, awe-inspiring architecture, or colorful iconography, valuable and necessary though they are. We're talking about beauty fully integrated with what is good and true at the heart of the liturgical celebration, a beauty that almost eludes articulation. So you see, we're talking about all sorts of different levels of beauty. Included in this, obviously, is the very transforming beauty of the Gospel message. Services, whether simple and stark, or solemn and quite elaborate, manifest this beauty, a beauty that brings together young and old, rich and poor, schooled and unschooled, past and present and future alike. They help us celebrate and enter the friendship of the living, present Christ.

"Think about it this way: when we experience beauty even in art and science, we're conscious of its power, even if we can't verbalize it. We know it has touched us in a unique way. It creates a new inner strength to deal serenely and constructively with the unexpected turns of daily life. Sometimes these can be severe. For example, what are we to say about liturgy celebrated in wartime, in concentration camps, in burned-out churches, amidst all kinds of suffering, hunger, and misery? Are we to say that there is no beauty in these liturgies, that beauty is somehow missing? Not at all, because here we're talking about something that transcends external, physical beauty.

"When we actively enter into the spirit of liturgical worship and dwell in its atmosphere of beauty, we soon find our highest desires and aspirations revealed, reinforced, and refined in us. This is why we take such pains to bring out the inherent beauty and sense of the liturgy, even in the humblest circumstances. This is why we try to eliminate anything that distracts or detracts from that beauty."

Through liturgy we articulate in word and symbol what we believe, while at the same time discovering in it *what* we believe — and in periods of doubt — *that* we believe. At one point during the retreat conferences Bill confessed, "There was a period in my life when I wasn't sure of anything. I was depressed — no, maybe 'angry' is a better word — and confused. But I kept going to church . . . I don't even know why. Now as I look back, I can see that just being there, with all those other people, helped get me through the darkness, and when the trial passed, my faith was stronger."

E MPIRICAL SCIENCE itself sheds light on the influence of liturgy on our spiritual growth. Studies have shown, for example, that we perceive and react to what we hear more quickly and immediately than to what we see. "That's one reason sacred chant has such an uplifting effect on us," Brother Marc explained. "Researchers point out the difference between two types of sound. *'Discharge'* sounds cause fatigue, *'charge'* sounds reenergize us and increase health and resilience. The particular sound frequencies and tonalities produced in chant physically energize us. They affect more than simply our ears. The entire body grows stronger, and the mind becomes quiet and alert, which is why we feel so refreshed by it."

"So once again we touch on worship as therapy?" asked Tim.

"Yes, though again, that's not the primary reason we engage in it. Liturgy is an integral part of a healthy spiritual life, and this naturally includes the healing brought about by all the aspects of the liturgical celebration, chant included. The harmonious effect of voice, music, and speech — like all the other elements of liturgy — instantaneously changes our very neurological responses and hormonal balance. And this is just one example."

"Absolutely," continued Father Laurence. "We really need to be open to these realities, pursuing a fuller understanding of them. Naturally if we don't believe or at least want to try to believe in what's going on, liturgy will mean little or nothing to us. We're blocking its effects. Often this is the very problem with people who think that they get nothing out of liturgy. It's not enough to have been born into the church, to be a 'cradle Christian.' At some point, each of us has to make our own personal commitment to the faith. Human nature being what it is, that's when our work *really* begins. Our decision commits us to working steadily toward a mature faith. As we begin to understand what's going on, we will acquire an intuitive feel for the mind-set at the core of the church and the liturgical celebrations. We'll gain both a better appreciation and a deeper experience of the significance of liturgy for a stronger personal inner life, as well as a more powerful and nourishing communitarian life."

As the conference was drawing to a close, Father Laurence was reminded of a final point. "Liturgy disavows any sort of false triumphalism. To worship, to believe, hope, and live in the church demands our love, not only for those whom we know, but an openness and charitableness *toward all people without exception simply because they are our fellow human beings.* As members of the body of Christ we are Christ for the world. We bear the hope that the desires, aspirations, yearning at the heart of human existence will somehow be realized and fulfilled. Faith, hope, and love are called theological virtues precisely because they lead to God and the fulfillment of the divine purpose of all life. . . . God bless all of you!"

W E STARTED THIS CHAPTER with the experience of darkness. In the face of darkness, humans learned to control and use fire for their benefit and began lighting lamps to replace the fading daylight.

The early Christians, too, perceived that light itself is God's most precious gift, for it allows us to see all of his other blessings. It seems quite natural that they took light as a symbol of Jesus Christ. Saint John the Evangelist placed this insight on the lips of Christ himself:

> "I am the light of the world; whoever follows me will never walk in darkness, but will have the light of life." (John 8:12; translation New Skete)

> "Whoever sees me, sees the one who sent me. I came as light into the world, so that those who believe in me need not remain in the darkness." (John 12:45, 46; translation New Skete)

More than just poetry, this use of light as symbol illuminates a profound, eternal reality. It is precisely because the early church experienced Christ's enlightening presence so powerfully and joyfully that it connected this with the evening lighting of lamps. The earliest Christian worship included a rite of light, or *lucernárium* (the Latin term for the ancient lamp-lighting ceremony). This was appropriately used at the very beginning of vespers, before the evening offering of incense, since lights were needed for chanting the service. We still sing today the ancient hymn *"Phôs ílarón"* that always accompanied this:

> Radiant light of the holy glory
> of the immortal, heavenly, holy, and blessed Father:
> O Christ Jesus!
> Now, as we come to sunset, as we see the evening lights,
> we sing to God, the Father, Son, and Holy Spirit!
> At all times are you worthy to be praised by undefiled
>   tongue,
> O Son of God, who give life to the world:
> For this, the whole world praises you!

In the fourth century Saint Basil the Great wrote that this hymn was already so old that nobody could remember who composed it. Its power is archetypal. As often as we sing this with its haunting chant melodies — while we light the candles to slowly dispel the darkness — we are rejuvenated by its calm vision and unending hope that this world darkened by the horrors we perpetrate on each other has in fact been redeemed. This present moment becomes a link in the working out of this cosmic mystery. Christ himself did not invent or decree these realities: he recognized them and proclaimed that they lay at the root of human existence. We, too, can actually see in an experiential way now that this is so. Here in this hymn sunset and lamps and candles become the symbols of our deeply experienced knowledge of Christ, our never-fading enlightener and path to divine life.

It does not take extraordinary insight to perceive the cumulative effect of this rite on a community of believers that daily celebrates vespers. This liturgical event dramatizes the necessity of doing works of light — any and all of the good things that we are not ashamed to let the world see — instead of works of darkness, those things we are rightly ashamed of, that smack of deception and dishonesty, divisiveness and injury to others, of selfishness, greed, and ulterior motives calculated to justify and aggrandize ourselves, even at the expense of others. This defines our struggle, for the destiny of our minds and hearts is to be taken up into light.

We praise and glorify you, O unsearchable God and
    master of all that is!
For though you are one God, you are worshipped in
    Trinity, Father, Son, and Holy Spirit;
and though you are three, you are still one, the only
    one from whom, in whom, and by whom,
all that was and is and ever shall be, in heaven and on
    earth, finds its being.
At all times, make us conscious of your presence.
Grant that we may live each day before you with
    courage and confidence,
and enable us to please you in all things.

Prayer of the litany for Theophany matins

ELEVEN

What Does Love Look Like?

W HEN A LONGTIME FRIEND of our monastery came for his yearly retreat, he described an insight about his personal relationships that had profoundly affected him over the previous year. He is a leader of a close-knit church community in an impoverished neighborhood. For as long as we've known him, he's wrestled with trying to live according to spiritual values in a tough urban culture. In fact, he inspires us as he balances prayer and spiritual discipline with charitable work in the community. "I was meditating one day," he said, "when suddenly the thought came to me, 'What does love look like?' This was really strange. The question was not, 'What is love?' or 'How should we define love?' but 'What does love look like in actual living?' Now much about my life became clearer. I saw how I must grow."

Love is admittedly a very complex reality: rich, elusive, mysterious. Yet, we speak about love. We experience love. We know how good and necessary it is to be loved and to love, and as we mature in life, we gain all sorts of insights into what the love of a human being is about. Such maturity brings with it an awareness that the definition or description of such love is not necessarily the one we find in the dictionary, much less the image conveyed by television and movies.

Another friend of ours recently spoke with us after he and

his wife celebrated their twenty-fifth wedding anniversary. "When we first married, I think both of us, without even being aware of it, were seduced by the fantastic unreality of Hollywood love. We didn't understand the difference between our deep feelings for each other and true love, and this created expectations that made the first years of our marriage disappointing and rocky to say the least. For us, the real saving insight came at a weekend retreat we made here several years after we were married, and in particular during a private talk with Father Laurence. I'll never forget what he said:

" 'Look, at this point what you feel doesn't matter. Feelings come and go: one minute you feel like you're on fire, the next nothing, or even worse. Monks know this as well as anyone. But beyond what you feel, beyond what you know, beyond everything, is what you're *willing to do* for one another. Each of you controls that. Once you realize that you can *will* to love — *to act for the good of the other for its own sake and not simply for what you might get out of it* — then your love will mature and ripen. Then your love will really mean something. Before that, it's not really worth talking about.' That remark so startled me that it helped me take a fresh look at the whole idea of love."

At that his wife poked him playfully and quipped. "Yeah, *'Good Lord, what did we get ourselves into?'* "

Understanding love requires a lot of experience, listening, and reflection, plus the realization that, like many other things in the human condition, we can never fully understand it.

What *does* love look like? Actual love is the willingness to give the other what we would like for ourselves — the golden rule — continually going out from our own limited selves toward the other, unhampered by whatever we might happen to be feeling at the moment. Jesus also teaches this:

"Now I am giving you a new command — love one another.
Just as I have loved you, so you must love one another . . ."
(John 13:36)

Jesus wasn't making a suggestion, something to apply only to
our friends or to those we like. He was giving us a command,
a new commandment — one that already presumed adherence
to the great commandment, "You shall love the Lord your
God with all your heart, mind, and strength, and your neighbor as yourself" — and he backed this up with the example
of his own life. His love was unrestricted, extending to all,
even to those who hated him.

We might well think of dramatic situations in which the
challenge of this commandment is severely put to the test:
during the civil rights movement, for example, when Dr.
Martin Luther King Jr. repeatedly exhorted his marchers and
demonstrators to love their oppressors, and not to respond
violently to those who beat and abused them.

Such love seems almost unreasonable or impossible, yet we
can see that the moral integrity manifest in such behavior is
powerful and compelling. However, the breadth of this command also extends to the most seemingly banal and insignificant of events as well. This is why such love so changes and
transforms us: it affects the whole of life.

*The Seeker vividly recalled wrestling with this obligation to love both
during and after the visit of a particularly obnoxious guest, a monk
from Europe, who had spent several days at New Skete. After the
monk had left, the Seeker was helping clean the guest house with
Brother James, the guest master, when he asked casually, "So what
did you think of our recent guest?"*

Brother James pulled the cover sheet over the bed and replied, "Oh, let's just say that he wasn't my cup of tea," and tucked the sheet under the mattress. "Why do you ask?"

The Seeker was dusting. "I was just wondering because you had to spend so much time with him." The Seeker shook his head. "How do you do it? To tell you the truth, I can't recall when I've disliked a guest so much. He embodied everything in Orthodoxy that I loathe: narrow-mindedness, arrogance, and pharisaism. Just listening to him talk, with all his self-righteous priggishness, made me want to tell him off. But then when Father was talking in his sermon yesterday about love, all I could think of was my attitude toward this detestable monk, and how incongruous that was with real love!"

Brother James listened closely and then replied, "Incongruous? Aren't you really talking about your feelings? You know, you can't afford to confuse what you might be feeling with love. As I recall, you did a decent job of counteracting those feelings at table by being respectful, courteous, and helpful."

"Yeah, but it all felt so phony. Here I am, feeling as though I'd like to make mincemeat out of him, and all I can do is listen to the conversation politely, attend to his needs, and ask 'Would you like decaf or regular coffee?' when he was finished eating."

"But you were willing to do the right thing, weren't you? And you weren't being polite simply to deceive him," observed Brother James. "That's hardly being phony. You were doing what love was asking of you at that moment. That sort of willingness takes us into a different dimension from mere feelings. That's what love is really about."

Brother James motioned to the Seeker to check the refrigerator stock of fruit and water and then looked over the rest of the guest house quickly. Satisfied, he expanded his thought. "We feel what we feel whether we want to feel it or not, and no matter how much we'd like to feel something that we don't feel, we just don't feel it. But when we're given a command to do something, what we're commanded may

have little to do with what we feel, but it has everything to
our intent and will. It'd be ridiculous and unjust for God to co
something beyond our power to carry out. It seems that's why ʝⱼus
can speak about love as a new commandment: because it's precisely a
matter of our willingness to love as he loved. C'mon, do you really
imagine Jesus felt the same way about everyone? Yet I also believe
that he willed to do his best for their good independent of whatever he
felt. In the same way, it's within our capabilities to do this, and to ask
ourselves what love looks like in our own lives."

Up to this point, while we have repeatedly emphasized the
holistic character of spirituality — that spiritual life isn't a
category of life, but is life itself — we have focused primarily
on establishing a conscious inner life. We have seen that each
of us is drawn to the spiritual journey because of a hunger
that is part of our nature. If we look at ourselves honestly,
whether we are believer or unbeliever, Jew or Christian,
Buddhist, Hindu, or Moslem, we will recognize this desire
for spiritual wholeness, for integrity, by sheer virtue of our
humanness. In an effort to give the reader clearer insight into
how to respond to this inner attraction, we have looked at
different facets of the spiritual journey — repentance, discipleship, asceticism, sacred reading and meditation, prayerfulness,
and liturgy — all of which must be cultivated if we are to
grow in a balanced and integrated way.

The natural result of such growth, however, is not a clos-
ing in on ourselves, but a movement outward, toward others.
This is why we want to focus now more explicitly on the
outward manifestations of healthy spiritual living, and on the
essential link they have with the inner life.

The more we mature spiritually, the more we consciously
try to harmonize all of our actions with the transcendent
aspects of life. The inner disciplines put us in touch with the

absolute reality we call God. But what is more important than the name we give to it is the recognition that this reality is absolutely and ultimately benevolent toward us. This inspires us, in turn, to pursue an ever-expanding attitude of benevolence toward others.

Benevolence — from the Latin *benevolentia,* meaning *good will* — means a universal disposition of good will toward others, regardless of external circumstances. We will never achieve this automatically, or by virtue of the way we spontaneously feel toward others; it takes the repeated, conscious decision or act of our will to make this virtue a part of our life. It is very hard work, and a continuous struggle, yet it is the only real foundation of healthy and lasting relationships.

As they walked up the hill from the guest house, the Seeker remarked to Brother James, "I think I understand what you're saying, yet somehow I've always had difficulties picturing love as a willpower thing. I guess what bothers me is that it makes love sound so antiseptic, almost clinical and cold."

"I don't see why at all," responded Brother James. "Look, you know me well enough to know that I'd never minimize the fact that human beings are emotional, feeling beings. God forbid! But that's not the primary focus when we're speaking about love. What's confusing you is that love and feelings, while separate realities, usually go together. Granted, we don't have a thermometer to indicate how much feeling accompanies the exercise of our wills, but it's still true that some sort of human feeling usually colors our choices and decisions. And true love, a deliberate, thoughtful, and habitual willingness to act right, still carries with it all kinds of feelings. Usually, they're pleasant, invigorating, pleasurable, affirming, encouraging — in some way, life-enhancing. But they can also be just the opposite, as when we experience disappointment in love or are angry with a loved one, or when

we feel stung by a friend's careless remark. Still, usually we wouldn't say we no longer love the person, even though our feelings are hurt. True love is more than just feelings."

S O WHAT EXACTLY is this love? For all of the ink spilled on love throughout the centuries, we are surprisingly vague about it. The ancient Greeks had many different words for what we call love, each word touching on a different aspect of the reality. *Agápē* means the benevolent love of a person as a human being, *agápētos* is the beloved, *agapênor* is to love in a strong, virile way, *philía* is love as friendship and affection, *éros* is driving, passionate love, *ímeros* is the craving and obsession one has for someone who is present, *storgê* is the love one has for blood relatives, *philóstorgos* is tender love and affection, just to mention some. English is far less nuanced; the single word love is used for all of these and more, often in ways that are foreign to the essence of the reality.

Most Christians have heard Saint Paul's immortal passage on love:

> If I speak with the eloquence of men and of angels, but have no love, I become no more than blaring brass or clashing cymbal. If I have the gift of foretelling the future and hold in my mind not only all human knowledge, but the very secrets of God, and if I have that absolute faith which can move mountains, but have no love, I amount to nothing at all. . . .
>
> This love of which I speak is slow to lose patience — it looks for a way of being constructive. It is not possessive: it is neither anxious to impress nor does it cherish inflated ideas of its own importance. Love has good manners and does not pursue selfish advantage. It is not touchy. It does not keep

account of evil or gloat over the wickedness of other people. On the contrary, it shares the joy of those who live by the truth.

Love knows no limit to its endurance, no end to its trust, no fading of its hope; it can outlast anything. (1 Corinthians 13:1–7)

The problem is, this passage is so familiar (and, we should add, frequently reflected on so superficially), that it often ends up carrying all the power of a greeting card. "We've heard it all before: there's nothing new here!" We tend to think of love as a kind of theoretical ideal, an abstract concept, which perhaps sounds good, but meanwhile our smugness hides from us the actual, life-giving experience of practicing authentic love. Love is not a warm, fuzzy feeling toward the thought of humanity in general. It is easy to "love" the poor and homeless, the suffering, from the comfort of one's home, but how about the less spectacular, everyday love of the people we actually live with, that normally lacks such lofty feelings?

Brother Christopher made this point responding to a question Brother Gregory asked in novice class about how society tends to misuse the word "love." "Hasn't it ever struck you how casually we talk about love? We hear the word everywhere so much that we've come to use it carelessly — even to trivialize it. Who doesn't just *love* the latest rage in fashion . . . this stand-up comedian . . . this mystery . . . ? More and more, 'love' is *what we feel* about something, rather than our deliberate attitude and conduct toward others. Rampant emotional immaturity, blatant narcissism, and broken relationships in our society have resulted in a great deal of confusion about the true nature of love."

He leaned back in his chair and shrugged philosophically. "Do we think we know what love's all about simply because we say we love, because we've got some vague notion or strong feeling of love? Perhaps we think love is our feeling for those whom we like, respect, or need very much. All that does is reduce love to its dictionary definition: taking pleasure in someone or something, a matter of positive good feelings. That's not what the New Testament is talking about. Obviously such feelings are an important part of life, but they come and go, unbidden, like the wind. They certainly don't constitute an act of the will, and they may well end up controlling us."

Making a living, planning our next vacation, having fun with our pet, looking for a good buy on a new car — these and other concerns all merit our considerable attention. Our days are literally crammed with things to attend to, and many of them we might take genuine pleasure in doing; we "love" them. Indeed, who doesn't "love" getting a new car, or "love" playing with their dog?

First, we want to make it clear that here we use "love" solely with regard to other people. For this is the principal meaning of love — what the New Testament calls *agápê* — *the constant willing of good toward others,* to identify with one's neighbor so that we no longer treat him or her as an "object," but indeed as an other self.

Second, though we may indeed desire to know God as the one from whom we have come and to whom we shall return, the only way we can authentically and healthily show our love of God is through the infinite network of human relationships that make up our lives as flesh-and-blood creatures. Saint John the Evangelist puts it in clear and startling terms:

> No one has ever seen God. Yet as long as we love one another, God remains in us and his love is brought to perfection in us. . . . God is love, and those who remain in love remain in God, and God remains in them. . . . If someone

says, "I love God," and hates his brother, he is a liar. For any-
one who does not love the brother he can see cannot love
God whom he cannot see. (1 John 4:12, 16b, 20; translation New
Skete)

The message of Jesus and the New Testament is unam-
biguous: love must extend to all. There is no one we are per-
mitted not to love. The manner in which we love the various
"others" that make up our life — our spouse, our closest
friend, a casual business acquaintance, the person sitting next
to me on the bus — will vary according to the nature of each
relationship. More important, acting for the good of others
can and must transcend our romantic or sentimental feelings
and affection, what we ordinarily seem to think love is. Furthermore, this is within our power to accomplish, by virtue
of our free will.

This is the central struggle of an integrated spiritual practice: to will the highest good for each person we meet, without exception. Our attitude and actions must be based on
this decision and intent to do good for the other — for all
others — whatever we may happen to feel at the moment.
Well then, what does this love look like?

IF SOMEONE WERE to ask us, "How do you show your
love?" many of us might not be sure how to answer. We
lack the straightforward assurance of how to speak about the
love we have for others. We know, for example, that part of
religion is about being good to one another, yet why is it that
we often grow self-conscious in the very presence of the
word "love"? Are we embarrassed, or do we sense that we fall
short? Maybe we tell ourselves, "Oh, they know how I really

feel about them," while failing to demonstrate the truth of our love?

"What I want to know is, how are we supposed to communicate this understanding of love to others?" asked Sister Helen in novice class. "I'm thinking of a conversation I had not too long ago, in which a woman stunned me by saying, 'What do you know about love? After all, you're a nun.'" Sister Helen laughed at the recollection, then continued, "So many people today seem unable to take seriously a love that doesn't express itself erotically, and so they miss out on anything monastic life might be able to teach them. The irony (at least if I understand Father Laurence correctly) is that monastic life is supposed to be a school of love, which insists on the primacy of love over everything else in spiritual life."

"That's right, which is why I'm not sure there's any point in arguing about it," replied Brother Christopher. "Either people will see it in the way we live, in the very concrete way we are, or they won't. But the person who's thoughtful isn't going to write off the witness of love from a person like Staretz Silouan, the highly respected Orthodox monk, or Mother Teresa of Calcutta, for example, simply because they were celibates. They'll recognize in them a force that transcends any particular state in life, which expresses itself concretely, in all sorts of simple acts of love.

Brother Christopher hesitated. "Yet that said, I do think we monks and nuns would do well to think about how we actually do express our love, instead of simply presuming that it's understood. At times, I get the impression that we're awkward and embarrassed about this, and so take each other for granted. For example, because of the sexual taboos that have surrounded monasticism, I think many of us are too stiff and uptight with each other, afraid that our friendliness and good will are apt to be misunderstood. Our love needs to be chaste, but it should also be human as well."

Brother Gregory added, "I think another reason people might be skeptical when monks and nuns talk about love is that we stay in the monastery, and so don't go out into the world to serve in active ministry."

"No doubt that's so," agreed Brother Christopher, "but still, learning how to love is all that this life's about. It's just that we do it here, in this particular context. People today often don't see the relationship monastic life has with the overall health of the church, that monks and nuns serve the church and society in one way, while clergy and the laity serve in another. Each group needs the other, because no one individual or group can do everything. Each of us must make choices as to how we're going to love and serve, and then do that to the best of our ability. Regardless of our state in life, the issue is how authentically we love."

Brother Christopher continued, "But it will always show in our relationships. There's a principle to keep in mind that I remember coming across in Dorotheos of Gaza, a sixth-century abbot from Palestine. He told his monks to imagine a circle with a center point, noting that the center point would naturally be the same distance from any point on the circumference of the circle. 'The circle represents the world,' he said, 'and the center point, God.' Then he told them to imagine straight lines drawn from the edge of the circle to the center. 'These represent the lives of human beings.' Dorotheos then pointed out that to move toward the center, to God, the task of each of our lives, is equally to move closer to one another. 'The closer we come to God,' he said, 'the closer we become to one another, and the closer we are to one another, the closer we are to God.' Regardless of the context, the other is our path to God.

"I bring this up because often we're unconscious of people around us. We don't realize the implications of taking them seriously as independent human beings. We don't intend not to love, but can we really say we love without being consciously and truly present to the other?" The novices listened intently. "For example, when someone doesn't hold our interest at the moment, when we give him or her only scant attention or a quick brush-off, our relationship to that person is careless and mindless. When we allow ourselves to be preoccupied with other things, we fail to realize that we're being distracted from the person right in front of us, the one we are supposed to love, the immediate key to our enlightenment. Our mind is adrift, and so is our love."

Sometimes this syndrome even happens with those we are closest to, whom we would never wish to hurt. In not giving them the full attention of benevolent love, our lack of awareness allows hidden emotions to affect our behavior. How often does submerged anger, the fight I had with my boss this afternoon, for example, script my present behavior, controlling and manipulating me simply because of my careless mindlessness? If I am unconscious that I am held in the grip of anger and a bruised ego, I can easily find myself lashing out at my spouse without even being aware of where the anger is coming from. Instead of being in the present, intent on the tenor of our relationship with him or her, I end up "not myself," stuck in the past. After such a scene, "What does love look like?" becomes a mocking refrain. It certainly doesn't look like my disordered attitudes and behavior.

It is not easy to work constantly at being aware of ourselves. To leave the past, with its history of emotional turmoil, in the past, staying conscious of the actual interaction and circumstances we are engaged in right now, in the present, is hard work. Without such an alert consciousness, we will repeatedly drift into unconscious ways of acting, habitually making the same mistakes, and being chronically unhappy. When we correctly and wisely will to love, we progressively leave behind the sense of isolation brought about by exaggerated individualism and self-protection. Our intentional thoughts and acts of love create a further readiness to love within us, which in turn, enables us to form the habit of loving, to practice the art of loving. This fosters our own spiritual integration. It makes us better able to give our best in each situation of life, to change things for the better. This is the challenge of a fully human life, of an authentic and spiritual inner life, and the real meaning of happiness.

As our awareness expands and our relationships change for the better, we will find that we are moving toward our goal of knowing and experiencing the creative, universal, and unifying love of God. A monastic tale from our community is related to this idea of being awake:

> Once, a young man who had traveled throughout the world came to the monastery to speak with the abba. After his arrival, while they were at table, the abba asked the young man, "So tell me, what have you learned in your travels?"
>
> The young man looked intently at the abba, and after a short pause replied, "I've learned that the whole world is asleep!"
>
> At this, the abba burst out laughing and slapped his thigh. "You may stay as long as you like."

Before we can profitably envision what love looks like, how it shows itself, we have to be awake to all the particular contexts in which it can be expressed.

So what does real love look like? Obviously appeal to Christ as a living example of this love, recalling memorable encounters such as his defense of the woman caught in sin, his healing of the paralytic, and his forgiving his executioners. But we must also go much further. What does it look like today in my own life? All talk of love will remain coldly theoretical *to us* unless we actively work to make our love real in the furnace of daily living.

We cannot know that we have truly loved, or be sure that others know that we love them, without putting a face on love by our concrete behavior. We will not know what love looks like unless we grab hold of opportunities to demonstrate our love tangibly. We may think that we are putting love at the center of our spiritual lives. We might read, preach, discourse, or protest about how important it is. But invisible love is, when all is said and done, no love at all. If it is not, here and now, the cornerstone of our actions and attitudes, it will wither away.

By trying to visualize how love can embody itself every day with everyone we meet, and then repeatedly acting upon that, we will soon come to understand with our own insights what the love looks like that Saint Paul described to the Corinthians. We can expand and personalize Paul's insight by struggling to perceive and reflect on the new and infinite ways our love can show itself in our own lives.

Committing ourselves to work for love creatively in all of our relationships does not mean that we now have to look at the world through rose-colored glasses. Love is realistic, not sentimental. We naturally have our own likes and dislikes; we will not *feel* absolutely the same about everyone we meet, nor take to everyone equally; and finally, we will certainly have our share of legitimate disagreements with others. Because we are human, conflicts will arise. Because we are human, we will fail again and again. But true love always goes deeper. There are proper and positive ways of thinking and acting in every situation: we can learn how to love, how to will what is good for the other, in the midst of any scenario, no matter what our personal feelings might happen to be. As a saying has it, when we find ourselves in a boat with our worst enemy, will we drill a hole in his side of the boat? We can search for the truth of the matter at hand, for example, by being open and direct, responding with consideration and tact in a manner that shows respect without compromising our integrity.

How can this possibly be? Isn't it simply naïve to presume such a thing? Yes, it is, if we limit love to feelings. But once we realize that love is a deliberate act of our mind and will, of good will toward the other, then real love toward all is possible. The very act of resolving to love, no matter what our emotional state, is the crucible and school of love.

The Seeker vividly recalled a crucial period during his novitiate when Father Laurence was addressing the topic of love repeatedly — in community meetings, in his teaching and preaching, in various conferences he gave — trying to illuminate the many different ways love needs to express itself in our lives. For the Seeker, an insight began to come together for him in a memorable way toward the end of a Saturday evening community meeting. Father had been speaking about the inclusiveness of love.

"This is why love is a catholic reality, extending to everyone," Father Laurence stressed. *"'Catholic' is from the Greek* katá hólon, *which means 'whole,' 'entire,' 'meant for all.' Being catholic in outlook is the opposite of being defensive, uptight, or insecure. It is neither aggressive nor suspicious, but confident, generous, open, and sincere. It has room for everyone. This is certainly what love is all*

about. It's open to life, recognizing in it the opportunity to becc
truly happy in a way we could never imagine.

"Since true love seeks to become liberated from the sway of our feelings, a good place to begin observing it is from the perspective of each person we meet. What does our love look like to him or her? Think about that as you leave tonight."

The Seeker lay in his bed that night, reflecting seriously on Father Laurence's question, and it was some time before he drifted off to sleep. During the night he had a dream. He found himself at the edge of an enormous field, with a large hill in the center and people of all kinds and colors walking toward it. He heard a voice from the top of the hill talking, but from where he stood, he couldn't make out who it was or what he was saying. As he drew closer, he realized the voice was that of Father Laurence, though he looked much younger than the Seeker had ever seen him. In fact he didn't look like Father at all. He was dressed in a simple monastic tunic, and as he spoke, the Seeker realized the throng was listening intently, and Father's voice was composed and measured. He was talking about love.

"For example," Father said, "what does our love look like to the black, to the white, to the Chicano? What about to the gay, or the straight? Will the Protestant, Catholic, or Jewish person with whom we are dealing observe an honest benevolence in us? How expansive is our love when we're racist, sexist, or homophobic; when we despise someone because of his personality, preferences, or opinions; when we avoid him because of his idiosyncrasies or eccentricities? What does our love look like to the person whom we ignore as a nonperson, without at least an occasional nod or smile? . . ."

In his dream the Seeker saw the monk turn from side to side, calmly looking at the crowd. "What about those who don't love us, who have no real interest in us, who couldn't care less about our life? What does our love look like to them? How about the one who is jealous of us, who resents or despises us and tears us down? Would that person, if he looked, recognize anything like love in us? On the other hand, what does our love look like to the person who has a crush on us, but for whom we feel nothing special? In each of these situations, love can pierce through the mist and fog of feelings to show itself: using common sense, wisdom, and skill in willing the very best for each of these. Do you do this?

"This demands relentless alertness and self-discipline. So then, doesn't love look like self-control? It's able to handle the unexpected emotional turmoil that arises when life doesn't go our way. Instead of giving free reign to our emotions, we immediately exercise the great power of deliberate love, moving past our agitated emotions and feelings to size up the actual reality more clearly and objectively.

A large flock of birds flew over the gathering, bringing in their wake a soft wind. Father continued, "Love is peaceful. It is able to resist the temptation to tear others down with gossip, envy, and resentment. It is never threatened or defensive; it shows self-possession; it always delights in the goodness of another."

No one was asking any questions. The crowd was listening to every word, and it struck the Seeker as odd that there were people as far as he could see, yet they all seemed able to hear. Father didn't seem surprised by this at all, and felt no need to raise his voice, but continued in the same tone.

"There's nothing superhuman in this; it begins with our willing it from our hearts, then flowers when we conscientiously work at it. Because love is realistic, it focuses us on the need for change in our own life, instead of self-righteously pointing a finger at others, habitually judging them, labeling them, writing them off. Love admits and understands its own imperfections, that we're all together in this human condition, and thus it seeks to look compassionately on the faults of others. Such self-disciplined love lets go of past hurts — forgiving from the heart — instead of nursing grudges that give hatred an entrance into our lives. It's independent and liberated from what another does to me. Isn't it wonderful when we encounter a person *who appreciates us for who we are, instead of as a threat* ı

esteem? Love desires to do this for others."

Father's gaze was steady, though as the Seeker continued tơ him he began to disappear, as did the throng around him. Su؟ ؟nly the scene changed, and the Seeker found himself in a university auditorium, standing before a group of adults sitting in the seats, raising their hands and asking questions. The Seeker heard his voice begin to say, "Love? . . . love looks like generosity. It spends itself willingly (and wisely) for others, be it with time, attention, money, or simple concern." Where were the words coming from, he thought? But his voice kept speaking, and he relaxed. "Usually we associate generosity with people of substantial wealth, philanthropists whose fortune puts them in a better position to help others, but generosity is much more than donating large sums of money to the needy, no matter how noble and important such efforts are. Generosity has to do with giving — not only money to charity — but with the giving of ourselves, from the heart. That's the root of any work of generosity, whether it be volunteering at the local hospital or holding the door for someone, extending hospitality to a guest, or offering the gift of your full attention.

"A generous love is expansive. It is willing to be flexible and inclusive, not rigid. It gives freely for the sake of others, instead of always counting the cost and effort. Parental love is our primary experience of generosity: parents give of their very substance for the child, without making the child's gratitude a precondition. So love looks like a giver.

"Love looks like gratitude, too. It knows how to receive the love of others graciously, without embarrassment or discomfort, for it understands that we are always receiving. Love is not so presumptuous or proud as to suppose that it can do without the love of others; and so it appreciates even the smallest expression of concern from another. Love gives and receives freely, without expectation or demand. It recognizes that no price could ever be attached to it, that there can be no life without it. It shows appreciation."

The dream continued, and while the Seeker was aware as he slept that it was a dream, he was so fascinated by the fantastic nature of it that he wouldn't allow himself to awaken. Instead, he continued to listen to himself speak to the class in what now seemed to be the same measured tone he had heard Father use. "Love looks like friendliness. It gives to others the benefit of the doubt in favor of goodness, rather than suspiciously presuming hidden agendas. Though it is not naïve, it inspires others to a similar goodness by the example of its simple, straightforward lack of guile. Such friendliness is not a charade, sporting a lacquered smile meant only to hide its true intentions. It sincerely intends and evokes the good in others.

"A friendly person reflects a largesse of heart with enough room for those who are not part of his or her group, society, or religion. He or she seeks avenues of understanding that lead people together rather than ideologies that keep them separated. When we rise above purely partisan concerns, we embody openness and goodness that engenders healing and trust." And the Seeker woke up with a start.

During his early morning ritual of washing and getting coffee, the dream remained vividly in his mind, so after making his morning meditation, the Seeker recorded the dream in his journal and continued reflecting: "Love looks like being interested in those it meets, especially those with whom it is on intimate terms. It is fascinated with the beloved, wants to know all it can about the person, dedicates time to further the relationship, establishes an open context where mutual respect, insight, and creativity thrive.

"What passion we can bring to a subject that we are taken up with, the research involved, combing the library for every last word on the subject! The sense of wonder it evinces in us drives us to understand everything we can about it. What happens when we bring such passion into our human relationships (and here we are not speaking of sexual passion)? Is this not the basis of real friendship? Don't friends enjoy being in each other's company? Given the uniqueness of each relationship and personality, how much richer

life becomes when we show genuine interest in everyone we encounter, when we focus on them and listen!"

No human being is totally devoid of love, but our capacity to love is substantially greater than what we show others. Yes, it takes courage and persistence to expand the scope of our love. The ways in which it becomes manifest in our lives are infinite, if we allow ourselves to use creativity, spontaneity, and ingenuity. But love is not abstract: it must be concrete. Perhaps this will mean massaging your spouse's back or feet after a difficult day at work, or paying attention to a recap of his or her day. Maybe it will be giving a hand to a busy colleague at work or sending a thank-you note. Small things? Yes, but each has the look of love.

We've gotten to know the parcel post driver who makes regular deliveries to our monastery. Occasionally his wife will send him a card in care of us, to surprise him in the middle of the day with an expression of her love. It was not surprising to hear this man say, "I'm married to a wonderful woman; she's my very best friend!"

Love sees what is needed, what is missing, and seeks to respond. It is true contemplation and thoughtful perception of the other, whether God or our neighbor. This is why love is the supreme characteristic of the interior, contemplative life, and not just in a monastery. We cannot hope to act correctly — lovingly — without first facing what reality is asking of us right now. Love is the root of every virtue and good. Love has no limits. This is why love is not only the source of our humanity, it is the crown of the mystical life: in our striving to become conscious of the reality of all realities, love opens for us the ultimate, infinite reality that permeates everything, what we call God.

Whence New Skete?

> You brought us to this wilderness of joy.
> *Hymn for the synaxis of New Skete*

As we recounted in the first chapter, Father Laurence and those with him who were the first members of New Skete originally belonged to the Byzantine Rite Franciscans. This was a part of the Roman Catholic Order of Friars Minor and had been formed in the 1940s to work in the United States among Eastern Rite Catholics from eastern Europe. In addition they were to prepare themselves as missionaries for the moment when the Iron Curtain would finally fall.

During the ferment of the Second Vatican Council in the early 1960s, this group of Franciscans extensively discussed how best to implement the directives of the council in their own life and work. Of first importance to most of its members was the necessity of bringing their own practice as a community into harmony with the authentic principles of Eastern Christian tradition. This meant once and for all laying aside the specifically Latin Rite characteristics of the community, in its liturgy, theology, prayer, and rule of life, which it had inherited from the Franciscan order.

The higher authorities in the order refused to sanction the vision of the majority of the members of the Byzantine Franciscan community. At this point Father Laurence and those who went with him asked for and received official canonical permission to leave the Franciscan order for good, with a view to starting a new foundation. The purpose of this new monastic community would be to realize as much as possible the spirit and ideals of Eastern Christian monastic tradition in and for the contemporary American setting. So it was that in May 1966, New Skete was established.

Among the many difficulties involved in beginning this new community was the issue of canonical recognition by the church. By reason of similarity of rite, New Skete should have been recognized by one of the Eastern Rite Catholic bishops. Because of political problems, these were unwilling to do this, and so Rome placed us under the jurisdiction of the nearby Latin Rite bishop of Albany.

During the next ten years it became clear to us where we were actually finding the sources and inspiration of our way of life. Our research, discussion, teaching, reflection, and practice showed that our roots lie primarily in the spirit and traditions of the Eastern Orthodox Church, particularly as they were expressed in its first millennium of existence as well as in the best of its theology and practice today. The real rationale of our own religious life, in other words, had not so much to do with allegiance to Rome as it did with our desire to pursue the authentic life and spirit of the Christian East. It was not that we had come to see Rome as somehow wrong or the Orthodox Church as exclusively the true church. This was not our thinking on the matter at all. It was more a question of finding our rightful place in the universal Church, of participating in the living tradition and human community of the churches of the East that we had chosen to serve from the beginning.

Finally in 1979 New Skete was received into the Orthodox

Church in America, one of the many Orthodox jurisdictions in this country today. We believe now as then that we can best serve God and the whole of the church and Christianity by calling ourselves officially what we believe we are in our praying, thinking, and living: Orthodox Catholic monks.

Suddenly the judge will come and all our works will be uncovered.
Let us throw off sleep and laziness,
And with reverence let us sing the song the angels sing,
"Holy, Holy, Holy are you O God."
By the prayers of all the saints, have mercy on us.

Lenten hymn from matins in Tone Three

TWELVE

Good Work

ONE DAY A BISHOP was visiting our monastery. During his brief and cordial stay he attended church services and meals with us, was given a tour of the monastery, and was able to observe the work we do. After marveling at how quickly our community had been able to establish itself, and expressing his respect for our monastic life, he remarked, "It's just too bad you have to work with dogs. You really can't find something else more suitable?"

The bishop meant no offense by his remark; it seemed obvious to him that breeding German shepherd dogs could only interfere with the religious and church-related character of our life. He undoubtedly presumed it to be unspiritual work, perhaps necessary in order to live, but having no intrinsic worth or value in the monastic search for God. "After all, dogs only are animals," we could envision him saying. "But also, being involved with sexual matters and reproduction, with all the very earthy demands of breeding and raising dogs, seems entirely at odds with your more spiritual concerns."

Our purpose in recounting this story is not to extol dog breeding as a means of support. Historically, monks have engaged in other forms of labor that are far more idiosyncratic than this. Rather, we suspect that our friend the bishop would have been equally disturbed with us were we designing computer software, producing honey or wine, making custom wood furniture — anything he would consider nonreligious. He thought monks should be above all that, untainted by profane (*pro*, "outside," plus *fanum*, "the temple") work, which takes them away from what is holy. The only work he would think suitable for monks would be more traditional, pious forms of activity like painting icons or producing candles and liturgical vestments. Then monks and nuns would remain separated from crass and worldly concerns. As this thinking goes, pedestrian work is distracting and strictly counterproductive to the life of the spirit. No doubt the bishop, as well as other religious figures, also believes that if it were possible for us not to work at all, if we could give ourselves more exclusively to prayer, we would be more pleasing in God's eyes.

This story highlights a presumption and mentality all too common today, and not only among those of the cloth, that the responsibilities of work by their nature take us away from the search for God and from the values of a higher spiritual and religious condition. This is a fallacy.

Rarely do people today seem to appreciate the relationship that work, even in its most allegedly menial forms, has with spirituality and with healthy living. We are reminded of a businessman ordering our dog biscuits recently who quipped, "You could make a fortune with these if you didn't have monastic ideals to worry about." Like him, many think work and spirituality are two opposing sectors of life, and that to tie them together only results in hopeless confusion, to the detriment of both. "Spend time with your family on the weekend, go to church on Sunday morning if you have to," a typical CEO might counsel, "but Monday to Friday you belong to us." The implication of all this is that someone who sees it differently, who is unable or unwilling to sustain one code of ethics for the workplace and another at home, is in for big trouble.

It is not a mystery why so many people experience dissatisfaction in their work when we divide ourselves in this way. The fortunate minority who genuinely enjoy their work, who earn enough money to live comfortably, and whose job is also a source of deep personal growth is vastly exceeded by the great majority for whom work is alienating, whether they make loads of money or not. A recent guest, when asked what she did for a living, replied, "I work with social services," and her eyes glazed over. "I hate it. . . . Next question?"

It isn't simply that so many people seem alienated from their work — they truly loathe it. Work has become an inescapable drudgery, a soulless exercise, meaningless except for earning a living. In this climate it is easy to conclude that work is the regrettable inheritance of Adam's fall in paradise: *"Cursed is the ground because of you; in toil you shall eat of it all the days of your life."* One painfully misguided retreatant told us this when he announced his interest in becoming a monk: "Adam messed up in paradise, and we've been paying for it ever since. At least monastic life provides an out. One of the things that really attracts me about becoming a monk is not having to work so hard." Needless to say, he had to be set straight on many counts.

Those who use such logic to define work — that it is a punishment — will see no alternative to bravely toughing it out with resignation or cynicism. After all, we need that blessed paycheck. Is this also the real reason we throw so much money away on lottery tickets: hoping in one glorious moment of good fortune to escape the demands of work? If we endure our work as a necessary evil at best, if we spend a third of our adult lives at this, then how can we not expect our life to be alienated, fragmented, unhappy.

Many of us also see work and leisure as two unrelated

spheres of life. We work so that one day we won't have to work, but in the meantime, it can be pretty unbearable. What a dead end! It is possible, though, to transform our experience of work by transforming the way we think about it.

Misguided, cynical thinking hides from us the inherent dignity of work. It squelches the inspiration that can free us not only to view work more positively, but in fact to use it as a way to put into practice our own spiritual convictions. Work is not punishment. Whenever we exert ourselves, whenever we strive to accomplish something, whether for ourselves or others — whether we get paid for it or not — we are in the realm of work. Beyond providing for material necessities, it presents an opportunity to make our love and humanity more visible — spiritually speaking, to put our money where our mouth is. We can thus transform even the most menial task into an avenue of growth and self-transcendence.

Certainly none of us is bound to a specific type of work, as if in some slave state. We are free actively to pursue work that pays better and that best reflects our talents and real interests. But it's a further principle that is so crucial: In public and private, in our workplace and at home, whether we like what we're doing or not, work can be made into a holy activity, something satisfying and enhancing to the whole of our lives.

To fully grasp the intrinsic dignity of work, and that this is not just pie-in-the-sky romanticism, let's return to the retreatant with monastic aspirations. When he was complaining about his job, Brother Barnabas remarked, "You know, it seems to me you're missing the entire point of that story in Genesis."

"How do you mean?"

"Well, I don't think work was Adam's punishment. I mean, God isn't a sadist, is he? Yet that's what you're implying. We human beings were created in the image of God, to prolong God's work of creation by sharing in his creativity. Work has its own dignity from the start. Go back to Genesis and read it for yourself: God placed Adam in the garden of paradise to cultivate and care for it. Work is a sacred trust; certainly God didn't intend for Adam to be in paradise doing nothing. It's a privilege to work in and with the divine creation."

The young man still wasn't convinced. He still felt that work was the penalty for Adam's sin, and that we couldn't really expect it to be anything but unpleasant. "I mean, do you really think we'll be working in paradise?"

"Look at the story," replied the monk. "Adam's disobedience, his being expelled from paradise, meant that he no longer enjoyed the intimacy he used to have with God. Living in God's presence is what paradise is, a state of being, not some place free of work. The fall was, in fact, when he forgot this. What now made work a burden was his willful separation from God, not the fact of work."

Reflection shows us that work is necessarily a normal part of human life. But like everything else, it is to be done with understanding and integrity, with an awareness of God's presence. What does being truly alive mean if not this? If we are to recover for ourselves this natural and graceful sense of harmony and balance, we must find a way to connect our work with our spiritual life. When we begin thinking differently about our tasks, this step alone can make our work more bearable, more truly meaningful. To achieve this demands, first of all, that we do away with the division we make between sacred and profane, between the so-called natural and supernatural, between contemplation and action; that we come to some tiny appreciation for the total oneness of reality. Our work and play, church activities and leisure, study and rest, can all be used to manifest our higher goals and awareness. Then we will be on the road to creating inner stability and peace in every circumstance.

A friend who taught business management at several top undergraduate and graduate faculties, and who attended services at the monastery, often remarked that what he observed within our monastic community were the very same principles larger corporations needed for success. Once while participating in a retreat with us, he spent the morning helping out in our food shop during the Christmas mail order rush. The work and concentration were intense, yet the atmosphere was companionable and energized. The monks were working together efficiently and harmoniously, and he was able to fit in and help out easily. Later at lunch he observed, "From my vantage point as a professor, I see that the worlds of business and spirituality have a lot to say to each other. It simply takes a bit of openness to recognize similar concerns in both." He pointed out how easily it can be demonstrated that less-anxious workers whose positive view of their work is supported by deeper values will not only be happier, but consequently more alert, responsible, and productive — a benefit to both company and employee.

A corporation is hardly a monastery, yet many of the values do overlap, and shared insights can help shed new light in each context. Both require that people work together for a common good while striving for personal satisfaction and fulfillment. Certainly modern industry finds its roots in the ancient monastic establishments. Wouldn't it be ironic to see the business world rediscover the ancient connections between good work and human values, and with an enlightened understanding of both?

M ANY PEOPLE ARE surprised by the notion that monks could ever teach them anything about work. The father of a monk in our community, a successful contractor, was distressed when he learned that his son was intent on entering the monastery. Unlike many parents who feel upset over the prospect that they won't have grandchildren, or who want to see their own values confirmed by their children's success in the world, his concern was different. Being a prosperous, self-made man, he worried that since monks "didn't do anything of practical worth," such a life would only coddle what he feared was a streak of laziness in his son. "What value can such a life possibly have?" he pleaded with his son. "Don't you see that you're throwing your life away? Here you have the chance of inheriting the business, building a life for yourself, and what are you going to do? Sit on your ass all day and pray?" It wasn't until after several visits to the monastery, where he witnessed all the work being done (the monks did the building themselves), the spirit of hospitality, and the obvious camaraderie between the monks, that he gradually changed his mind. Toward the end of one of his visits he took our abbot aside and said, "Father Laurence, I have to apologize. I thought you monks would only be unrealistic philosophy majors. But seeing all the work you've done here, I'd have to say my visits have given me an entirely different perspective." In fact, he was so impressed that from time to time through the years he proved himself a helpful friend of ours as well as the father of his son.

Just as we saw in the story of the bishop, the picture most people have of a monk is of a cerebral individual totally given over to pietism and prayer, who couldn't be bothered with the practical demands of everyday living. Such a stereotype is utterly foreign to authentic monastic tradition, whether Christian or not, which has always been conscious of the integrated nature and balance of the whole of life.

A certain brother went to see Abba Sylvanus on the mountain of Sinai. When he got there, he saw the brothers working hard, so he said to the monks, "Why are you working for bread that perishes? (John 6.27) Was it not Mary who chose the better part, namely to sit at the feet of the Lord, and not to bother with the work?" (Luke 10.42) Abba Sylvanus said to his disciple, "Zachary, give the brother a book and show him to his cell."

When the ninth hour came, the monk reading in his cell began watching the door, expecting someone would be sent to call him to the meal. When no one came, he got up, went to find the abba, and said to him, "Have the brothers not eaten today, Abba?" The old man replied, "Oh, certainly, they just finished dinner." The brother then said, "Well, why didn't anyone call me?" The old man said to him, "But you're such a spiritual man, surely! You don't need food that perishes. We, being carnal, want to eat, which is why we work. But you have chosen the better part; you read the whole day long and can get along without food." When he heard these words the brother said, "Forgive me, Abba." The old man said to him, "Mary needs Martha. It is really thanks to Martha that Mary is praised."

Jesus may have chided Martha for being upset that her sister Mary was listening to Jesus teach instead of helping her with the chores of hospitality, but Jesus was in no sense disparaging work. He was correcting Martha's attitude of self-pity and complaint, as well as commending Mary's attentiveness. Similarly, Abba Sylvanus makes his point by creatively adapting the story to show the balance that must exist between Martha and Mary, symbols for the contemplative and active aspects within each of us. The true contemplative is the one who lives in balance, infusing his activity with a spirit of respectful thoughtfulness and attention. This is as true for the Wall Street executive or the clerk bagging groceries as it is for the monk. Not all of us can do the same work, but each of us can work in a spirit that transforms whatever work we happen to be doing.

BOTH THE BIBLE and monastic tradition recognize the inherent dignity of work. The Apostle Paul, who supported himself as a tent-maker, considered manual labor a moral and social virtue. He saw the value of honestly earning one's living, of not living off the sweat of someone else's brow, and of being in a position to help those in need. Similarly, the consensus of Christian monks over nearly two thousand years is that work is essential in the spiritual life of every human being. The early monastic rules of Saint Basil and of Saint Benedict put work on the very same plane as meditation. In fact, much of the growth and development of civilization in medieval Europe (both western and eastern) is the result of the quality of the monastic work ethic, as even the most antimonastic historians grudgingly concede. Our own rule at New Skete says,

> Throughout history, our predecessors in monastic life have taught us that work is not only required to sustain oneself and the community, but that it is equally important as a means of self-discipline and individual growth as an adjunct to prayer and worship. Work, therefore, is part and parcel of our life, first of all, because it is essential to monastic life.

After receiving a tour of the monastery recently, an ast
ished visitor asked our guest master Brother James, "With all
that you have to do, when do you have time to pray?"

Work *is* one of the ways we pray. Prayer is not just verbal.
Without some form of healthy physical work our prayer will
inevitably be impoverished. "We're by no means worka-
holics," replied Brother James to the woman, "and each of us
takes time for meditation, prayer, and study. But good work
expresses prayer, which is how abbeys were built, farms
tended, land managed, art and skills nurtured, and culture
passed on. Monasteries didn't just appear: monks built them,
by the sweat of their own labor. Their work was their prayer."

The fruit of this marriage of work and prayer is a serene
atmosphere that radiates beauty and peacefulness. Another
visitor in the same group observed, "You know, Brother, I'm
an architect, and I resonate with what you're saying very much.
I see the elegant landscaping, the buildings, and the thoughtful layout. For me, these make me aware of God without anyone having to say a word."

Here we should say that every thought, word, and action
of the monastic life is an expression of the awareness of the
presence of God and of our fellow community members, of
the intention to dedicate the day to the glory of God and
making a good response to whatever each moment presents.
This in itself is a definition of prayer. This means that the
morning rising, study, meditation, choral services, common
meals, manual labor, and other responsibilities such as meetings, classes, and visiting with guests — all become an extension of the social and personal dedication of the monks'
prayer. Each of these daily functions resonates with and reveals
that prayer. If they did not, the disharmony would immediately be apparent. If these did not flow from each individual's

life of prayer and if in turn that prayer was not fed by them, the monks would be forced to disband.

So the monk does not see work as an intrusion into his prayer, but as a support and balance. Work causes the monk to grapple with issues provoked by its demands; it also gives him the opportunity to overcome latent attitudes of selfishness, egocentricity, and self-pity (which we all have to some degree) that would otherwise not be visible. When we work, we see what we are made of — just as in prayer. When a novice takes his turn cleaning, it is not unusual for him to feel resentment. "Why do I have to do this?" he may think, or "Aren't there better things for me to be doing? And anyway, isn't this kind of demeaning?"

No doubt all of us have had similar feelings, yet if we stop and think, we can see what the novice doesn't yet understand. He still thinks there are different grades of work, that some work is better, more sophisticated, less degrading, than others. He can envision himself being the cook, perhaps, so his immature self rebels: "Where is God to be found in cleaning toilets? Is there anything that could be more ungodly?"

If he's open, he'll discover God waiting for him right there in those toilets he was assigned to clean. God is not some object to find, but a living presence. And when we are able to break out of our own restricted world, to view things in the light of God's presence, we find ourselves able to make peace with even the least pleasant tasks.

WE ARE THE FIRST to profit from applying the meaning and values of our inner realm to all our work. A monk who storms around the cloister muttering about how much he detests his work is just as negative as a steelworker moaning about how horrible his job is as he downs a late-afternoon beer at the local bar. The attitude in both is grossly deficient. How they react to the way they feel about their work is a symptom of very real immaturity. By refusing to deal with reality, they make happiness unattainable.

When we have the correct attitude, it shows in our work. We are not passive at all; we pay attention to everything. Holiness requires that we creatively harmonize with all the aspects of life. So Saint Benedict gives the astonishing admonition for his monks "to treat the utensils and tools of the monastery as if they were sacred vessels of the altar."

When people make a retreat for more than a couple of days, we often give them some work to do. Guests have found this helpful as a balance for the intensity of their monastic stay. Recently Father Laurence was saying goodbye to a guest and she said to him, "Thank you so much for allowing me to visit, and even more so for letting me work during my stay. I hope you don't feel offended if I say that the work that I did was one of the most valuable aspects of my visit."

What could be so special about raking leaves or linking sausage? She went on to explain, "I guess helping the brothers affected me so much because I wasn't expecting it to. Free of the pressures of my ordinary job, I was able to experience work in a different light and actually to enjoy raking leaves. I suppose it helped that the weather was so beautiful. But it was more than just enjoying the work. I found that I really paid attention to it. I wasn't being distracted with all sorts of thoughts and anxieties, as usually happens at my job. In fact, because of the negative feelings I have about my work in general, I rarely do these sorts of chores at home, and I now see that this is a mistake. I'm missing out on something. Although I didn't experience anything so dramatic as 'finding God' while I worked, I did experience a peacefulness that made me somehow aware of his presence. Simply having the chance to work while I was at the monastery taught me something important about *how* to work; it helped me to see work differently from the way I do at my job. I mean, what if I could work that way at the office?"

When we pay attention to our work, use our tools carefully, deal with our coworkers respectfully, remember who we are and our desire to grow, rather than just dilly-dallying and chafing at the bit, our attitude changes. We discover a new sense of appreciation and contentment that carries over to the rest of our life. This exemplifies the monastic principle that whatever we do, when we do it in a manner that glorifies God, it promotes a unity and strength in our everyday life.

The monk strives to be eminently realistic. His first thought is, "What needs to be done?" and he sees the will of God in that necessity. This attitude allows him to respond freely and appropriately to the demands of the moment whatever they may be. It is not a matter of self-esteem. Nor does it mean that he does not have personal preferences, or that he does not enjoy one type of work more than another. A mature outlook recognizes that certain realities demand our absolute attention, a positive response that can set aside personal feelings and eventually modify them.

The way we work can change our state of mind. If we clean house conscientiously, even lovingly, our spiritual intentions become evident and are reinforced, and anxieties and petty concerns are put in perspective. Try this and see. Don't fight the task; just carefully and calmly do good work, simply because the house needs to be clean. When your attention strays, focus again on the task at hand, for the quality of your work is also slipping. This exercise results in the satisfaction of having an orderly and clean house, and though you may be

tired, you might even feel psychologically refresh
very doing of this, you will experience how even t
life is worthy of respect. When you apply this to wha....
your life asks of you, your attitude toward everything is transformed.

S PECIFIC THINGS each of us can do, small things to begin
with, can make work less an exercise in drudgery and
more an exercise in personal creativity. The most obvious, no
matter what our state in life, is to strive for excellence, which
points us beyond what we have done so far. It transforms us
because it never lets us rest content with sloppy work; it
always goads us toward what is higher and better. When we
give our best, we can take legitimate pride in our work, and
we can also feel confident in seeing it as a service to others, to
enrich their lives.

Our work can dramatically affect the lives of others while
also reflecting on us, often without our being fully aware of
its scope. It's crucial to keep this in mind. We leave a part of
ourselves in our work. We can choose whether it will be a
good reflection or bad. The quality we bring to our work
continues to communicate long after the sweat has dried and
the effort is forgotten. It reflects us just as if we had placed the
final brush stroke on a canvas, or dotted the last "i" in a
manuscript. Does not the functioning of a new car reflect on
the factory workers that assembled it, on the engineer who
helped design it? If they had been careless, a malfunction
could be deadly. To recognize how our work affects the lives
of others is a powerful incentive always to give our best.

There is not much glamour operating a forklift, selling
furniture, answering calls for a phone bank, taking care of
income tax returns. These activities quickly become routine.

Even here at the monastery we have to work hard not to allow training dogs or any other part of our life to become monotonous and boring, much less slipshod. We've had to be both creative and conscientious in finding ways to renew our enthusiasm and interest. This in turn makes the work a more natural extension of ourselves. The effort we expended in trying to make our own work more interesting resulted in our writing two books on dogs and making a videotape series on their care.

Good work of any kind starts when we remind ourselves of the fundamentals of life. This is what the Seeker explained to a guest who was watching him socialize some of the puppies one morning. "When I practice the discipline of remembering the presence of God, I respond by the way I do my work — and it shows. However I might feel at any particular moment, I can make the task the focus of my religious and monastic dedication. If I'm really conscious of God's presence, would I be satisfied with simply getting by, doing mediocre work? Even if it's working with puppies! This isn't to say God's standing over me like some taskmaster; but I genuinely want to act out of my own best side. On the practical side of things, I also remind myself that the pups I'm working with now will be a reflection on our community, good or bad. If the puppies leave well socialized, with a positive head start in life, and if we do a conscientious job of explaining to the owners how to continue the pups' development at home, this will significantly improve the quality of life of these people. That's nothing to dismiss. It's a concrete way to serve others."

WHAT CAN WE DO about it when we are forced to do work that we dislike or do not want? What if you and your family are buried in bills? And you lost your job when

the company downsized, and are now flipping hamb?
a local diner? Are you destined to a meaningless life or ??
pity and alienation?

The answer is a resounding no! When we view work as a
vital part of our spiritual practice, what we do is less important than how we do it. If we cultivate the correct attitude,
everything can be transformed into a tool for growth and
integrity. With the right frame of mind, we can even attain
a certain satisfaction with work we enjoy the least. Even
though we always try to secure work that not only pays well
but also engages and challenges us, at times we may have to
settle for much less. Yet from a very practical point of view,
unless we wish to allow the work we hate to crush our psyche
and spirit, we're going to have to face the fact that we have to
find a positive way to view it, to make it work out for us.

Even in the monastery, the work is often menial and repe-
titious. At some time or another every monk will have to
wrestle with this: "All my education — for this?" he may
think. Brother James gives a conference for novices about his
own experience of dealing with distasteful work. Recently he
explained to them, "When I first came to New Skete, I used
to have to feed and clean up after the dogs in the boarding
kennel every other week. To me, that was hell on earth. The
barking dogs were hell, the unavoidable smell of the kennel
was hell, the old building, ditto. I dreaded the very thought of
it. My feelings grew worse the more I dwelled on them. My
whole life seemed to revolve around kennel work. Was I a
monk or a kennel boy?

"I began to see that if this was going to be part of my life,
then I had to find a way of living with this thing that I hated. I
had to come to terms with it in a positive, constructive way, or
it would destroy my chance of any genuine spiritual living."

He wisely decided to see this as life's challenge for him: he trusted in this way of life and was willing to work with what it presented him, like the alchemist seeking to transform lead into gold. The gold here is wholeness and integration. "Each day of each week that I was on kennels, as I walked to work I would remind myself, 'Okay, instead of focusing on how much I hate this, I've got to fortify myself with a mental review of all of the issues that I'm working on in myself: self-centeredness, anger, lack of generosity.' I considered how they affected the work staring me in the face, how the work provoked me. And so as I cleaned up and scrubbed the runs, fed the dogs, did the assigned chores, I was conscious of my own issues. And I asked myself, 'Where was I with these the last time I was on kennels? What did I see about myself then?' The effect of all this was dramatic. I was obsessing less over how much I hated the work, and instead it became the occasion for self-examination. When I grew impatient with the barking dogs, I reminded myself of the way I wanted to be — free. Thus kennel work became a tool for meditation. And you know what? In doing this I discovered it was no longer hell. It's easy enough to feel connected to God in paradise. It's in hell that we really have to work to be connected to him."

The guy with a master's from MIT grilling burgers has to deal with exactly the same issue. The present moment is the only one he can be sure of. While waiting (and planning) for circumstances to change, he has the opportunity of using the situation for his own growth. No doubt issues will arise that he did not have to face in his previous employment. Will he use them to discover aspects of himself that he is ignorant of? Instead of wallowing in negative thoughts about his job, he can see he is at least providing for hungry customers. He still can take pride in his work by being on time, by dressing with self-respect, by being cooperative and pleasant with his coworkers and customers, and by doing his job well. The opportunity and choice are his, just as they were for the monk working in the kennels.

R ECENTLY a middle-aged lawyer, exhausted from stress, made a retreat here trying to recover a sense of balance in his life. Clearly unhappy, he told us how frustrated he was at regularly having to act against his deepest convictions because his job depended on it. "I have five kids to put through college, a big mortgage to pay, all sorts of other bills. There's no way I can get out of this. I feel trapped, like I'm sinking in quicksand. Yet my partners continue to hand me messy divorce cases because I'm successful with them. But I hate these cases. They make me feel dirty, like I'm in league with the devil."

The lawyer had allowed himself over the years to be victimized by his job, with the inevitable result of a fragmented life. He failed to perceive that he was the one who let his work tyrannize him, that he was the one who failed to integrate his legal work and his spiritual practice. Whether or not our work is dehumanizing depends on how we approach it, and the vigilance we sustain throughout our careers. Even this man's problem could be seen as an occasion for growth if he dealt with it actively and thoughtfully.

"Isn't there another way of looking at your work, so that your public and private lives can come together?" asked Brother Christopher as they took a walk in the woods. "Maybe you can work in a new way that better reflects your own values."

"You just don't understand," the lawyer replied. "I've been forced into being unethical. I've fudged things for the sake of my clients, when I knew it was dead wrong."

The monk replied, "I don't think you're seeing it right. Does your profession *really* require you to be unethical — no matter who or what pressures you to be so? If you've happened to fall into this trap, no matter whose responsibility it is ultimately, some reflection might show you what you have to do about it *now*. If you honestly feel forced to quit, then do so. But it seems that such a drastic solution is not really necessary. The mind-set you bring to your work is the crucial factor here."

This man failed to perceive how his own attitude helped to bind him, to make his work alienating. He alone made the decision to use unethical means, and if he really considered the matter, ultimately this didn't serve either his client or himself. Shouldn't a lawyer serve the interests of his clients always within the parameters of the law, both civil and moral? Is it impossible to practice the law ethically? His integrity might mean that some clients would be uncomfortable with his representation, and he might not earn as much money, but he would not compromise the foundations of his own spiritual development, and his self-respect would be intact. Obviously this would require both the guilelessness of the dove and the cunning of the serpent (cf. Matthew 10:16).

Brother Christopher continued, "Every day contains new possibilities, and there are specific things you can do to regain, or even rebuild, a sense of integrity in your life."

"Such as?"

"For one thing, you can begin to practice a regular, daily period of reflection, considering the demands of not only your family and profession, but of your own humanity. You can't expect to discern the subtle intricacies of your job, the correct way to approach specific situations, without developing a consistent awareness, a broader consciousness of how and where your life is moving, especially in the eyes of God.

Do that at the beginning of your day, and you'll be much more effective in doing what is best in spite of the pressures that arise later on. Perhaps you'll also see the need for more regular spiritual guidance, to check your view of yourself against that of someone you respect and trust."

The monk motioned the lawyer to gaze to his right, where an overlook offered a splendid view of Vermont. They were silent for several moments, contemplating the mountains. Finally Brother Christopher said, "Don't misunderstand me. You have a challenge ahead of you that is going to require a lot of courage and perseverance; but if you work at it, you'll be the first to enjoy the fruits of your efforts, and your work will no longer torment you."

THE MONASTIC WAY shows us that work itself is neither degrading nor alienating, neither all-consuming nor something to be avoided. It is a natural and necessary part of human life. Most of us have to work to survive, but all of us have to work if we are to become whole. Some of us have more control than others over the kind of work we are employed at and the quality of the workplace. But the effect work has upon us is up to each of us alone. With the right attitude, even scrubbing floors can help us grow. The key is being conscious of who we are and where we are going.

Most Christians were raised with the pious admonition of doing the best they can for the love of God. But we should notice that we ought to do the best we can because that's how the thing ought to be done, whether for the love of God or not. It is foolish to think that someone who doesn't happen to believe in God (for whatever reason) is thereby excused from doing his best. How could that be right? Can we say that heart surgery may be done less conscientiously because the surgeon doesn't happen to be a believer? None of us will ever find peace, happiness, and fullness of life if we do not give our best in all our endeavors.

When we decide to work conscientiously, honestly, whole-heartedly — at whatever we might do — we will gradually find inner peace, because we no longer permit ourselves to be affected by outward circumstances and our own negativity. This process isn't easy, but it certainly is possible. That is the real meaning of good work.

For my sin is only too clear to me; my sin is ever before me.
Against you, you alone, have I sinned; what is evil in your
   eyes, this I have done . . .
Purify me: I shall be cleaner than spring water;
Wash me: I shall be whiter than snow . . .
O God, create in me a pure heart, in my belly, a new and
   constant spirit.

Psalm 51[50]:3, 4, 7, 10

THIRTEEN

A River of Mercy

ONE AUTUMN AFTERNOON, a young woman rang the front doorbell of the monastery, asking hesitantly if there was a priest she could speak with.

"I'm a priest," replied Brother Marc. "How can I help you?" The woman paused for several seconds, trying to compose herself, but she could not prevent the tears from streaming down her cheeks.

"Father, . . . I was raised Orthodox and, . . . God, I'm sorry," she said haltingly, fighting the tears back. "The last thing I wished was to . . ."

"Hey, there's no need to be concerned," Brother Marc replied calmly as he took her gently by the arm. "Here, come with me," and he escorted her to the conference room. After getting her a cup of tea, he sat with her silently for a few minutes, giving her time to collect herself. Finally she began, looking up at the ceiling because of her shame. "Father, I've had an abortion . . ." For the next half hour, between fitful moments of sobbing, the woman explained the story of how she had become pregnant, of how both her boyfriend and parents did not want her to have the baby, and how she had eventually come to the painful conclusion that her only real option was to have an abortion.

Brother Marc listened closely, asking only a few additional questions to clarify what she said.

The woman continued, "I didn't talk to our priest about it because I was afraid of how he would react. You see, our family has known him quite well over the years, and . . . well . . . I just couldn't tell him." She rolled her tearful eyes and sighed. "God what a mess!" She wiped her eyes with a handkerchief. "Before I had it done, I thought I was pretty much in control. I had no idea how it would affect me. But afterward . . . God, I've been so besieged by guilt. I keep trying to tell myself, 'It's okay, it's okay,' but it's not okay, and I don't know what to do."

"How does your boyfriend feel about this?"

"I don't really know," the woman admitted. She shrugged her shoulders. "We broke up shortly afterward and since then he's done his best to avoid me." She glanced sideways. "I get the impression he can't really deal with it."

Brother Marc was silent for a few moments. "What you've done is very serious, something you'll likely feel the effects of for years to come. Yet what is even more certain is the reality of God's mercy, his forgiveness if you ask it from him, if you're truly repentant."

The woman blurted out in tearful frustration, "Yet how can God forgive me when I can't even forgive myself?"

Brother Marc replied, "That's pride talking. Each one of us is sinful, in need of God's mercy and compassion — myself no less than you. You're not the greatest sinner ever to have walked the earth, and even if you were, the possibility of God's forgiveness would still be offered to you. That's because God is love — unconditional love. You say you can't forgive yourself, but that's simply another way of saying that you're better than everyone else."

"What do you mean?" asked the woman in an incredulous tone.

Brother Marc continued, "Because you're putting yourself above the rest of us. While others fall into sin, make mistakes, apparently you think yourself different, or at least that you should be different." The woman was silent. "It's true, you made a big mistake and that should never be minimized. But you need to move forward, and the first step is to seek forgiveness, both from God and yourself, and not to engage in a subtle and insidious form of pride. So long as you're repentant, so long as you intend in your heart to change, you can experience the healing that comes with God's forgiveness."

"But isn't that somewhat easy for you to say?" She sobbed. "I mean, you're a monk. How often do you really have to face this sort of offense? I killed my unborn child!"

Brother Marc replied, "You don't think monks and nuns know the pain of falling into serious sin? You think this talk of forgiveness is pie-in-the-sky romanticism?" He looked her straight in the eye. "Let me tell you a story about a monk named Abraham and his orphaned niece, Maria." The woman tried to dry her eyes and calm herself as the monk began his story. "It seems that this monk, Abraham, had a brother who had a young daughter named Maria. The brother died, leaving Maria an orphan with no one to take care of her. When told of the situation, Abraham had an additional room built for the girl at his hermitage, and so she stayed with her uncle. Now the years passed, and Abraham gradually taught Maria how to pray; in time she displayed a real love and dedication for monastic life. She spent twenty years with Abraham.

"Anyway, it happened that a certain monk would visit Abraham from time to time, and well, you can guess that he began to be very attracted to Maria. Without Abraham's knowledge, this monk would speak words designed to spark Maria's lust and desire, and one night, she succumbed to his temptations and she slept with him.

"Well, afterward, she was appalled by her action, hitting her forehead with her fist, weeping uncontrollably, and feeling as though she were as good as dead. In fact, she reacted very much like you. Convincing herself that she had irreparably angered God and dishonored her uncle, that her life, in fact, had come to nothing, she fled to a distant town where she changed her appearance and became a whore!

"Naturally, Abraham was devastated when he discovered Maria had fled, but it was revealed to him in a dream what had really happened. Still, it took two long years for Abraham to locate Maria. When he finally did, he immediately changed his monastic habit for secular dress and set out for the town."

The woman was now listening intently to the story. Brother Marc continued, "Well, Abraham found the brothel all right, and when he entered it, he posed as a client. Looking around, he noticed that Maria wasn't present, so he inquired of the owner about a particular girl he had heard about, whose beauty was as great as anything nature could create. 'You must mean Maria,' said the owner, and he went to fetch her.

"Now Abraham had disguised himself, so when Maria saw him, she didn't recognize him, but as they sat together drinking, she smelled the scent of the desert on him and grew nostalgic. Tears welled up in her eyes, but to avoid her recognizing him and making a scene, Abraham got up and gave the owner a sack of money, saying, 'Fix us a very good meal, for I want to have this girl tonight!'

"After the meal, Maria took the old man to her chamber, where Abraham sat on the bed. The girl began to unfasten his trousers, but Abraham said, 'Make sure the door is locked, first.' When she came back to the bed, the old man made as if to kiss her, but as she drew close to him, he whispered, 'Maria, don't you know me? I am the one who raised you, who took care of you. Who so greatly hurt you that you had to run away? Why, after you had sinned, didn't you tell me? I would willingly have done penance for you to keep you from so wretched a fate. Maria, I've come to take you back home.'

"Naturally, Maria was totally stunned at Abraham's disclosure, and she wept openly as she explained why she hadn't been able to come to him. She was too ashamed. How could she pray to God again after being defiled with such a filthy sin as hers? She was fit only to be a whore. Then the old man said to her, 'On me be your sin, Maria, and let God put it on my account! But only come back with me. Please, I beg you, don't ever doubt the mercy of God.' Then he said something each of us must take to heart. He told her that sin is only part of being human, but so is our ability to change and mend our ways. We must never despair, for God's mercy and compassion are endless. Maria believed him. As things turned out, she returned with her uncle and resumed her former way of life, having come to taste the forgiveness of God and the wisdom that sets us free. And there isn't a person alive who's not in the same situation."

When the monk finished the story, tears were still running down the woman's face, but now they were of a different sort. She thought silently for a time, then finally nodded her head and said to Brother Marc softly, "Thank you, Father," after which she asked, "Before I go, would it be possible for you to hear my confession?"

B EING FORGIVEN is an extremely powerful experience, we might say an essential human experience, which empowers us to become better human beings, more compassionate and understanding of both ourselves and others. As we have seen, when it occurs at the beginning of our spiritual journey, its effects are liberating, and we experience an inner revolution. The wiping clean of all our past misdeeds — the guilt that we feel in our hearts — allows us to breathe the fresh air of new possibilities. God's forgiveness gives us the chance to make our lives better, without laboring under the guilt of past misdeeds; the energy it engenders is remarkable.

Yet forgiveness is an equally important issue throughout our spiritual journey as well. While many presume that our need for forgiveness wanes the further we progress spiritually, actually this is not so. Mercy is something we always need. It is not that we look to commit more sins — hopefully, that is never the case, despite the fact that serious mistakes may indeed occur in the lives of each of us. It may also be that the more refined our understanding becomes, the more clearly we see other things in our past that merit forgiveness. As we grow spiritually we become more conscious of those occasions when we have chosen, or do choose, to act in a way that displeases God. This has a further effect: recognizing our need for God's mercy will also keep us mindful of our need to be merciful to others as well. This invites us to become more responsible than we were at an earlier, less conscious age.

The result of this process of maturation is a deepening awareness that in life we are always pilgrims. What characterizes this pilgrimage is that while we often take two steps forward, we also easily take one step backward. We never fully arrive at our destiny this side of death. As we journey further and further, we become increasingly aware of our need for God's continuing forgiveness. Should we doubt this, the legacy of numerous monks, nuns, priests, pastors, and rabbis, and their persistently deep and dedicated interest in God and spirituality should tell us something. Their lives clearly manifest their continuous dependence on the mercy and compassion of God to support them. Any honest consideration of our lives prevents us from believing the illusion that religious faith transforms us magically into perfect human beings. In fact, the struggle is harder in the light of religious faith, precisely because now we should be more conscious of how we think and act.

Discovering the disconcerting truth that we are still very imperfect and fallible, that at times we act less than perfectly, perhaps even reprehensibly, confronts us with a daunting challenge: "Can God, or my spouse, my friend, my child, possibly forgive me for my folly? What happens when my worst secret sees the light of day?" Sexual indiscretions, violent acts, hypocrisy, mean-spiritedness — what happens when such failures occur? Despair?

We are never without hope. Nevertheless, like tired soldiers having seen too much of their own reality, the excuses we make for our shameful behavior do often sound hollow and pathetic. "We should have known better . . ." only makes us all the more depressed, weighed down under the knowledge that the spiritual ideals that originally animated us now seem to mock us for our hypocrisy. In such circumstances, we can easily entertain thoughts of "What's the use?" which, left unchecked, only increase our sense of alienation. This is a long way from the complete renewal of conversion. Now, instead of being freshly reborn, we seem like weathered pieces of art requiring major renovation.

Without denigrating the intensity of this experience, we need to perceive what is really going on. It is never the case that we are totally lacking in inner beauty, but the original beauty can be obscured by the distortions we have brought into our lives, not unlike the centuries of dirt and soot clinging to Michelangelo's frescoes on the ceiling of the Chapel until they were cleaned.

F ORGIVENESS IS exactly what it sounds like: to give up the repayment (real or imaginary) due because of an offense. By extension it means to be freed from the guilt of the misdeed. Through the act of forgiveness, the rupture in the relationship created by the offense between us and God, or between one person and another, is healed. The debt brought on by the offense is canceled. The linguistic background of forgiveness comes to us from the Greek *apheínai,* "to send away," and from the Latin *absolvere,* "to cut loose." The same idea is present in Church Slavonic, *razrešati,* "to cut through" (in the sense of freeing: the sinner is no longer imprisoned by the guilt). When we say that God no longer calls the sin to mind, we are saying, effectively, that he has exiled it: he does not hold it against us. *"Far as east is from west, such is the distance he has removed our sins from us"* (Psalm 102[101]:12). Further, even more radically, it is not that God forgives us when we entreat him for this: he has already forgiven us. He exists in a mode of being that is eternally forgiving.

If this sounds too good to be true, it is only because our inclination as human beings is to do the precise opposite: to hold on to the faults of those who have sorely offended us. Our reluctance to forgive makes us distrust the reality of God's forgiveness. We think that, like an elephant, God never forgets. Now as a matter of fact, God — being God — forgets nothing; but he does not hold the offense against us.

An early monastic tale sheds light on the "reasonableness" of forgiveness, which when understood, makes believing in forgiveness possible. An abba was asked by a certain soldier if

God would forgive his many sins. The abba did not answer him directly, but instead asked: "Tell me my friend, if your cloak was torn, would you throw it away?" The soldier replied, "No, I'd mend it and put it back on." The elder said to him: "If you take care of your cloak, how much more will God take care of his own image by forgiving you?"

This is as true for the young woman mourning her recent abortion as it is for the soldier who had participated in the unspeakable horrors of war, as true for the fallen monk as it is for the person enmeshed in the self-destructive behavior associated with substance abuse. No matter who we are or what we have done, by virtue of our common humanity each of us has not only the ongoing need for forgiveness, but the possibility of receiving it.

THROUGHOUT THIS BOOK we have emphasized the essential role that change, *metánoia*, has in any healthy life. We have seen that *metánoia* is a law of the spirit that plays out throughout the whole of one's life: each of us will change whether we want to or not; the fact that we are religious or not has no bearing on this. Change is a fundamental reality of living: either our life moves forward or it degenerates, but it never stays the same. It is up to each of us to direct the process of change deliberately for the good of ourselves, as well as everyone else. This means learning the power of forgiveness in both its forms: forgiving others, as well as receiving forgiveness from God and our neighbor.

For many, this invites serious misgivings. What happens when people experience this reality of forgiveness time and again, when they seem to abuse it? In a community gathering one Saturday evening at the beginning of Lent, the liturgical season in the Christian year dedicated in a special way to repentance and forgiveness, Sister Helen asked Father Laurence, "Isn't a potential problem with such an understanding of forgiveness the fact that a lot of people will simply end up taking advantage of it, living only for themselves, since they know that ultimately they'll be forgiven? I mean, don't we need the threat of eternal punishment to keep people honest?"

Father conceded, "No doubt there are those whose lack of any true understanding and appreciation of the reality we call God might make them think that somehow they can outsmart God, that they can do what's wrong with impunity. Needless to say, this is sheer madness. Such a person may well reject the thought of retribution in the next world, but we'd do well to notice that heaven and hell begin in this world, not the next. The personal agony and anguish, the guilt, the obsession that many a human being suffers, are often the direct result of living in a way that violates the nature of reality. We're worried about hell in the afterlife without realizing that it begins here. Thus, regardless of what we might think, reality will make us pay for our misdeeds, and we won't get off without paying the last cent."

Father looked around the room and continued, "But see, I don't think that this is what normally happens. I think that more often there's a misunderstanding on the other side, that God's forgiveness depends upon what *we* do. We've got loads of Christians who think like this and it leads to a conception of God that is seriously defective."

Sister Sarah raised her hand. "I'm not sure exactly what you mean."

"No? Just take a look at the way people go through Lent every year. Christians realize that Lent's the forty-day period prior to the Church's celebration of Easter. They know *that*. But are they aware of the real purpose of Lent?" Father shook his head. "I have my doubts. See, the purpose of Lent is to remind us of the ongoing need for us to change in a conscious and deliberate way. That was the sense behind monastic tradition declaring that a monk's life was to be perpetually Lenten in character: continuously oriented to positive, life-enhancing change.

"But if you look around, we seem a long way from that sort of understanding. A lot of Christians give me the impression that they think of Lent more as a limited time of fasting and asceticism that earns God's forgiveness, simply because it earns their satisfaction! It's almost as if one says, 'For forty days I'll work like mad on myself, making myself miserable by denying myself, following all the rules, so that at Easter I can stand before God with a clear conscience.' Then they go right back to living the same way they always have. There's no real lasting interior change. Such a mind-set colossally misses the point. Lent is not about earning God's forgiveness by doing this or that. It's about changing ourselves for the better because we realize just how compassionate and merciful God really is, and how much we need that compassion and mercy. Besides, God's forgiveness is absolute. He gives it freely, unconditionally. Before the idea to ask forgiveness even enters our minds, we're already forgiven. Forgiveness is a state of being we live in, not something we earn."

"Are you saying that what the church stresses during Lent — the penitential practices — actually can get in the way of the real meaning of the season?" asked Sister Anne.

"Absolutely." Father's expression grew more animated. "When we focus on such dubious practices as extreme fasting, sleepless vigils, and interminable church services, we use those as a smoke screen, congratulating ourselves on how dedicated we are, instead of really changing from the inner self, where I am who I am. We think we earn God's forgiveness, never grasping the deeper truth that his forgiveness can never be earned. It's entirely unconditional, proceeding from a love that's quite simply beyond our power to comprehend. That's the insight that should make us want to change, and to make lasting changes.

"Think about this for a minute. It's traditional for us Orthodox to call the vespers service that opens Lent 'forgiveness vespers.' At the end of this particular service, at least in the Russian tradition, every member of the congregation goes around and asks the others present for forgiveness. Wherever this ritual is done, it's supposed to symbolize the willingness to forgive not only those present, but every other person, without exception. We don't do this here, not because we don't strive for the same goal, but simply because it's not our custom. But whether one engages in the ritual or not, it's got to be more than an exercise in emotional satisfaction for having asked for and received forgiveness. There has to be lasting change, and that's what is too often missing. The ritual is being milked for all its emotional worth without precipitating a real change of heart and mind for those who engage in it. Without sincere change, there's a real danger of hypocrisy, or at any rate of totally missing the point.

"Now I'm sure the casual onlooker might be moved by the apparent sincerity of this ritual, one that seems to take forgiveness so seriously, which is all well and good. But I wonder, even after centuries upon centuries of such gestures, how deep they really go. What does it mean when year after year people manifest the same rigidity they've always had, the same self-centeredness in their behavior, the same failure to change? If we really do forgive one another, why is it that we allow the same misguided acts and attitudes to cling to our lives — like lint on a suit coat? Why is it that we continue to manifest the same disdain for those we dislike as always?"

Father peered at the community gravely. "A question each of us should ask ourselves during Lent is how different are we from the previous year. As an example, to what extent have we really forgiven, have we really let go of one another's offenses? Do we manifest an honest willingness to forgive others serious things, not just peccadillos? Were I someone's worst enemy, or if someone were present at the service who had really offended me, would I make the gesture to them, and if so, what would this expression mean? Would it mean that I'm ready to forgive that person . . . really?"

Father Laurence continued, "My experience is that while the intention concerning these rituals at forgiveness vespers may be good, the understanding of their real dynamic leaves a lot to be desired. In the trench warfare of daily life, most of us show only limited understanding of the proper role that our emotions play in forgiveness. Think about it. We find it impossible to forget hurtful offenses, concrete events that fester and rot in our souls. They enslave us. Because we still feel their effects, we presume that it's simply impossible for us to forgive. We haven't learned to distinguish between the remembrance of the offense along with the feelings we have about it . . . and the *intent* we have to forgive it. These are two different realities. Thus, the real outcome the service intends to foster is frustrated."

Brother Luke raised his hand. "But what does it mean when we intend to forgive someone, yet we still find ourselves feeling angry with him, or hurt? Does that mean we're just kidding ourselves?"

Father shook his head immediately. "Not at all. You see, we live under the mistaken impression that forgiveness depends upon how we feel about a person. Now there is a certain connection here, but it's very subtle. If I will to forgive the other, part of that package is my intent to try to work on

my feelings. The authenticity of my forgiveness lacks
thing if I allow myself the luxury of wallowing in my
tive feelings without trying to do something about them.

"On the other hand, just because we don't feel immediately approving of another, or we don't immediately like him,
doesn't mean that we can't forgive that person. That's simply
not true. But such a mentality is common and underscores
the fundamental confusion many people have about forgiveness. How many times have I heard the categorical declara-
tion, 'Father, I just can't forgive so and so . . .'?

"That's baloney! What the individual is really saying is
'I don't want to forgive him, because what he did is too horrible. If I forgive him, then I let him get away with it.' Meanwhile, the resentment and hatred the person carries around
with him eats him alive. Forgiveness doesn't necessarily mean
that the person who committed evil is going to get off scot
free. That's a valid issue for consideration, but it's not the same
thing as being unable to forgive."

Father looked at the entire community. "Forgiveness is
entirely a conscious act of the will, not a feeling. But it also
carries with it the resolve to work on changing our feelings.
So we can forgive in spite of feeling the terrible effects of
injustice, contempt, and hatred. When we forgive, we consciously choose to hold nothing against the other, even while
acknowledging that the other may have done something truly
reprehensible. We let go of any claim to revenge or the holding of grudges."

To forgive may be divine, but it is also a distinctively
human phenomenon. One of the principal effects of forgiveness is an increase in the humanness of the forgiver as
well as of the one being forgiven. The perennial popularity of

Jesus over and above institutional religion is the peacefulness and serenity of his life, the way he treated others, the magnanimity of his heart, and his ability to say, "Your sins are forgiven" — not "I forgive you," but "Your sins are already forgiven" — restoring the individual to serenity of mind and peacefulness of soul. As much as anything else, this is what Jesus embodied.

Brother David raised his hand and asked if he could pursue a related issue. "I'm still not entirely clear on the psychology of forgiving. Why do we find it so hard to forgive, to let go, particularly since each of us realizes that we have been forgiven too?"

"This whole subject of forgiveness is extremely complicated," explained Father, "for when we try to exercise forgiveness, there are all kinds of psychological realities mixed together with the divine invitation to forgive. But to go on to your question, besides not understanding what forgiveness really is, I think many of us also see forgiving as the act of a weak person, one who lets the offender get away with murder, especially when the offense was against someone we love. To forgive what another has done against us is one thing. But to forgive someone who did something unspeakable to a loved one — a rapist, for example — that seems like an act of betrayal to the loved one. This isn't the image of ourselves we want to entertain. We want to see justice done.

"But forgiveness gets beyond this sort of thinking, recognizing that while a criminal should be brought to justice and pay for his offense, we still must be willing to forgive. We must be willing to let go of the offense, despite the fact that we may feel anger, contempt, and hatred. While these may be natural reactions to the pain and hurt we've experienced, we can't afford to cling to these destructive feelings. We can't allow them to fester inside us forever. We've got to work to get beyond them. Over and above these understandable feelings, each of us has the ability to forgive, to be willing to let go of the whole experience, to treat the other — the offender — as we would want to be treated ourselves. Far from an indication of weakness, forgiving is the act, or better, the frame of mind of a brave and courageous person, of a person whose strength, character, and integrity the world isn't ready to appreciate. Certainly this is the way that God has treated us — or better — the way God always treats us.

"Naturally, for us this isn't easy. We're still smarting from whatever the offense happens to be, dealing with the thoughts that race through our minds on the heels of the experience. But the truth is that each of us is in need of being in a relationship of forgiveness with God, and this can only occur as we stand in a relationship of forgiveness with others. Nothing is ever beyond the scope of forgiveness. Nothing. Obviously we know what inner turmoil is about, what resentment is. Nevertheless, we have to get hold of ourselves; we have to face up to these emotions, these feelings, these angry thoughts lest they destroy us. We have to calm ourselves inwardly and outwardly and come to the realization that there will be no peace in the world unless there is peace in our hearts and that forgiveness is one of the greatest creators of peace in the world. Remember what Jesus said when Peter asked him, 'If my brother goes on wronging me, how often should I forgive him? Would seven times be enough?' 'No,' replied Jesus, 'not seven times, but seventy times seven times!' which is Jesus' way of saying that we must *always* forgive."

TODAY WE LIVE in an increasingly secularized society, in which the concepts of sin and separation from God have less and less meaning to more and more people. For this reason, the notion of sin (and the related phenomenon of forgiveness) gets little attention. This is not because sin is any less present than it ever was, it is simply labeled differently: compulsion, dysfunctionality, and other neologisms. In a way, we fancy ourselves too sophisticated for sin, so we live in denial of its reality. Admittedly, past thinking about sin has included a lot of nonsense, but we wonder whether denying its existence simply by giving it a different name is not equally nonsensical. We shall leave this for psychologists and theologians to argue about.

Nevertheless, what is worth noticing is that whether we are believer or unbeliever, whether we believe in "sin" or not, if we are basically healthy, we cannot but feel the effects of wrong behavior. We still wrestle with guilt, if even by trying to blot it out with the help of mind-altering substances, or simple denial. But there is such a reality as guilt. This brings us to an important question: how are we healed of our guilt? How do we come to know forgiveness as a personal fact? Precisely because of the psychological issues involved in forgiveness, knowing forgiveness requires the presence of the other, the forgiveness of one who says, "Go in peace, your sins are blotted out." We cannot simply forgive our own sins and expect to be healed. Trying to do this will only make forgiveness feel all the more empty and unconvincing.

I JUST DON'T SEE why we have to go to confession," a middle-aged retreatant recently complained. "If God forgives us unconditionally, then why do we have to bother confessing to another?"

Brother James responded, "The paramount importance of the sacrament of penance, wherein we confess our sins to a priest and receive absolution, has nothing to do with the juridical fact of forgiveness. It's the attitude in the heart that is important. Is the person truly repentant, truly sorry for his or her sins? Do they intend to do their best to change their lives? As with all the sacraments, confession is both the opportunity for, and external sign of, our repentance — as well as God's forgiveness. Remember, we are flesh and blood beings: we need these sorts of tangible signs."

The monk went on, "God has forgiven us absolutely, and this isn't dependent upon confessing our sins to a priest. As a matter of fact, we don't confess to the priest at all; we confess to God, and the priest represents God. On the other hand, most Protestants don't engage in auricular sacramental confession, yet I certainly don't believe that their sins aren't forgiven. Hardly. But psychologically, confession is indispensable."

"Why is that?" asked the retreatant.

"Because sin tears at our conscience," replied Brother James, "that is, at the very fiber of who we are. It leaves wounds that are serious and long-standing, and with many implications. To find freedom from the burden of our faults, from our denial of them, having the compassionate reassurance of another person is invaluable. The priest is not there to humiliate us. Just the opposite — hearing the priest pardon and absolve us in the name of Christ supports our belief in the reality of God's compassionate mercy. Confessing destroys the sense of isolation, the alienation that sin has created." Brother James gestured with his hands. "Confession is a kind of spiritual surgery; it cuts to the very source of our faults, pulling out the sin by the roots."

The Seeker was reading over a letter he had just finished writing to Jack, his friend from college. Since Jack's visit for the Seeker's profession, he had returned periodically to the monastery, and his own spiritual practice had grown more serious. In a recent letter, Jack had asked the Seeker what he thought the most important aspect of monastic life was, and what relationship that has with those outside the monastery. The Seeker ended up thinking a lot about that question, and in his reply he explained, "After thinking about your question, I have to say I was surprised by the answer I came to. It's not what I would have first anticipated.

"Obviously, the first thing in a monk or nun's life is the liturgy, the opus Dei, or "work of God," as the Latin tradition calls it. This doesn't mean that we always like to worship. It simply means that we recognize that this is what we owe to God as his creatures.

"In a similar way, private prayer for a monk or nun is also central to what our life is about. Solitude and contemplation help us to fill out our relationship to God as members of this particular believing community. This is what defines us as monks and nuns.

"Then there's our work. Though our lives are not consumed by work, we have to sustain ourselves, especially in these days of particular financial stress. What else is there for us to do but work?

"Then, receiving guests and retreatants, for example, allows us to receive Christ, and has always been a central monastic responsibility. Receiving guests also permits us to share the fruits of our whole life with others.

"Yet when all is said and done, it is living faithfully in community — which embraces and requires all of the above virtues without separating any one of them from the whole — that most truly characterizes monasticism.

"But it's crucial to remember, Jack, that it would be utterly impossible to do any of this without the qualities of compassion and mercy whereby we forgive one another. Forgiving others the hurts they inflict on us, just as we depend on those same others to forgive us the wrongs we visit on them, is absolutely necessary for successful community living. That's the only way we can live peacefully.

"*When you live as closely as we do with one another, situations are bound to arise in which someone is hurt or offended. Unless we can be humble enough to speak to each other about these occasions, to communicate honestly because we trust each other — and then be willing to forgive whenever necessary, the bonds that keep us together will become strained and our love for one another will grow cold.*

"*Living in the monastic community, we discover that none of us reaches a state of perfection in which we never hurt or offend another brother or sister. Obviously there are times when this occurs unintentionally, but unfortunately at other times, our demons drive us into behaving less nobly. There will always be situations in which we get irritated, or in which we've been hurtful. That's simply part of being human. What's more important than that these things occur is that we are ready always to apply the salve of forgiveness when they do, that the healing and mercy characteristic of God may bring about in us a bit more of the kingdom.*

"*As far as what this has to do with the world outside the monastery, I suspect that the world too often forgets about this type of forgiveness. When I've had to go out on community business, I've noticed a few bumper stickers that say, 'Want Peace? Work for Justice.' But I've never heard of forgiveness — forgiving your neighbor — being used on a bumper sticker. How are we going to build a truly just society without real forgiveness? We are all too ready self-righteously to sacrifice our brothers and sisters on the altar of justice without considering what is included in such justice. Isn't there something in scripture that reads, 'What I want is mercy, not sacrifice . . .'?*"

More About New Skete

You bestowed on us all a legacy.
Hymn to Saint Basil the Great

For many people the most obvious feature of New Skete is that it is controversial. Those who know us can also see clearly our passionate desire to live the monastic life and to worship as Orthodox Christians authentically and intensely.

Our entire history has been characterized, in the midst of the struggle to keep body and soul together and to make a living, by our efforts to translate the essentials of tradition into ways of living that are enlightening, liberating, and transforming for us today. This has entailed pursuing the knowledge needed to wisely and intelligently foster a spirit of healthy simplicity and understanding in our community.

Monastic life does not mean simplistically following the platitudes ("Keep the rule and the rule will keep you") and bizarre exaggerations found in the past (e.g., in asceticism, dress, and personal hygiene), nor the nominalism of role-playing with its arbitrary externals (being tonsured without sufficient training or without an actual community to live in). These frustrate any authentic inner life. True monasticism has never made an idol out of observances and individual practices. It has rather emphasized right living, healthy change and renewal, and the goals of evangelical love.

This is perhaps the most alarming aspect of our approach for those who see us as controversial. Namely, we categorically refuse to be museum keepers, replicating and reliving the customs, formulas, and manner, whether real or imagined, of another century or of another ethnic culture.

The question is, how are we called to live here and now, in this time and place? No matter how golden another age may have been for the church or for monastic life, we are now still responsible for adapting for our own generations the teachings, inspiration, and the hard-won accomplishments of our whole tradition. This means a respectful yet uncompromising confrontation with religious and monastic stereotypes and ritualistic externals. It also means confronting our own personal weaknesses and often mindless attitudes, opinions, and ways of living.

No perfect, unchanging, and safe blueprint will ever exist for this task. On the other hand, we do not have to reinvent the wheel, so to speak, by trying to start from scratch or by following contemporary fads. We have the example of those who have struggled with this throughout history with wisdom, competence, and holiness. We are also fortified, instructed, and inspired by the generous and competent help of contemporary researchers and fellow workers.

Our life at New Skete, then, has sharply moved away from the artificial encrustations and baroque customs of former times that helped make monasticism unnecessarily institutional and impersonal. (This kind of return to simpler, more primitive ways can also be found in Benedictine monasticism, where there have been attempts to return to smaller community size, healthy manual labor, liturgical simplicity, and hospitality.) We feel we have embraced and harmonized with the dynamic insights and spiritual treasures of Orthodox monastic tradition all the more deeply by continuously distilling its wisdom in the light of the knowledge and experience readily available to us today.

And so it is within the normal course of our life that we have questioned and critiqued, and then either adapted or put aside, many of the ways of monastic and religious thinking from the past. We have spent our lives and resources discussing, publishing, and putting into practice our work of renewal, reform, and restoration in Orthodox liturgy. We monks, along with our community of nuns and that of the married people at Emmaus House, worship together daily, accompanied by those who attend from our small parish or as guests and visitors. We have grown by working, studying, praying, and eating together over the years. Though four of the monks have been ordained as priests and one as a deacon, all of us are addressed simply as Brother, except for Father Laurence, and the women as Sister. The monks support themselves through a variety of fine meat and dairy products, dog training books and videos, and by breeding German shepherd dogs. The nuns make their famous cheesecakes, icons, and vestments, and the married community also produces icons and all-natural, hard, gourmet dog biscuits.

Most of our members were born and raised in one of the Western Christian traditions, and yet somehow we were attracted to the traditions of Eastern Christianity. Because of this, we have always been especially sensitive to the divisions among the churches and in our own small way tried to be a bridge of understanding between all peoples. We are interested in and respectful of believers and unbelievers alike and welcome them into our home. We try to live our own lives simply and straightforwardly. And we are committed to doing whatever we can toward healing the centuries-old schism between the Roman Catholic and Orthodox Churches. Father John Meyendorff, a well-known theologian and friend of ours, once said to us, "You should properly be called western eastern Christians!" As a matter of fact, we have come to see that a truly Catholic Christianity is necessarily ecumenical, embracing differences while trying to be open to the entire human race.

"Lord," exclaimed Peter, "it is wonderful for us to be here!"

Matthew 17:3

In the End, Happiness

O N AUGUST SIXTH every year, we celebrate the Feast of the Transfiguration. This year at the eucharistic liturgy, Father Laurence gave this homily:

"Today is the Feast of the Transfiguration. We celebrate Christ's going up Mount Tabor to be transfigured in glory before his three disciples. Before their very eyes Jesus' appearance changed, his face became like the sun and his clothes white as light. To either side of Jesus were Moses and Elijah and they were talking with him. The disciples were so overwhelmed with what they saw that Peter offered to set up three tents, one for Jesus, one for Moses, and one for Elijah. Then suddenly a bright cloud overshadowed them, and when the disciples looked up again, they saw only Jesus.

"As we know, nobody talks about the Transfiguration without mentioning light, and as Orthodox especially, we make a big thing about the 'uncreated' light, the creative power of God, the divine energies. Yet I fear that in many instances we take this for some kind of physical light, granted us through New York Gas and Electric, or perhaps even the light of the sun. We don't realize that the light we're speaking of today means infinitely more than this: that in relation to this feast, light means God. You remember how the creed speaks of Christ as 'Light of Light.' This necessarily includes the fullness of truth, absolute clarity, freedom, and peace. Pure light. Where God is there is no darkness, there is nothing hidden, nothing dirty, nothing black, nothing dark, nothing but total light. That is why we are told to be children of light.

"But the one thing that nobody ever mentions about the scene on Mount Tabor is what we're going to consider this morning. And that is to say how happy the disciples were to be there. I've never heard any in-depth discussion of Peter's remark, 'Lord, it's wonderful for us to be here!' I'm sixty-four years old and I've never once heard any reference to the disciples being happy to have been there — to say nothing about the happiness that must have been Jesus' — not a word said about their happiness. Yet 'wonderful' means that they really loved the experience, despite the fact that on some level it was over-whelming, frightening, unnerving. It made them feel alive in an utterly new way. For in the light of God, which is to say the eternal light that God is, there is no such thing as sadness or sorrow or sighing, as the funeral service says. There is only happiness. And just as sure as night and day are what they are, so it is that human beings were made to be happy.

"Yet there are many people, religious people (not excluding teachers of religion!), who think that happiness is not only *not* what God wants for us, but that it is wrong for us to pursue it, because it signifies our unwillingness to accept our 'lot' in life. But this is foolishness. It's totally unreasonable to believe that God would make any intelligent being except for its happiness. Only a theologian could think up such a thing! No, happiness is ours for the taking. And we have to take it.

"Our problem is that most people do not understand what happiness really is. For example, many of us think happiness is an extra buck, lots of extra bucks! Many of us think happiness is a vacation, a beautiful house, or simply getting our own way all the time. We think it's having the last word, not being humiliated, not having a rough time in life, or not having illnesses to burden us. This isn't what happiness is about. Satisfaction, contentment, all of these are very, very real parts of human life, but they're not happiness.

"So what *is* happiness? If it's not success, contentment, having a good time, self-satisfaction — if it's not all the things that everyone thinks it is, well then, what is it? It would seem that happiness is something almost beyond description, beyond verbalization, which each one of us may experience to some degree, yet which we never seem really to attain. It somehow eludes us, because we aren't clear about what it is. As a matter of fact, happiness is something dynamic, a reality that must continuously be struggled for, but which, once we attain it, cannot be diminished by the external circumstances of life. Happiness is never dependent on these, which is why it's a reality that each of us can achieve.

"This is the way that God has designed things. *This is the way he has designed us.* We like to talk about all kinds of things that God has done, but we never notice the things that God has *really* done. We'd like to ascribe to God all kinds of magic and superstitious ideas that suit our needs and feelings, but we never want to see what God REALLY does! That is to say, that God has put into our condition, the human condition, the ability to attain those things for which we were created. And one of the things human beings were created for IS to be happy. Not just content. Not just satisfied. Not just not troubled. Not just not humiliated. Not just having one's own way. We were created for something much more. We were created for what human beings call happiness.

"If God made us to know, love, and serve him in this world, and to be happy with him in the next, if he made us to become like him, then it must be that we've got to become happy. Because God is absolutely, without doubt, the happiest

being around. You can't find a happier one. He's ete
everlasting peace and tranquillity, inner harmony, full
sciousness of everything that is, was, will be, could be, should
be. And here we have a hint of what our happiness comes
from. It comes from entering into whatever we have to do,
whether it's watching the kids, cleaning the stove, mowing
the lawn. Being happy means entering wholeheartedly into
everything — no matter what type of challenge it presents,
no matter what the possible difficulties involved — entering
into it body, soul, mind, and spirit. We have to enter into it in
such a way that we're no longer separated from what we're
doing. We *forget* ourselves at the same time that we give ourselves completely. And when we do enter into life totally and
completely, then, if we stop and reflect for just a moment,
we'll notice that somehow we're beginning to experience
happiness. This is what we're made for.

"We're not made for drudgery. Drudgery in life exists
because human beings are also weak. We're defective, we
make mistakes, we succumb too easily to negative attitudes.
We find it hard to reach our goal, our purpose. And yet, the
amazing beauty of God is that he doesn't even make it necessary for us to reach any goal to be happy. *It's entering into the
struggle to reach the goal that brings us happiness.* And so what he
says to us is to live life fully, completely, absolutely, without
ambivalence, to put our minds, our hearts, our souls, our
spirits, all our strength and determination, our whole being
into the pursuit of what we're doing, right here and now. Not
worrying about how it's going to come out, not worrying
about this or that difficulty, despite any problems we might
have to struggle with. This is where we will attain happiness.

"This means we have to know what we're doing, being
conscious of every passing moment. We can't be happy if we
aren't conscious. If we can't achieve a greater awareness in

life, then forget it — we'll never be happy. Happiness demands consciousness, being aware, being alert, awake. No wonder we can't seem to attain this, for half the time we're asleep. We're only spottily conscious. If we were to show on a screen, for example, a silhouette of our consciousness and put a lot of holes in it, as if it were a piece of Swiss cheese, this is what our consciousness is like. At best, it's spotty. And therefore our happiness is spotty.

"Happiness never comes to us; it can only be achieved. We have to attain it, which is why the tools of the spiritual life — *metánoia,* self-discipline, solitude, prayerfulness, acts of love and forgiveness — are necessary ingredients to that end. And by the way, don't doubt for a second the fact that if we're not happy in this world, which is where heaven begins, then hell begins here. We must come to understand that God has put it into our power to attain happiness, that this is what he wants of and for us, and that it is entirely up to us to obtain it. No one can or will provide us with happiness. If we truly desire happiness, then we must struggle to do the best we can at each moment of life. Our happiness doesn't depend on somebody else's action or on anything else. It doesn't depend on our success, but rather on the effort we're willing to put into everything we do. Even if people disappoint or fail us left and right, even if people turn against us, hurt us, lie about us, don't understand us, even if they think they know everything about us and judge us unfairly, they can't infringe upon our happiness. True happiness means that we have a deep-seated peace and tranquillity that transcends all the difficulties of life, that cannot be disturbed by the chaos and warfare that might touch our lives.

"We had a friend who was in a Nazi concentration camp in the Second World War, a dog breeder, and he was digging in the trenches with the psychiatrist Victor Frankl, and Victor

Frankl told him: 'This is where you've got to find your happiness — right here in this trench, in this camp.' It is a simple matter of fact: you can be just as happy in a concentration camp, horrific and terrible as it surely is, as you can in any other circumstance in life. Or should we say that Christ was unhappy on the cross? For this is where we're supposed to find our happiness — where we are now, wherever that might happen to be, in all that we do, in whatever circumstances we find ourselves. To experience happiness is to experience freedom. No matter what may happen in life, nothing will be able to touch true happiness.

"Being happy involves the intense struggle of entering intimately into all that we do. And that is in our very nature; it's what God has placed in us. This is what the Transfiguration is about. It's not some pious story about going up a mountain and having light shine on everything. It has to do with the apostles gaining an insight into who Jesus really is. The reason Jesus took them up Mount Tabor was probably to show them in person what we were created for: to be like God. And being like God is always light, it is always joy, it is always peace, it is always tranquillity, it is always total consciousness, it is always being intimately connected with life. God is not separated from anything, which is why we say, 'God is everywhere.' We can find him anywhere.

"So we have to come to understand that happiness is not only in our power to attain, but our *duty* to attain."

GLOSSARY

Abba   (Aramaic, father) An affectionate address of a child or disciple to a father. In early monasticism, experienced elders came to be called Abba because of their wisdom, discretion, and compassion.

Áskesis   (Greek, training, practice) From which we get the word asceticism. The lifelong training in self-discipline that is essential for spiritual growth.

Catholic   Can mean the Roman Catholic Church or belonging to it; also can refer to all the ancient churches of Eastern and Western Christianity — Roman, Orthodox, and Oriental; or can mean universal, conciliar, all-embracing, the full truth of faith, doctrine, sacraments, and liturgy, and the cast of mind that seeks to embody these attitudes and to transcend divisions of time and place.

Cenobitic   (from the Greek *koínos bíos,* common life) The form of monastic life in which members live together in community, holding all things in common, and supporting one another in the living out of their monastic vows. Contrasts with eremitical, in which monks live alone as hermits.

Contemptus mundi   (Latin, contempt for the world) Originally reflected the belief that human beings had to repudiate worldly existence through extreme asceticism, which led to unhealthy exaggerations. A more positive way of understanding this today would be the struggle to overcome selfish and egotistical attitudes that distort the true nature of our humanity.

Desert/wilderness   Both a physical reality and a symbol of the human encounter with evil and grace in the spiritual life. In the Bible, the Israelites were led from slavery in Egypt through the desert to the Promised Land. During this time, they were pruned of their selfishness and hardness of heart and taught to rely on their faith in God alone. In

Christian tradition, this desert period became a metaphor of the human being's journey to God. From the late third century, the first monks actually went out into the physical desert to relive this; however, the lessons we glean from facing our own demons and duplicity in the solitude of our hearts can take place anywhere.

Dogmaticon   (Greek) These rather lengthy hymns (*stichéra*) are sung at the end of the incense Psalms at Saturday evening vespers, and again on the following Friday evening vespers. They are so called because they celebrate the mystery and dogma of the incarnation of Christ.

Epistle   Also called a letter, an epistle is a form of written communication that was widely used in the ancient world. Of the twenty-seven documents in the New Testament, twenty-one are in letter form. In Christian liturgy, the reading from one of the New Testament letters is called the Epistle.

Eucharist   (Greek, thanksgiving) The central sacramental celebration of the mysteries of Christ's death and resurrection by the Christian assembly with praise, prayer, and thanksgiving. As told in the Gospels, before his death Christ identified himself with the bread and wine at the Last Supper when he gave them to his disciples, saying, "Do this in memory of me." Christians have been doing this regularly ever since. During the eucharist, the Holy Spirit is invoked upon the bread and wine, that they might become the body and blood of Christ, to be shared by all, thus strengthening our unity and communion with the Lord and with each other as the Church, the living body of Christ.

Gospel   (Old English, good news) Broadly, the liberating message of God's saving activity in Christ, and more narrowly, the formal accounts of this produced by the early Church, namely the four canonical accounts of Matthew, Mark, Luke, and John.

Heart   The core of emotion, appetite, and intelligence within the human person, where individuals are most authentically and uniquely who they are. It is the center of our moral life, from which we manifest our true selves. Against any sort of dualistic notions, it refers to the person as a whole.

Iconóstasis   (Greek) A screen or wall, usually of carved wood, for displaying icons, which separates the sanctuary (altar) from the nave in Eastern churches.

Incarnation   The doctrine that God assumed human nature in the person of Jesus Christ, whom Christians believe is the Divine Logos, the

Word of God. The incarnation can also be understood to refer to the moment when Jesus was conceived by his mother, Mary.

Kondákion   (Greek; pl. *kondákia*) A long, metrical, poetic homily of about twenty-four sections; or simply its opening stanza which today is sung alone or with its *ikos,* a sort of chorus with a matching final refrain.

Metánoia   (Greek, changing one's mind) The attitude of repentance and spiritual seriousness characteristic of one who commits himself to God and to ongoing spiritual renewal.

Narthex   The entrance area of a church.

Nave   The central space of a church.

Novice   A beginner in the monastic life, one who has not made permanent vows at a profession ceremony. Ordinarily the length of time the novice spends in this state varies from monastery to monastery. At New Skete, the length of the novitiate is ordinarily three years, following the Orthodox tradition. Being professed in vows as a monk is different from being ordained a priest, either within or outside the monastic life.

Orthodox   (Greek for right belief or worship) Usually refers to a conservative religious group. Here it means Eastern Orthodox Christianity, as distinguished from Roman Catholicism (the two became separated during the last thousand years) and from the Oriental Churches who became separated in the fifth-century dogmatic controversies. The Orthodox Catholic Church is comprised of sixteen national or ethnic church bodies in Eastern Europe and the Middle East, who are each administratively independent, along with smaller church bodies around the world, in union with the Patriarch of Constantinople.

Paschal candle   A large candle blessed each year at the Easter vigil, which symbolizes Christ as the light of the universe.

Psalms   A book of the Bible, the ancient collection of 150 Hebrew songs and poems traditionally used for religious worship in both Judaism and Christianity.

Resurrection   The Christian belief that we will be raised from death to a new life with God. It is rooted in the belief in the resurrection of Christ, that after his crucifixion and death Jesus was raised from the dead by God, and that he appeared for a time to his disciples before being taken up into heavenly glory.

Riássa   (Slavonic; Greek, *ráson*) The monastic choir robe of a professed monk or nun.

Glossary

Rite   In the sense we are using it (as in Byzantine Rite, Roman Rite), the term for a distinct liturgical family or Church, including all its liturgical rites, ceremonies, and customs. This includes the theological and cultural ethos that animates and sustains it, and which its ritual expresses as well.

Rule of Saint Benedict   A sixth-century monastic code attributed to Saint Benedict of Nursia, which became the model for monks in the Western church. Covering all aspects of life in the monastery and balancing the needs of the individual with those of the group, it remains a fresh and enlightened outlook even for today.

Saint Paul   The most prominent convert of the early church, Paul was initially a zealous Jewish Pharisee who persecuted the early followers of Jesus. After experiencing a dramatic conversion, he eventually became a missionary and "apostle to the Gentiles," and his writings and teaching had a profound effect on the development and spread of early Christianity.

Saints Sergius, Herman, and Nil   Three well-known Orthodox saints. Saints Sergius and Nil lived in Russia in the fourteenth and fifteenth centuries respectively; Saint Herman was a monk in Alaska during the nineteenth century.

Sessional hymns   These refer to the hymns called *kathísmata* in Greek, which are sung after the reading of sections of the psalter and elsewhere in matins. The Greek term derives from the verb "to sit," for these hymns were sung seated.

Soléa   The raised platform located in front of the icon screen in an Orthodox church. It is on the same level as the sanctuary and may be approached from the nave by a few steps.

Stichéron   (Greek; pl. *stichéra*) These are the hymns that are sung at various offices, for example at vespers each night between the last few verses of the group of incense Psalms, Psalms 141, 142, 130, and 117.

Sýnaxis   (Greek) Usually refers to the anniversary of the monastery founding or to a meeting of all the members.

Theophany   (Greek, divine manifestation) One of the twelve major feasts of the Christian liturgical year, commemorated on January 6, which celebrates the epiphany or the manifestation of the Trinity when Jesus was baptized in the Jordan.

Théosis   (Greek, deification) The understanding of Christian salvation wherein enlightened humanity fully shares in the life of God. By entering a state of perfect communion with God, becoming one mind and one heart with him, we become like God.

Theotókos   (Greek, God-bearer) This is a common title for the Blessed Virgin Mary in Orthodox tradition.

Tone   (*échos* in Greek) Traditionally, both in the East and in the West, the church's chant developed into a system of eight distinct musical modes, or tones, whereby its hymns could be sung by a cantor or the entire congregation.

Tradition   Comes from both the Latin and Greek verbs meaning "to hand over, to pass on." In the church, the word "tradition" signifies the Christian faith and that which expresses it: liturgy, the sacred Scriptures, the writings of the church fathers, the rulings of the Ecumenical Councils, and the witness of the saints. Thus, above all, tradition is a living, not static, reality.

Transfiguration   One of the twelve great feasts of the liturgical year, celebrated on August 6. It commemorates the event in the Gospels (Matthew 17; Mark 9; Luke 9) in which Jesus went up Mount Tabor with his disciples Peter, James, and John. Before their very eyes, his appearance changed and shone forth with brilliant light, revealing in him both divinity and a fully transformed humanity.

Tropárion   (Greek; pl. *tropária*) These were originally any nonpsalmic refrain to Psalm verses used in liturgical services. In other words, they were nonscriptural antiphons. Today this generally refers to the main hymn celebrating a specific feast or commemoration.

Typicon   A foundation charter, code, or rule describing the principles and way of life in an Orthodox monastery.

BIBLIOGRAPHY

Understanding Scripture:
Suggested Reading

Brother John of Taizé. *The Pilgrim God: A Biblical Journey.* Washington, D.C. Pastoral Press, 1985.

———. *The Way of the Lord: A New Testament Pilgrimage.* Washington, D.C.: Pastoral Press, 1990.

Brown, Raymond E. *An Introduction to the New Testament.* New York: Doubleday, 1997.

Charpentier, Etienne. *How to Read the Old Testament.* New York: Crossroads, 1985.

———. *How to Read the New Testament.* New York: Crossroads, 1985.

Gomes, Peter J. *The Good Book.* New York: William Morrow, 1996.

Monks of New Skete. *The Psalter.* Cambridge, N.Y., 1984.

Tarazi, Paul N. *The Old Testament: An Introduction.* Volume 1, *Historical Traditions.* New York: Saint Vladimir's Seminary Press, 1991.

———. *The Old Testament: An Introduction.* Volume 2, *Prophetic Traditions.* New York: Saint Vladimir's Seminary Press, 1994.

———. *The Old Testament: An Introduction.* Volume 3, *Psalms and Wisdom.* New York: Saint Vladimir's Seminary Press, 1996.

———. *The New Testament: An Introduction.* Volume 1, *Paul and Mark.* New York: Saint Vladimir's Seminary Press, 1999.

Index

Index

Benedict, Saint, 29, 151, 199, 215, 270, 273
Benedictine monasticism, 29, 150, 151, 270, 305
benevolence, 242, 243, 249
Bernard of Clairvaux, Saint, 199
Bible, ix, 270
  apparent negativities in, 85–86, 87
  bibliolatry and, 160–63
  change and development within, 161–63
  translations of, 160
  see also Gospels; Psalms; sacred reading; *specific books*
body, 181, 183
  of Christ, 219–21
  unity of soul and, 185–86, 192
breathing, 41, 101
  rhythmically with prayer word, 99
Buber, Martin, 116
business management, 267
Byzantine Rite Franciscans, 8–9, 258–59

Camaldolese, 199
Carthusians, 199
Cassian, Saint John, 5, 91, 151
catholic outlook, 252–53, 260, 306
celibacy, 88, 177, 247–48
cenobitic monasticism, 30, 112, 150–51
change, 48–67, 254
  and behavior, 251
  denial of need for, 64–65
  directing in positive and life-enhancing ways, 49, 50
  and feelings, 297
  forgiveness and, 286, 288, 292, 294–96, 301
  habit of, 64
  inevitability of, 49–50
  Jesus as proponent for, 59–61
  in monastic life, 28, 51–53
  other-centeredness and, 66–67
  as painfully unsettling experience, 51

process of, 65–67
  profound, initial emotional response to, 34–35, 36
  and reality of new situations, 74–75
  "religious" people's resistance to, 62–64
  repentance in, 59–62, 67
  sacred reading and, 164, 165
  teacher as catalyst for, 53–59, 62–63, 64, 66
chant, 136, 232
Christ, *see* Jesus
Christianity:
  apparent negativities in, 85–86, 87
  contemplative tradition within, 154
  essence of, 84
  as way of life vs. beliefs or duties, 75–77
Christmas, *stichéron* for, 173
Christopher, Brother, 33–34, 51–52, 114–20, 187, 244–45, 247–49, 279–81
Chrysostom, Saint John, 221
"church," use of word, 218–19
Cistercians, 199
civil rights movement, 239
Climacus, Saint John, 45, 151, 179
Cluny, 199
Columban, Saint, 151
community, 102–4
  cenobitic monasticism and, 112
  communion, 79, 87, 115, 223
  contrasted with spirituality for sake of individualistic agendas, 102–3
  essential in spiritual practice, 103–4, 107–8
  human need for, 207, 222
  liturgical, 210–11, 213, 215–18, 222–24
  living church as, 219
  public rituals and, 207–9
Companions, 13
compassion, 224, 302
Conferences (Cassian), 151

Index

Index

Index

Index

praxis (practice), 76–77, 83–84, 90–91
  and Greek word for asceticism, 79
  and right thinking about reality, 84
prayer, 53, 66, 76, 155, 198, 302
  "angelic" ideal and, 186
  while attending to other responsibilities, 97–98, 186–87
  attitude of, demonstrated in Psalms, 189–92
  focusing on quantity of, 186, 192, 193
  of incense Psalms at vespers, 202
  Jesus' teachings on, 105, 106
  of litany for Theophany matins, 236
  and living in presence of God, 187–97
  as means to deeper reality, 97
  "pray without ceasing" admonition and, 186–97
  private, liturgical worship vs., 210–11, 215–18
  sensual experience of, 33–34, 39, 41
  spirit of, demonstrated by Jesus, 192–93
  spiritual dryness and, 39, 41–42
  spontaneous bursts of, in sacred reading, 169–70
  techniques for, 95–99, 105–6, 108
  using Psalms for, 136, 139
  work as form of, 271–72
  in yoga positions, 99
  see also meditation; sacred reading
premodern cultures, symbols and rituals in, 203–6, 207
pride, 285, 286
Proverbs, v
Psalms, 105–6, 283, 291
  attitude of prayer demonstrated in, 189–92
  earthy honesty in, 138–39, 140, 190
  Hebrew, 205, 206
  individual responses to, 142–43
  prayer of incense Psalms at vespers, 202

sacred reading of, 136–44
  self-knowledge and, 138–39, 143
  stream-of-consciousness response to, 140–43, 144
  uninhibited sentiments in, 190–91
psychology, role of, in spiritual life, 127–30
puppies, 131, 276
purgation, 40

questions, most important in life, 116–17

reality, 90, 130
  and being in harmony with God, 50
  fidelity to demands of, 75, 87, 92, 257, 274
  prayer and, 97–98
  rituals and symbols in experience of, 203–7
  seeing beyond delusion to, 60, 66
Rebecca, Sister, 99–101, 106–7
relationship(s), 56, 224, 250, 299
religious "high," 33–38, 45
  see also first fervor
religious leaders:
  of Jesus' time, 60–61
  in spiritual growth and development, 55
repentance, 83
  in change, 59–62, 67
  forgiveness and, 285, 286, 293, 301
  Greek word for, 59–60, 67
  as ongoing process, 63–64
resentment, 139
Revelation, 176
reverence, 185
rituals:
  of ancients, 203–4, 205, 207
  divorced from religious moorings, 208–9
  and human need for communal celebration, 207–9
  lamp-lighting, 19, 234–35

Index

Index